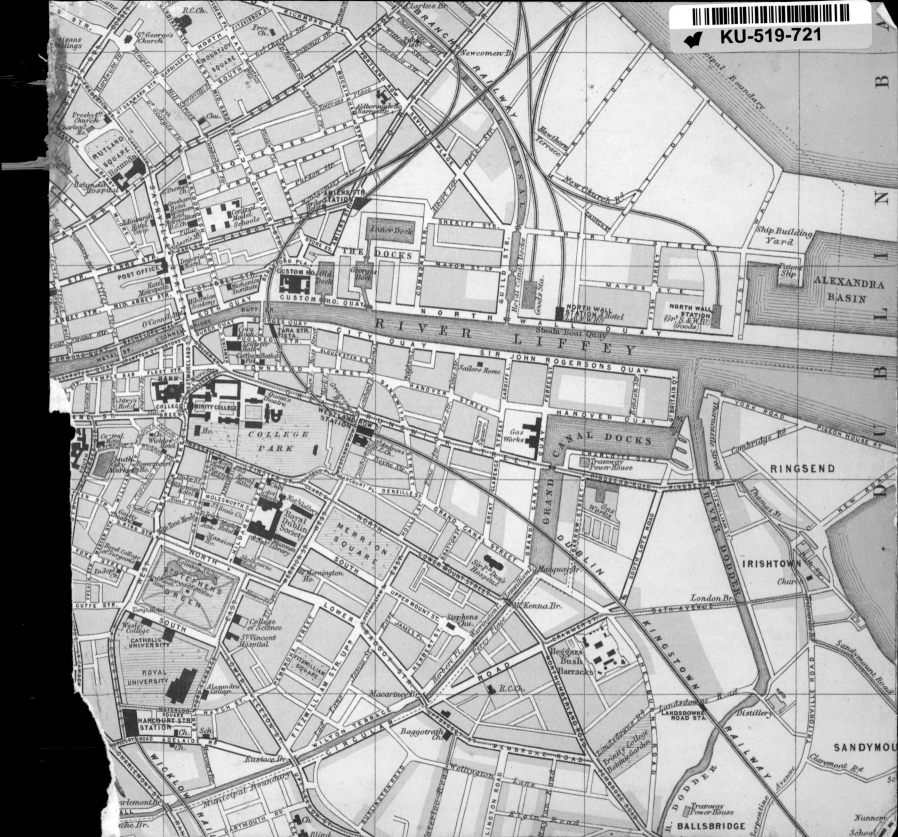

James Joyce's Ireland

David Pierce

With contemporary photographs by Dan Harper

1992

YALE UNIVERSITY PRESS

NEW HAVEN AND LONDON

For Jack and Mary Haugh of Liscannor, County Clare,
and for all my relations and friends west and east of the Shannon

In memory of my Irish Catholic grandmother Mary Kilmartin (1881–1973)
and of my English Jewish grandmother Esther Pierce (née Aarons) (1887–1927)

''*Tis as human a little story as paper could well carry.*'
(Finnegans Wake)

Front and endpapers: detail of Bartholomew's map of Dublin (see also p. 85). *Copyright* © *Bartholomew, 1990.*
Reproduced with permission.

Frontispiece: Liphitzki's photograph of James Joyce. *Courtesy of the Beinecke Rare Book and Manuscript Library, Yale University*

Copyright © 1992 by David Pierce

Designed by Mary Carruthers
Set in Linotron Bembo by Best-set Typesetters Ltd., Hong Kong
Printed and bound at Kwong Fat, Hong Kong

ISBN 0-300-05055-0

Library of Congress Cataloging-in-Publication Data

Pierce, David.
James Joyce's Ireland/by David Pierce.
p.   cm.
Includes bibliographical references and index.
ISBN 0-300-05055-0
1. Joyce, James, 1882–1941 – Homes and haunts – Ireland.   2. Joyce, James, 1882–1941 – Knowledge –
Ireland.   3. Authors, Irish – 20th century – Biography.   4. Ireland in literature.   I. Title.
PR6019.O9Z7817   1992
823'.912–dc20

[B]   91-29289
                                                                                              CIP

CONTENTS

ACKNOWLEDGEMENTS

JOYCE REWROTE THE PAST, but those who write about Joyce know that the past cannot in one respect be rewritten. As is apparent from even a cursory glance at the pages of this book, my work here is entirely dependent on the labour of others in the Joyce community, most notably the late Richard Ellmann. All I have done is re-arrange the material, suggest a different set of emphases, but always in the knowledge of a considerable debt to others in the field. I wish I could claim – as Joyce said about *Finnegans Wake* – it was 'the last word in stolentelling', but it is not, for I have added to the likelihood of errors in transcription the inevitability of misinterpretation.

Among those I am specifically indebted to are Dr Pieter Bekker, co–editor of *The James Joyce Broadsheet*, and Professora Rosa Maria Bollettieri Bosinelli of Bologna University, who kindly agreed to comment on the MS. Any errors still present in the text – those pervasive 'wandering rocks' common to all books on Joyce – remain mine to claim.

I would also like to record my debt to the following: In my own College: The Librarian and her staff and in particular Sandra Huxley; the Academic Board Research Committee for financial assistance.

In Britain: Dr Chris Ridgway; Professor Graham Martin of the Open University; Professor Tim Webb of Bristol University; Jane Lidderdale, OBE; Fliss Coombs at Zenith Productions; Janet Koss at the British Library; Brenda Maddox; John Jones of Leeds University; Dr Bill Shiels of York University; Kenneth Winch, Librarian at Bartholomew in Edinburgh; Clare Sunderland, Picture Editor at B. T. Batsford; Catherine Duncan at Waddington Graphics in London; Dr Mary Bryden, The Beckett International Foundation, Reading University; Professor Patrick Parrinder of Reading University; Professor Roy Foster; Trevor Jones, Fellow, Designer Bookbinders. Richard Hamilton was most generous. I am especially grateful to Catherine Carver, Beth Humphries and Rosemary Amos for their comments on the manuscript, to Robert Baldock, my Editor at Yale, for his timely interventions, to Sheila Lee, also at Yale, for her careful contributions to the shape of this book, and to Alice Macrell for the index.

In Ireland: Judge David Sheehy; Malachi O'Brien of Vance and Wilson, Main Street, Bray; Father Bruce Bradley SJ of Belvedere College; Robert Nicholson, Curator of the James Joyce Tower; Eilis Ni Dhuibhne, Assistant Keeper, Photographic Archives and Phil McCann at the National Library;

Henry Sharpe; Angela McEvoy at the Abbey Theatre; the actor Eamonn Morrissey; Bernard Meehran, Keeper of Manuscripts, Stuart O Seanoir, Assistant Librarian and Vincent Kinane Trinity College, Dublin; Rionach ni Ogain of the Department of Irish Folklore at University College, Dublin; Galway Corporation; the Western Region Tourist Office in Galway; Mrs Margaret Farrington and Elizabeth Ryan.

In Europe: I owe a particular debt to Dr Fritz Senn, Ruth Frehner and Christine O'Neill of the James Joyce Foundation in Zurich; to Professor Peter de Voogd, Rijksuniversiteit Utrecht; to Dr Grazia Bravar, Director, Civici Musei di Storia ed Arte, Trieste; and to Dr Carla de Petris, University of Rome.

In the United States: Vincent Giroud and Lori Misura, Beinecke Rare Book and Manuscript Library, Yale University Library; Sara Hodson, Curator of Literary Manuscripts, The Huntington Library, San Marino, California; Patience-Anne W. Lenk, Special Collections, Colby College, Waterville, Maine; R. Russell Maylone, Curator, Special Collections, Northwestern University Library, Evanston, Illinois; Sheila Ryan, Curator of Manuscripts at Southern Illinois University at Carbondale; Mark Dimunation, Curator of Rare Books at Cornell University; Robert Bertolf at the State University of New York at Buffalo; Debra Armstrong, Registrar, The Harry Ransom Research Centre, The University of Texas at Austin; Deirdre Bair; Wayne Furman, Office of Special Collections, New York Public Library.

In Canada: Jean Townsend-Field and Martina Field were especially generous.

I would also like to take this opportunity to record a special word of thanks to Dan Harper, of Cabrillo College, Aptos, California. In October 1985, we undertook an enjoyable trip round the literary sites of Ireland, and the photographs of his in this book were taken at that time.

My chief debt, as always, is to Mary Eagleton, long-suffering life's companion, who read and transformed everything from start to finish.

I would also like to thank 'The Society of Authors as the literary representative of the Estate of James Joyce' for permission to publish extracts from Joyce's work. Quotations from Joyce's work are from the following: 'Dubliners': Text, Criticism, and Notes, ed. Robert Scholes and A. Walton Litz. New York: Viking Press, 1969, repr. 1979. Stanislaus Joyce, The Dublin Diary of Stanislaus Joyce, ed. George Harris Healey. London: Faber and Faber, 1962. Exiles, St Albans: Granada, 1979. Finnegans Wake, London: Faber and Faber, 1939, repr. 1971. Richard Ellmann, James Joyce (revised edition), London: Oxford University Press, 1982. Stanislaus Joyce, My Brother's Keeper: James Joyce's Early Years, ed. Richard Ellmann. New York: The Viking Press, 1958. 'A Portrait of the Artist as a Young Man': Text, Criticism, and Notes, ed. Chester Anderson. New York: The Viking Press, 1968. Stephen Hero, ed. John Slocum and Herbert Cahoon. New York: New Directions, 1944, repr. 1963. Ulysses (Garland student edition), Harmondsworth: Penguin, 1986. Letters of James Joyce, ed. Stuart Gilbert. London: Faber and Faber, 1957. Letters of James Joyce, Vols II and III, ed. Richard Ellmann. London: Faber and Faber, 1966. James Joyce. Poems and Shorter Writings, ed. Richard Ellmann, A. Walton Litz, and John Whittier Ferguson. London: Faber and Faber, 1991.

Every effort has been made to ascertain and acknowledge ownership of illustrated material; any errors, absences, or oversights will be rectified at the earliest opportunity.

ABBREVIATIONS

D *'Dubliners': Text, Criticism, and Notes*, ed. Robert Scholes and A. Walton Litz (New York: Viking Press, 1969, repr. 1979).

DD Stanislaus Joyce, *The Dublin Diary of Stanislaus Joyce*, ed. George Harris Healey (London: Faber and Faber, 1962).

E *Exiles*. (St Albans: Granada, 1979).

FW *Finnegans Wake* (London: Faber and Faber, 1939; 3rd edn 1964, repr. 1971); page number followed by line number.

JJ Richard Ellmann, *James Joyce*, revised edition (London: Oxford University Press, 1982).

MBK Stanislaus Joyce, *My Brother's Keeper: James Joyce's Early Years*, ed. Richard Ellmann (New York: The Viking Press, 1958).

P *'A Portrait of the Artist as a Young Man': Text, Criticism, and Notes*, ed. Chester Anderson (New York: The Viking Press, 1968).

PSW *James Joyce. Poems and Shorter Writings*, ed. Richard Ellmann, A. Walton Litz and John Whittier Ferguson (London: Faber and Faber, 1991).

SH *Stephen Hero*, ed. John Slocum and Herbert Cahoon (New York: New Directions, 1944, 1955; new edn 1959; repr. 1963).

U *Ulysses*, Garland student edition (Harmondsworth: Penguin, 1986); episode number followed by line number.

Letters I *Letters of James Joyce*, ed. Stuart Gilbert (London: Faber and Faber, 1957; new edn. 1966).

Letters II *and* III *Letters of James Joyce* vols. II and III, ed. Richard Ellmann (London: Faber and Faber, 1966).

All map references are keyed to Bartholomew's 1900 Map of Dublin reproduced on endpapers and p. 85.

CHAPTER ONE
Joyce and Victorian Ireland
(1)

INTRODUCTION

JAMES ALOYSIUS AUGUSTINE JOYCE was born in Dublin on 2 February 1882 into a middle-class Catholic family. A day earlier he would have been born on the feast of St Brigid, the Mary of the Gaels, the saint who belongs as much to magic, animism and the fairies as to Mariolatry and organized religion. As it happened he was born on Candlemas, the Feast of the Purification of the Virgin Mary, the day when the candles are blessed in honour of the light that came into the world forty days previously, at Christmas. In the Church's calendar it is a happy feast day, for the Old Testament prophecy is fulfilled, a new covenant established, and the old man Simeon can now depart in peace. In the liturgy for that day the word 'light' has a special significance. *Lumen ad revelationem gentium*: light for the revelation of the people. The true light which *illuminas omnem hominem venientem in hunc mundum*, which illumines every person coming into this world. Early February is a fitting time for Joyce to be born, for among the outstanding qualities of his work are an attentiveness to female experience and to the traditional character of modern Ireland, and an intelligence that lights up everything it touches. At the very end of *Finnegans Wake*, his last book, Joyce writes, 'The Keys to. Given!' (*FW* 628.15). It is a highly charged moment, made more so by its New Testament associations. Just as Jesus gave the keys to St Peter, so Joyce hands us the keys to his subversive kingdom. Joyce is part of the great fulfilment of western literature, and his *Ulysses* constitutes, in the grand-sounding words of T. S. Eliot, a 'step toward making the modern world possible for art'.[1]

The weather forecast for that day, 2 February 1882, contained by Irish standards nothing exceptional: mist was promised with some rain, the wind south-easterly and southerly, fresh or strong, with perhaps a gale in the west. The political climate, on the other hand, was more stormy, for Joyce was born three months before the murders in the Phoenix Park of the Chief Secretary and the Under-Secretary for Ireland, and at a critical moment in the demise of landlordism in Ireland. Three years before, in 1879, tenant farmers under the leadership of Michael Davitt had formed the Land League to defend themselves against the threat of eviction from unscrupulous landlords. It was the beginning of the Land War in Ireland, which lasted until 1882. In a short space of time, especially after Charles Stewart Parnell, leader of the Irish Parliamentary Party at Westminster, pledged

1 The unveiling of a statue of Queen Victoria outside Leinster House, Dublin in 1908. Such a ceremony seems with hindsight an extraordinary piece of optimism, for within fifteen years Leinster House ('Royal Dublin Society' on map F5) had become the seat of the new Irish Parliament. Joyce was born into Victorian Ireland but he lived to see the emergence of a new Irish Free State and the breaking of the British connection. Ireland today, to the British, is often seen as separate and different; it requires an imaginative leap to realize that, in the nineteenth century Ireland was not only part of the 'Victorian' Empire but also in many ways essentially Victorian. The letter-boxes were red and carried the initials 'VR'; the country was administered by the British Crown from Dublin Castle; and MPs were elected to serve at Westminster. *Courtesy of the National Library of Ireland, courtesy B. T. Batsford.*

his support for the League, the land question and the nationalist issue became to British defenders of the Union dangerously entwined.

The atmosphere of the time is well captured in the following account, appearing in the *Times* of London on 2 February 1882, of an address by the MP for Lynn to his Norfolk constituents:

> The capital blunder which the Government made from the first and persist in to the present moment was and is in not believing the Land Leaguers when they told them candidly that they meant revolution. . . . Nothing will satisfy them but abolition of landlordism and separation from England. Abolition of landlordism means Communism in its most naked form; the separation from England means revolution. . . . The condition of Ireland has made a deep impression on Europe. . . . They say, 'What title has the Government which now rules in Ireland to preach to others on the condition of their country? Is there less crime and less weakness of Government in Ireland than in Asia Minor?' Gentlemen, it is difficult to hear these questions asked without a sense of deep humiliation. . . . The government of Ireland has caused us to become a byword among the nations.

Joyce is part of the Irish revolution which in the years between the Land War and the Government of Ireland Act of 1921 made Ireland ungovernable from Westminster. Joyce and the making – or, as I later suggest, the *un*making – of modern Ireland go hand in hand.

Because Victorian Ireland was both Irish and British, Joyce's work looks both ways. Advanced nationalists in Ireland sought to separate the two, but it is to Joyce's credit that he cut through the narrow-minded nationalism of his day and endeavoured to widen the scope of Irish identity. Because he exposed the cant and prejudice in Irish life, he was for many years cold-shouldered by the Irish, and it is only recently that he has received positive acclaim in his own country. In an article in *Scrutiny* in 1938, for example, Grattan Freyer declared, 'James Joyce continues to live in Paris, though any attempt to return might well be prevented by the stones of a priests' mob';[2] in 1963, Joyce's sister Eileen complained bitterly in an interview with the Dublin *Evening Herald* that she had 'heard many, many people saying he was damned'.[3] But if the British take comfort from Joyce's liberalism, they should not forget that the person who is partly or largely responsible for rewriting modern 'English' literature is Irish. In this respect Joyce's work provides a powerful critique both of the 'condition of Ireland' question and of the 'English' connection. On 2 February 1922, forty years to the day after he was born, Joyce was presented in Paris with the first copy of *Ulysses*, a book which not only 'made a deep impression on Europe' but which also marked a key moment in the formal separation, in the cultural sphere, of Ireland from Britain.

JOYCE'S FAMILY AND CHILDHOOD

There was no time for Joyce to enjoy his childhood free from history and politics. From the beginning, he was entangled in a centuries-old historical conflict and in the last stages of a colonial encounter. His family ensured him little protection from this public world. His father, John Joyce, the only son of a 'gentleman' from Cork, came to Dublin in 1874–5 with no thought of work, and spent his time sailing, drinking, and giving the occasional vocal concert.

of mortgages on his inherited properties' (*JJ* 21).

When James, the eldest of ten, was born, the family lived in Rathgar, a respectable suburb on the south side of Dublin. The author of the *Times's* obituary in January 1941 was mistaken in describing Joyce as 'one of a large and poor family'. Only after he was born did the Joyce home become the 'House of the Bare Table', as Joyce's brother Stanislaus called it (*DD* 30). The impression of poverty was partly created by the frequent changes of address. At first this was for convenience – they wanted more space, to be near the sea, to be further away from John Joyce's wife's family – but later of necessity. In 1884 they moved to Castlewood Avenue in Dublin, in 1887 to the seaside resort of Bray, south of Dublin, then in 1892 to Blackrock where, according to Stanislaus, 'the disintegration of our family set in with gathering rapidity' (*MBK* 46–7). Soon they were unloading again, this time back into Dublin north of the river to Fitzgibbon Street (F2) off Mountjoy Square. Debts continued to mount for the debt

2 Joyce in a sailor suit, 1888. Arguably his most winning photograph. *Courtesy of the Beinecke Rare Book and Manuscript Library, Yale University.*

Around 1877 he invested money in a distillery in Chapelizod. Then, in May 1880, as a reward for his support of Liberal candidates in the general election in April of that year, he was given a well-paid position in the office of the Collector of Rates for Dublin. With an annual salary of £500, a gentleman's office hours, and ample time for gossip, no occupation could have been better suited to John Joyce. That same month he married May Murray, the daughter of a wine and spirits agent. Thereafter, as Richard Ellmann succinctly puts it, 'John Joyce applied himself with equal diligence to the begetting of children and the contracting

3 The Victoria Hotel, Cork, in 1898. This is where Stephen Dedalus and his father stay on their visit to Cork, and where Stephen hears his father sing '' 'Tis youth and folly / Makes young men marry'. The hotel bus waits at the door, and the standard is in place for the new electric tram wires. *Courtesy of the National Library of Ireland.*

3

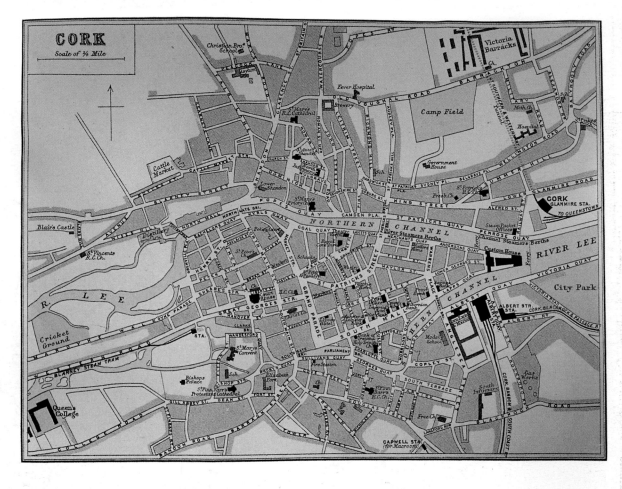

4 Map of Cork City in 1900. In *A Portrait*, Stephen returns to Cork with his father to sell off the family property. They stay in the Victoria Hotel (at the corner of St Patrick's Street and Cook Street), walk along the Mardyke to Simon's old university, Queen's College, and pass some cricketers. Later they meet up with Simon's old friends, who unearth traces of a Cork accent in Stephen's speech and get him to admit that the Lee is a much finer river than the Liffey. In his youth, according to Mrs Dedalus, Simon spent 'all his time out after the hounds or rowing on the Lee' (*SH* 85). John Joyce also sang in concerts at the Theatre Royal and took part in university theatricals, often receiving a mention in the city newspapers. James Joyce, 'eldest surviving male consubstantial heir of Simon Dedalus of Cork and Dublin' (*U* 17.537–8), was very fond of his father's city and had a picture of Cork (with a cork frame) hanging in his flat in Paris. *Copyright © Bartholomew, 1990. Reproduced with permission.*

5 River Lee softly flowing with St Finbarr's Cathedral in background. 'On this I ponder, where'er I wonder, / And thus grow fonder, sweet Cork of thee; / With thy Bells of Shandon that sound so grand on / The pleasant waters of the River Lee.' In the Picture Gallery chapter of *Finnegans Wake*, Cork is converted into 'Dorhqk' and is the answer to the question: which city has 'the most expensive brewing industry in the world' (*FW* 140.11). *Photograph Dan Harper.*

collector, and in 1894 they relocated to Drumcondra, where their neighbours were navvies and farmhands. Later that year, again for financial reasons, they took a house in North Richmond Street (F2), a 'blind' street where the houses, 'conscious of decent lives within them, gazed at one another with brown imperturbable faces' (*D* 29). Between 1898 and 1901 they changed address three times in Fairview alone; then in 1902 they moved to 7 St Peter's Terrace, Cabra (D2), just off the North Circular Road. According to Stanislaus they acquired nine addresses in eleven years. 'In the beginning two furniture

vans and a float were frequired for the moving; in the end it was just a float' (*MBK* 50–1). Their frequent moves and social decline fed James's later sense of being on the outside of things: long before he left Ireland Joyce was an exile. 'Here's the Bayleaffs' (*FW* 421.12) as he remarks in a humorous passage recalling the addresses of his childhood: '13 Fitzgibbets', '12 Norse Richmound', 'Fearview', '8 Royal Terrors' (Royal Terrace), '3 Castlewoos' (Castlewood), '2 Milchbroke' (Millbourne Ave), '7 Streetpetres. Since Cabranke' (Peter Street, Cabra), '60 Shellburn' (Shelbourne

6 Stanislaus Joyce in Trieste in 1905. Stanislaus was indeed his brother's keeper, and for his pains was memorialized in a series of uncomplimentary fictional sketches. Stanislaus is the subservient Maurice in *Stephen Hero* (a 'lying autobiography', according to Stanislaus), the staid Mr Duffy in 'A Painful Case' (named after 'Pisser' Duffy, a roughneck who taunted the Joyce boys when they were living in Drumcondra), and Shaun in *Finnegans Wake*. The Shaun figure is invariably associated with order, control, and moral uprightness; he is disadvantageously contrasted with the more human 'low hero' (*FW* 184.11) Shem, the writer who owns up to being a 'sham' (*FW* 170.24), that is Joyce himself. Perhaps there was a modicum of truth in the portrait, for in his *Dublin Diary* Stanislaus confesses: 'I have never dared to act as I please, but think in a little way "what will be thought of it?" ' (*DD* 33).

Road). 'Gee. Gone . . . No such no . . . At sea . . . Place scent on . . . Drowned in the Laffey . . . Seized of the Crownd . . . Blown up . . . Too Let . . . Razed. Lawyered. Vacant. Mined.' (*FW* 420.17–421.14).

Of all his brothers and sisters, James was closest to Stanislaus. Stanislaus has left us a remarkable portrait of Joyce as a young man in his companion studies, *My Brother's Keeper* (1958) and *The Dublin Diary of Stanislaus Joyce* (1962). The first recalls family life up to Mrs Joyce's death in August 1903, the second provides a series of vivid glimpses of the Joycean household in the two subsequent years. 'It is astonishing that a father with so little character could beget a son with so much' (*MBK* 29). This crystallizes Stanislaus's attitude towards James and his father. John Joyce was at home 'a man of absolutely unreliable temper': he referred to Mrs Conway ('Dante') as 'that old bitch upstairs' (*MBK* 35, 39), called 'all his children bastards as a habit' (*DD* 17), and took for one of his maxims 'Never apologize' (*MBK* 32). James, his father's favourite, was less affected by the disintegration of the family, possibly because for three years, from 1888 to 1891, he was at boarding school, by which time he had assumed a more detached view of his family. He never developed the hostility towards his father manifest in Stanislaus's attitude. Indeed, 'The two dominant passions of my brother's life were to be love of father and of fatherland' (*MBK* 238). It was then a short step towards preferring 'people whom the world rated as failures' (*MBK* 217).

As to James's character, Stanislaus noted in 1903 that it was 'unsettled', 'developing', that he possessed a 'vicious selfishness', 'extraordinary moral courage', and fierce scorn of the 'rabblement' (*DD* 13, 14). 'I think', wrote his brother, 'there is little

courtesy in his nature'; 'few people will love him' (*DD* 15). As to Joyce's beliefs, the 'guiding theme of his life' was freedom (*MBK* 108), but this could be located only outside the Church. According to Stanislaus, 'as a kind of interim religion' (*MBK* 131) James toyed with theosophy, but he never underwent 'any crisis of belief' (*MBK* 130). His political leanings were towards socialism, and in Trieste in 1905 he 'still called himself a socialist' (*MBK* 170). Stanislaus cautions against the view that Stephen Dedalus in *Ulysses* is an accurate autobiographical portrait, for his brother had a 'lively sense of humour and a ready

7 Bray Esplanade looking towards Bray Head. It was here that John Joyce took up rowing again. He also enjoyed walking along the promenade with his uncle William O'Connell ('Uncle Charles' in *A Portrait*) and reminiscing about Cork. *Courtesy of the National Library of Ireland.*

laugh' (*MBK* 187). As to James's sexual attitudes, he thought women the *radix malorum*, the root of evil (*MBK* 254), 'affecting to regard them as dirty animals' (*DD* 20). At the same time, 'there was never any real hostility between my mother and my brother' (*MBK* 237); he declared that he 'believed in only two things, a woman's love of her child and a man's love of lies' (*MBK* 91); and as for his love poems, 'the fact is that when he did fall in love, he stopped writing them' (*MBK* 152).

As will be apparent from the chapters that follow, Joyce the writer constantly recycles material from his own life.[4] At the begin-ning of *A Portrait*, he summons up a scene from early childhood when his family were living in Martello Terrace, Bray:

The Vances lived in number seven. They had a different father and mother. They were Eileen's father and mother. When they were grown up he was going to marry Eileen. He hid under the table. His mother said:

– O, Stephen will apologise.
Dante said:
– O, if not, the eagles will come and pull out his eyes.

7

8 Martello Terrace, Bray. From 1887 until 1892 the Joyce family lived in the end house at 1 Martello Terrace, next to the boat-house. In September 1888, Mrs Hearn Conway, known as 'Dante' on account of her Cork accent which makes 'auntie' sound like 'dante', became the children's governess. She left the family on 29 December 1891, presumably after the Christmas dinner row recorded in *A Portrait*. A frequent visitor to the house was John Kelly of Tralee, the 'hillside man' who became the model for John Casey in *A Portrait*. Kelly was in prison several times for Land League agitation, and while there he was visited and befriended by John Joyce. *Photograph the author.*

9 This chemist shop in Main Street, Bray, was owned by the father of Eileen Vance, Joyce's childhood sweetheart and playmate. The two used to play 'tig' in the hotel grounds near by. In later life, Eileen recalled being beaten over the head by Joyce with a child's wheelbarrow because she was a 'Prod', and he was going to burn her. Real life is often stranger even than Joyce's fiction. According to Malachi O'Brien, current owner of Vance and Wilson, Eileen emigrated to Saskatchewan in Canada in 1923. There she worked as a nurse in the TB sanatorium, and later joined a group of singers and dancers who toured Canada. She married twice, and on her hundredth birthday in 1981 received telegrams of congratulations from the Queen and from the Canadian Prime Minister Pierre Trudeau. *Photograph the author.*

Pull out his eyes,
Apologise,
Apologise,
Pull out his eyes.

Apologise,
Pull out his eyes,
Pull out his eyes,
Apologise.

Among their neighbours at the time were the Vances, a Protestant family who owned a chemists' shop in Main Street, Bray. John Joyce and James Vance became friends, as did James Joyce and Eileen Vance, who were the same age. The scene in *A Portrait* suggests a half-realized, half-understood moment in Joyce's childhood. It is difficult to know what the young boy has been doing: some critics suggest he has been peering up Eileen's skirt. Joyce is honest to a fault, apologizes for nothing, and makes himself at once unassailable and more vulnerable. Possibly, the boy took time to respond, trapped between his mother's strictures, his aunt's threats, and John Joyce's maxim 'Never apologize'. The path from Joyce's life to his fiction is both inviting for his readers to construct and frustrating for them to effect or verify. Often, what Joyce includes is uncomplimentary both to himself and to his family and friends, but his remarks invariably require careful sifting. All kinds of tension are at work in Joyce. His memory is rarely faulty, but like Actaeon in the Greek myth, he sees what he should not have seen and, in his case, writes about it; like a good Catholic, he shamefacedly owns up to what he was experiencing. Shame, however, prompted two separate responses: it made him more self-conscious, but it also emboldened him to attempt a clean break with his past. Equally, writing unearthed its own set of problems, for it was perhaps associated with the devil's work, part of the secret world of sin and guilt which Joyce felt impelled to share with other fellow mortals and sinners. In this sense – like the overreacher Faust – he was tempted by 'supernatural' powers. On the other hand, writing was perhaps like the sacrament of confession, a means of atonement, less a substitute for religion than an entry into a higher form of being in the world.

In 1888 Joyce was sent as a boarder to Clongowes Wood College (see map on p. 217), the Eton of Catholic Ireland. John Joyce wanted his eldest son to receive the best education, and the Jesuits, as Simon Dedalus tells Stephen, were 'the fellows that can get you a position'. 'Christian brothers be damned!' (*P* 71). Ironically, just when the family's star was about to fall from the sky, James was learning the art of mixing with the sons of gentry. In retrospect, his family's decline was, though not in the most obvious way, an enabling experience. The downward spiral could have spurred him into succeeding materially in life, into becoming a journalist, a lawyer, or a doctor, as his father hoped. Instead, he became ill-equipped to deal with the world on its terms, and perversely sought instead to make the world fit for his imagination.

10 Henry Sharpe's drawing of Joyce at the entrance to Clongowes Wood College. (From Robert Nicholson, *The James Joyce Daybook*, Dublin: Anna Livia Press, 1989.) *Courtesy of Henry Sharpe.*

CLONGOWES WOOD COLLEGE

At Clongowes Wood College Joyce was known, on account of his age, as 'half-past-six'. He was tiny, popular, conscientious about his work and, as Kevin Sullivan suggests, 'more delicate than brilliant'.[7] He was also conscious, if we are to believe Stephen in *Ulysses*, of his inferior social position, telling the Clongowes gentry he had 'an uncle a judge and an uncle a general in the army' (*U* 3.106). He was assigned to Elements, the first class, which in 1888–9 had thirty-eight pupils, most of whom were much older than Joyce; he remained in this class for three years, probably on account of his age. To prevent mixing across the age range, the school operated a Line system: the

Third Line included boys under thirteen, the Lower Line those from thirteen to fifteen, and the Higher Line those from fifteen to eighteen.

Life at Clongowes revolved around the classroom, the dormitory, the refectory, the playground, and the chapel. In winter, the boys played gravel football, in summer the English game of cricket. In Father Power's class ('Father Arnall' in *A Portrait*) the boys were divided into two rival groups, the House of York and the House of Lancaster, and encouraged to compete with one another. Joyce quickly learned about

11 The class of Elements at Clongowes Wood College, 1888–9. Joyce is sitting on the grass in front of Father William Power. In the back row, Rody Kickham is sixth from left, Christopher ('Nasty') Roche fifth from right. In the front row, Wells is second from right and a boy named Francis Pigott fourth from right. Pigott's father was the author of forged letters which the *Times* of London used in 1887 in an attempt to discredit Parnell – an event to which Joyce returned when he came to write *Finnegans Wake. Courtesy of Father Bruce Bradley SJ.*

bullying, breaking rules, punishment, and being ill. His name appears three times in the punishment book, once for wearing outdoor boots inside the school, once for using 'vulgar language', and once for 'forgetting to bring a book to class': he received six 'pandies' for the first, four for the second, and two for the third (*JJ* 30). But there is no record of the incident described in *A Portrait* where he is punished by the prefect of studies for being a 'lazy idle little loafer' (*P* 50).

The regime was strict, uncluttered, and uncompromising:

   6.30 Rise
          Holy Mass
          Breakfast
          Free until study
          Two hours of class
 12.00 Lunch
  1.00 Two hours of class
  3.30 Washing and dinner
          Free until 5.15

  5.15 Beads in chapel
          Study
  7.00 Supper
  8.15 Night prayers for small boys
          Bed

Such routine was designed to inculcate a strong sense of interiority in the boys. Silence was the norm, whether in the dormitory, in chapel, in the classroom or in the study. The externals of life were catered for in order that a spiritual life could be fostered. The Jesuits taught pupils to be at once self-reliant, selfless, and selfish, a powerful mixture of virtues and vices that stood Joyce in good stead when he became the centre of the world's attention in Paris in the 1920s. At Clongowes, Joyce developed an interest in plainchant and church music, his intellectual curiosity was stirred, and the foundations were laid for his remarkable stamina, long-term commitment, and, what Stanislaus so admired in him, 'a purity of intention' (*DD* 50). *Ulysses* took seven years to write, from 1914 until 1921, *Finnegans Wake* some fifteen years, from 1923 until 1938. Few writers in modern literature have imagined their work on such a time-scale. From 1914 until 1938 Joyce's writing was always in this regard 'Work in Progress', the title he gave to *Finnegans Wake* while it was being composed. Only someone driven at an early age to conceive time in large uninterrupted chunks – as weeks, months, terms, academic years, and holidays, as seasons in the Church calendar – could have assembled the necessary habits and the perspective for such an undertaking: 'First came the vacation and then the next term and then vacation again and then again another term and then again the vacation' (*P* 17).

At Clongowes Joyce was taught the habit of self-control and it never left him: looking at a photograph of him, you see that he rarely gives anything away. But self-control also took its toll. The body and time became associated with hurdles to be overcome; transformed into enemies, they threatened his spiritual life and his heavenly prospects. Joyce was constantly assailed by the Jesuits' militaristic discipline and by the example of St Ignatius of Loyola, the sixteenth-century Spanish soldier who left the battlefield to become a soldier of Christ and to launch the Society of Jesus (SJ). At Clongowes, the boys read the Ignatian *Spiritual Exercises* and followed the *Ratio Studiorum*, the Jesuit system of studies. They were taught that in the battle of life there were two standard-bearers, one Jesus, the other the Devil. The Jesuits delighted in confronting their audiences with the need for decision: the choice was starkly presented, invariably implied a moral imperative, and left little room for intellectual doubt. Joyce constantly faced, therefore, the prospect of falling by the wayside:

The snares of the world were its ways of sin. He would fall. He had not yet fallen but he would fall silently, in an instant. Not to fall was too hard, too hard: and he felt the silent lapse of his soul, as it would be at some instant to come, falling, falling but not yet fallen, still unfallen but about to fall.

(*P* 162)

In his teens Joyce did fall, but, ironically, in his rejection of Catholicism he paid his Jesuit masters a kind of homage in reverse, for it was they who had forged his conscience. The Jesuits, the shock troops of the Catholic Church, stressed a muscular form of Christianity, and Joyce seems to have left the Church not because the Jesuits were cruel or because of disagreements with Church dogma but because he could not live up to the moral demands of the Church, especially regarding its teachings on sexuality. In passing the sentries of his childhood, Stephen rejected the call of the Jesuits and obeyed instead a 'wayward instinct' (*P* 165). His sister Eileen, on the other hand, insisted that he remained always a Catholic in his heart.[6] One thing is certain: he never relinquished his admiration for the intel-

12 A photo of the Jesuit community at Clongowes taken in 1889–90. In the centre is the Rector, Father John Conmee, who later moved to Belvedere College in Dublin. Father Conmee makes an unforgettable appearance at the beginning of 'Wandering Rocks' as the representative of the Church breathing unctuously on the world. 'The superior, the very reverend John Conmee S. J. reset his smooth watch in his interior pocket as he came down the presbytery steps. Five to three. Just nice time to walk to Artane. What was that boy's name again? Dignam. Yes. *Vere dignum et iustum est*' (*U* 10.1–4). *Courtesy of Father Bruce Bradley SJ.*

11

lectual and moral power of his 'masters'. As he proudly proclaims in his poem of defiance 'The Holy Office', his soul was 'steeled in the school of old Aquinas' (*PSW*, 99). According to Buck Mulligan, Stephen has the 'cursed jesuit strain' in him, 'only it's injected the wrong way' (*U* 1.209), and the first words addressed to Stephen in *Ulysses* are about shaking off his Jesuit upbringing: '– Come up, Kinch! Come up, you fearful jesuit!' (*U* 1.8).

The formative nature of Joyce's childhood and schooling can be gauged from the imaginative accounts to be found in his fiction. His work affords a striking picture of male power in a variety of institutional settings – the family, the school, the office, the Church, the State. Like Dickens, Joyce is at his best when defending the sanctity of childhood against the cruelty of adults, whether at school or inside the family. The ending of 'Counterparts', when Farrington takes out his frustration on his son Charlie, no reader forgets: 'O, pa! he cried. Don't beat me, pa! And I'll . . . I'll say a *Hail Mary* for you. . . . I'll say a *Hail Mary* for you, pa, if you don't beat me. . . . I'll say a *Hail Mary* . . .' (*D* 98).

Joyce's early reputation as a writer in Ireland suffered because of his candid treatment of sexuality, but the same vociferous puritan opposition failed to notice his discerning critique of the Irish family, his understanding of the at times desperate and possibly misplaced recourse to religion, and his level-headed awareness of the link between failure at work and at home. The cruelty of adults is also a theme that runs through *A Portrait*, from Dante's taunts about pulling out Stephen's eyes, through the classroom scene with the prefect of studies and Stephen's subsequent interview with Father Conmee, to the hell-fire and damnation sermons of the retreat.

The classroom scene in particular is a compelling, and again instructive, account of the exercise of male power, this time at school. 'The door opened quietly and closed.' Father Dolan in his role as prefect of studies enters. Immediately a hush goes round the class. The intensity of the scene is established at once. With skills honed from his study of word order in Latin, Joyce writes not 'the door opened and closed quietly', but 'the door opened quietly and closed'. We are inside the classroom, participating as much as observing: '– Any boys want flogging here, Father Arnall? cried the prefect of studies. Any lazy idle loafers that want flogging in this class?' (*P* 48).

JOYCE AND PARNELL

Joyce's stay at Clongowes ended in the winter of 1891 when, possibly for financial reasons, he was withdrawn from the school: a debt of £30 is still outstanding under John Joyce's name. That same October, Parnell died and his remains were brought back to Ireland for burial. In *A Portrait*, dates are shuffled round, so that the Christmas dinner scene, Stephen's first Christmas at home, is made to coincide with the death of Parnell. For Joyce, Parnell represented a public world that had failed. Even at the age of nine he had absorbed enough from his father to write a poem (only fragments of which remain – see *PSW* 71) entitled 'Et Tu, Healy', accusing Timothy M. Healy, an erstwhile member of Parnell's Parliamentary Party, of treachery against 'the uncrowned king of Ireland'. Joyce never lost his fascination with the figure of Parnell, and everything he wrote was in some sense 'under Parnell's star'.[7] What impressed Joyce about Parnell was his aloofness

13 and 14 Parnell and Mrs O'Shea. Parnell was a very private person whose temperament was strikingly at odds with his public image. When he lived in Brighton, his favourite pastimes were giving his dogs a swim in the sea, browsing in bookshops, reading about mechanical engineering, riding over the Downs, and watching the sun set over Shoreham harbour. The 'uncrowned king of Ireland' was, according to Mrs O'Shea, intensely superstitious (he objected to travelling in a railway carriage numbered 13), constitutionally lazy, obsessed with hobbies such as making model boats, and in temper 'quiet, deep and bitter'. Moreover, he disliked the colour green, entertained no religious convictions, and was not enamoured of the Irish pastime of attending funerals. According to William O'Brien in his *Recollections* (1905), Parnell once said, 'How could you expect a country to have luck that has green for its colour!' He remained a patrician at heart. On one occasion, unable to have a carriage to himself on the Brighton line, and forced to travel in Pullman class, he refused to acknowledge the other passengers furtively staring at him from behind their newspapers. He used to sign his letters to Mrs O'Shea, who was his 'Wifie' and 'Queenie', 'Your own King and Husband'. His attackers wrongly assumed that, because her first name was Katharine, his use of 'Kitty' was a familiar form of address – hence the venom behind '*Kitty O'Shea* and the rest of it' to which Mr Casey refers in the Christmas dinner scene – but in fact neither he nor her family ever used her full name. (From Katherine O'Shea, *Charles Stewart Parnell*, 1914.)

and moral courage. 'No one could flatter Parnell, neither could anyone humiliate him,' wrote Mrs O'Shea.[8] To Joyce, Parnell brought dignity to Irish politics and he was forced from office by lesser mortals. Joyce liked to think of himself in a similar vein, for he too sought to add dignity to Ireland's cause – to write, as he says of *Dubliners*, a 'chapter of the moral history of my country' (*Letters* II. 134); but everywhere he felt betrayed by former friends and acquaintances, and propelled into exile by the 'old sow that eats her farrow' (*P* 203). Pride, remoteness, refusal to bend the knee, resolution – all these are qualities that unite the Protestant landowner and MP for Cork and the Jesuit-educated son of the son of a Cork gentleman.

In each of his prose works Joyce dwells on different aspects of the Parnell story. In *A Portrait*, he enlists Parnell to ground his semi-autobiographical novel in history and to underline Stephen's similar heroic stature; in *Dubliners*, he addresses the paralysis that overcame Irish politics after 1891; in *Ulysses*, he plays down the tragedy of Parnell's fall, and at one point humorously imagines Parnell returning to life to award Bloom the freedom of the city; but in *Finnegans Wake*, he returns to familiar territory, this time enforcing an identity between Earwicker and Parnell.

While for Yeats the fall of Parnell cut a space for literature to develop free from politics, for Joyce it meant that the context for his work was inevitably both historical and political. On the very first page of *A Portrait* there is a reference to the maroon

15 Michael Davitt (1846–1906) was the son of an evicted tenant farmer who at the age of four was exiled from Mayo to Haslingden in Lancashire. While working as a child in a cotton mill, he lost his right arm. In 1870 he was sentenced to 15 years' imprisonment for Fenian activities, but was released in 1877 on ticket-of-leave. In 1879 he founded the Irish National Land League, with Parnell as President. The combination of direct action and Parliamentary agitation proved highly successful but it was short-lived. During the Home Rule crisis of 1886, Parnell showed himself more interested in constitutional reform than in the land question.

and green brushes that Dante keeps in her press, the one for Michael Davitt, author of a book significantly entitled *The Fall of Feudalism in Ireland* (1904), the other for Parnell. It is a small detail, but enough to suggest a specific moment in Irish history – the early 1880s – when Davitt and Parnell were allies. By the end of the first chapter, after the Christmas dinner scene, the innocuous sound of 'pick, pack, pock, puck' has taken on a distinctly political meaning as the old order passes 'like drops of water in a fountain falling softly in the brimming bowl' (*P* 59). There is a similar highly charged moment in Chekhov's *The Cherry Orchard*, when the sound of a string snapping is heard offstage; the sound evokes

directly the plight of Mme Ranyevskaia, the impending sale of her estate, and more widely the collapse of landlordism in Russia. In the first volume of Yeats's autobiography *Reveries over Childhood and Youth*, which was published in the same year as *A Portrait*, history is treated as background – noises offstage – but in the opening chapter of *A Portrait* such noises come to occupy a more central position, for history to Chekhov and Joyce (and to Yeats in his poetry) is – what external reality is to Stephen in 'Proteus' – 'ineluctable' (*U* 3.1).

In the Christmas dinner scene, Joyce recreates the divisions into which Irish politics sank after Parnell's fall. Stephen has returned home from Clongowes Wood for the Christmas vacation; he is still very young, a child poised on the edge of consciousness. After the coldness and lack of intimacy at boarding school, the warmth of the Christmas dinner is inviting – and deceptive:

A great fire, banked high and red, flamed in the grate and under the ivytwined branches of the chandelier the Christmas table was spread. . . .

All were waiting: uncle Charles, who sat far away in the shadow of the window, Dante and Mr Casey, who sat in the easychairs at either side of the hearth, Stephen, seated on a chair between them, his feet resting on the toasted boss. Mr Dedalus looked at himself in the pierglass above the mantelpiece, waxed out his moustache-ends and then, parting his coattails, stood with his back to the glowing fire. . . .

Bless us, O Lord, and these Thy gifts which through Thy bounty we are about to receive through Christ Our Lord. Amen. . . .

It was his first Christmas dinner and he thought of his little brothers and sisters

14

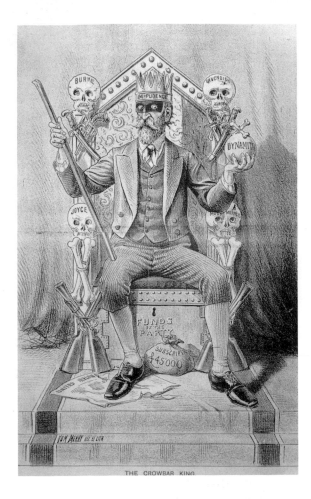

THE CROWBAR KING

the right of priests to preach politics from the pulpit, and denounces Parnell as a 'public sinner'. Simon Dedalus and Mr Casey blame the clergy for betraying Parnell and rending him 'like rats in a sewer'. When he is accused by Dante of being a 'renegade catholic', Simon takes this as a cue for a song:

> O, come all you Roman catholics
> That never went to mass.

The attack is continued by Mr Casey, who recalls a political meeting he attended in Arklow and how he was taunted by the anti-Parnellite gibes of a bystander:

– Well, I let her bawl away, to her heart's content, *Kitty O'Shea* and the rest of it till at last she called that lady a name that I won't sully this Christmas board nor your ears, ma'am, nor my own lips by repeating.

He paused. Mr Dedalus, lifting his head from the bone, asked:

– And what did you do, John?

– Do! said Mr Casey. She stuck her ugly old face up at me when she said it and I had my mouth full of tobacco juice. I bent down to her and *Phth*! says I to her like that.

He turned aside and made the act of spitting.

– *Phth*! says I to her like that, right into her eye.

He clapped a hand to his eye and gave a hoarse scream of pain.

– *O Jesus, Mary and Joseph*! says she. *I'm blinded! I'm blinded and drownded*!

(*P* 36–7)

This is too much for Dante, passions flare, fists strike the table. Stephen watches from a distance, hearing everything. Pitched into a no man's land between childhood and adolescence, he discovers the known world suddenly made strange and an adult

who were waiting in the nursery, as he had often waited, till the pudding came. The deep low collar and the Eton jacket made him feel queer and oldish: and that morning when his mother had brought him down to the parlour, dressed for mass, his father had cried. That was because he was thinking of his own father. And uncle Charles had said so too.

(*P* 27–30)

A row erupts between Dante on the one hand and Mr Casey and Stephen's father, Simon Dedalus, on the other. Dante defends

16 Tom Merry's vicious political cartoon of Parnell as 'the Crowbar King' appeared in *St Stephen's Review* on 27 December 1890. Under his right foot is a torn copy of *United Ireland* and behind him are the skulls of those caught up in the web of violence associated throughout the 1880s with his policies. Cavendish, Chief Secretary for Ireland, and Burke his Under-Secretary, were assassinated in the Phoenix Park in May 1882. Viscount Mountmorris, a County Galway landlord, was murdered in September 1880, a week after Parnell launched the boycotting campaign. The name 'Joyce' affords a delightful historical coincidence, since it provides a visual link between the names of Joyce and Parnell. In August 1882 in Maamtrasna, a village in County Mayo adjacent to the appropriately named 'Joyce's Country', a family was murdered in their cabin, seemingly without motive, by a band of unknown assailants. One of those falsely arrested and hanged for the crime was a Miles Joyce. In *Finnegans Wake* Joyce incorporated this incident into the Parnell / Joyce theme, for Festy King, 'a child of Maam' (*FW* 85.22–3) and '*elois* Crowbar' (*FW* 86.7–8), is arraigned in court for an indiscretion in the Park, and, being a Gaelic speaker – like Miles Joyce in the actual courtroom drama and not unlike what James Joyce does in *Finnegans Wake* – 'murdered all the English he knew' (*FW* 93.2).

17 Avondale, County Wicklow, home of Charles Stewart Parnell, the Protestant landowner whose skilful leadership of the Irish Parliamentary Party at Westminster nearly won Home Rule for Ireland in the 1880s. His downfall commenced when he was cited as co-respondent in a divorce case. As a result, his relationship with Mrs O'Shea, conducted for much of the time at her home in Eltham, Surrey, and in Brighton and Hove, became public knowledge. Under pressure, firstly from Methodist opinion inside Gladstone's Liberal Party, and secondly from the Catholic Church in Ireland – which was not to be outdone – he was forced to resign in 1890. Within a year he was dead. *Photograph Dan Harper.*

world outside his comprehension. This, his first Christmas dinner with the adult members of his family, ends miserably in a row about religion and politics. Dante leaves the table and shouts from one end of the room, 'We won! We crushed him to death! Fiend!' (*P* 39). The door slams behind her. Mr Casey begins weeping for his poor Parnell, 'My dead king!'

Joyce could have ended the scene at this point, but chooses not to. He returns to Stephen, the silent witness of Ireland's divisions after Parnell: 'Stephen, raising his terrorstricken face, saw that his father's eyes were full of tears' (*P* 39). Joyce records this moment with care. He does not write 'Stephen raised his terrorstricken face and saw that his father's eyes were full of tears', for this would simply 'round off' the scene.

Rather, he finishes on an understated but charged moment that brings Stephen's perception of events to the foreground, a moment that stays close to the original experience and that refuses to be incorporated into a comfortable narrative.

When this last sentence is read aloud, the reading voice searches for the right pitch on which to end, unsure of the appropriate tone to adopt. This mirrors precisely Stephen's contradictory emotions; he is terror-stricken by what he has just witnessed, by the ferocity of the argument, its unpredictability, by the open hostility between adults in the family. He is also confused: he is wearing his Eton suit for the occasion, it is the family's Christmas dinner, the first time he has been permitted to join the adult members of the family, and it ends not just awkwardly but in breakdown. The situation is heightened for Stephen when, though overcome himself, he notices his father's tears. For the second time that day, he sees his father revealed not as a god but merely human, and subject, like himself, to powerful emotions.

'Ivy Day in the Committee Room' is Joyce's version of what happened to Irish politics after the fall of Parnell. Politics became paralysed, little more than gossip exchanged in a cheerless room. The *Dubliners* story is set on 6 October, Ivy Day, so called because, on the anniversary of Parnell's death, his supporters wore a sprig of ivy in their lapels. The place is a committee room of the Nationalist Party in Wicklow Street (E4), the event a local election. (It was in Committee Room 15 in the House of Commons on 6 December 1890 that Parnell's party turned against him.) Time passes, but nothing significant happens. The canvassers, without a corkscrew, spend their time listening to the sound of '*Pok!*' as the bottles of stout placed near the fire release their corks. It is a deliberately downbeat view of Irish politics, written by someone who, ironically, was 'never in a committee-room in his life' (*MBK* 206). We learn in the opening sentence that Old Jack, the caretaker, 'raked the cinders together with a piece of cardboard and spread them judiciously over the whitening dome of coals' (*D* 118). The fire that once burned in Irish hearts when Parnell was alive is now but cinders; all that remains of Irish politics is the debris of a once-impassioned past. The room becomes a stage without footlights where people play at politics but have only walk-on parts, drifting unconsciously towards the fire for warmth.

The cast come in one by one. Mat O'Connor, the first to enter, is a canvasser for Mr Henchy, the agent for the Nationalist candidate Mr Tierney. He is succeeded by the Parnellite Joe Hynes, who is wearing a sprig of ivy and who supports Colgan, the working-class candidate. Henchy himself appears, followed by Father Keon. Father Keon, we are told, as if to underline that it is a play we are watching, resembles a 'poor actor'. His facial expression registers the only bit of surprise or excitement in this story, yet even this is accompanied by disappointment: 'He opened his very long mouth suddenly to express disappointment and at the same time opened wide his very bright blue eyes to express pleasure and surprise' (*D* 125). The eyes and the mouth, like a face that has been struck with paralysis, transmit contradictory signals, suspended between hope and disappointment. This is a vignette – or, alternatively, a parody – of the whole story. From inside the culture, politics after Parnell lacked charisma. The memory of Parnell continues to stir people, but not enough to shake them out of their cynicism or their conservatism.

Crofton and Lyons, canvassers for the Nationalists, enter. After the withdrawal of the Conservative candidate, Crofton has transferred his loyalty to Tierney, since Tierney is 'the lesser of two evils' (*D* 131). The discussion turns to Parnell. Henchy is uncomfortable, but Lyons, persisting, reminds him that 'we have our ideals'. The Tory, Crofton, a 'very fat man' who 'considered his companions beneath him', adds that his side of the house respects Parnell because he was a gentleman. Hynes returns and strikes a more serious note by reciting a personal tribute to Parnell, entitled 'The Death of Parnell'. It is an awkward moment, and the company are initially unsure how to respond:

When he had finished his recitation there was a silence and then a burst of clapping:

17

even Mr Lyons clapped. The applause continued for a little time. When it had ceased all the auditors drank from their bottles in silence.

(*D* 135)

Joyce's use of the word 'auditors' in this context is precise,[9] for Hynes's audience have not only been listening, they have been auditing the political account, and this in two senses. They have been drawing up a balance sheet of Parnell's place in history and at the same time they are anxious to draw a line and consign Parnell for ever to history. Everything in this story is two or three steps removed from full engagement with reality – the cinders in relation to the fire, modern politics *vis-à-vis* Parnell, the relationship of canvasser to agent to candidate, even the use of free indirect speech. Joyce gives the final word to Crofton, a man of few words, and, appropriately, that word is non-committal, yet another indirect mode:

> – What do you think of that, Crofton? cried Mr Henchy. Isn't that fine? What?
>   Mr Crofton said that it was a very fine piece of writing.

(*D* 135)

Ulysses contains several references to Parnell. Mr Deasy, in conversation with Stephen in 'Nestor', voices a commonplace prejudice when he remarks that it was a woman 'brought Parnell low' (*U* 2.394). Parnell receives more sympathetic treatment in 'Hades', when the funeral cortège winds its way to Glasnevin Cemetery (D1), where he is buried. While passing the foundation stone for a statue of Parnell near the Rotunda (E3), Bloom's thoughts momentarily link Paddy Dignam and Parnell: 'Breakdown. Heart' (*U* 6.320). A little later, he remembers Rudy, his son who died as a child – but not Parnell's and Mrs O'Shea's daughter

Claude Sophie who died in infancy. The living soon forget the dead: 'Even Parnell. Ivy day dying out' (*U* 6.855).

At Glasnevin, Bloom is approached – fittingly – by Hynes. He is taking the names of the mourners, and, in journalistic fashion, mistakes the man in a mackintosh for 'Mr M'Intosh'. Also in the cemetery, a group of mourners walk round to the grave of Parnell – the 'chief', as he was affectionately known.

> – Some say he is not in that grave at all. That the coffin was filled with stones. That one day he will come again.
>   Hynes shook his head.
> – Parnell will never come again, he said. He's there, all that was mortal of him. Peace to his ashes.

(*U* 6.923–7)

There are also allusions to Parnell coming again. Simon Dedalus imagines being elected to Parliament and Parnell being there to escort him out of the chamber; the cabman in 'Eumaeus' believes Parnell never died but went to South Africa to fight as a general with the Boers, that he will one day open his paper and see the headline 'Return of Parnell'. And then there is the strange figure of Parnell's brother, John Howard Parnell, with his 'haunting face', whose presence acts as a constant reminder of the chief's absence.[10]

In 1887 the *Times* of London, in a series of scurrilous articles entitled 'Parnellism and Crime', attempted to ruin Parnell by associating him with agrarian and political crimes and outrages. In particular, it printed a letter purportedly written by Parnell after the Phoenix Park murders in 1882, in which he expressed regret for the murder of Cavendish but, he said, 'cannot refuse to admit that Burke got no more than his deserts'.[11] The forgery was later exposed in

THE ILLUSTRATED LONDON NEWS.

REGISTERED AT THE GENERAL POST-OFFICE FOR TRANSMISSION ABROAD.

No. 2245.—VOL. LXXX.   SATURDAY, MAY 13, 1882.   WITH TWO SUPPLEMENTS   SIXPENCE. By Post, 6½d.

1. SCENE OF THE MURDER OF LORD FREDERICK CAVENDISH AND MR. T. H. BURKE, IN PHOENIX PARK, DUBLIN.
2. CONVEYING THE DEAD TO STEEVENS'S HOSPITAL.—SEE PAGE 454.

18   The Phoenix Park murders, as seen by the *Illustrated London News*. The bodies were discovered by two tricyclists in front of the Viceregal Lodge (A2): Mr Burke's throat had been slit, Lord Cavendish 'stabbed through the right lung'. Only that afternoon the son of the Duke of Devonshire had been sworn in at Dublin Castle and he was walking back to his lodge in the Phoenix Park. It was evening but still light. 'Mr Burke, following in a car, overtook Cavendish about the Park gate (B4). The Under-Secretary then got off the car, which he dismissed, and the Under-Secretary and the Chief Secretary walked together on the left-hand path. . . . About 200 yards from the Phoenix Column they were murderously attacked. . . . The attack was so sudden and silent that it scarcely attracted any notice. A common hackney car appears to have driven up and four fellows jumped off it, the driver remaining in his seat. Lord Frederick Cavendish was on the outside of the path, and Mr Burke was next the grass. The assailants rushed upon them with daggers, and a fierce struggle for life took place. But the murderers killed their victims in a few moments, and then drove off by a side road in the direction of Chapelizod, and rapidly disappeared.' When Bloom and Stephen stop off at the cabman's shelter in the 'Eumaeus' episode of *Ulysses*, Bloom whispers to Stephen that Fitzharris, the owner, is thought to be 'Skin-the-Goat', the driver who remained in his seat while the murders by the Invincibles were being committed. *Courtesy of The Illustrated London News Picture Library*.

court when Richard Pigott, the perpetrator, was asked under cross-examination to write the word 'hesitancy', and instead of the 'a' wrote 'e', as he had done in one of the forged letters. When he began composing *Finnegans Wake* in the 1920s, Joyce must have recognized that in the Pigott trial and the Parnell divorce case he had all the elements of a master narrative. Here was a fall from grace, a forgery, a courtroom drama, the narrow line between victim and guilty party, and a critical episode in Anglo-Irish relations. Joyce makes much of the links between Parnell and HCE or Humphrey Chimpden Earwicker, the multi-faceted hero of *Finnegans Wake*, and whenever the word 'hesitency' appears in the text, spelt thus, the historical figure and the fictional character are simultaneously evoked. Indeed, inside the very initials HCE there is an allusion to Pigott, Parnell and the Phoenix Park murders, and just in case we missed the connection Joyce at one point inscribes a capital E in the word 'hesitency' along with an H and C – 'HeCitEncy' (*FW* 421.23).

The parallels between Parnell and Earwicker are continued in the incident in Phoenix Park when Earwicker is approached by the menacing figure of the cad. Earwicker's response recalls the person who uncharacteristically delayed for over a year before publicly denouncing the Pigott letters as forgeries:

Hesitency was clearly to be evitated. . . . The Earwicker of that spurring instant, realising on fundamental liberal principles the supreme importance . . . of physical life (the nearest help relay being pingping K.O. Sempatrick's Day and the fenian rising) and unwishful as he felt of being hurled into eternity right then, plugged by a softnosed bullet from the sap, halted,

quick on the draw, and replyin that he was feelin tipstaff, cue, prodooced from his gunpocket his Jurgensen's shrapnel waterbury. . . . Shsh shake, co-comeraid! . . . there is not one tittle of truth, allow me to tell you, in that purest of fibfib fabrications.

(*FW* 35.20–36.34)

The very wordiness of the reply carries with it a measure of guilt. Not unlike Parnell, Earwicker realizes that he should avoid hesitation, for in hesitating he appears to be hiding something. Parnell was a country gentleman. He was educated at boarding schools in England before going on to Cambridge, and spoke with an educated Irish accent – perhaps not unlike a 'British to my backbone tongue' (*FW* 36.32). Like Earwicker also, he was a constitutional reformer, hated violence, but – at least in the case of the *Times*'s allegations – was unsure how to defend himself, producing from his pocket in Joyce's version not a gun but a Waterbury watch.

In the encounter between Earwicker and the cad, Joyce dramatizes a long-standing debate in nineteenth-century Ireland, between those who sought to win Home Rule for Ireland by peaceful, constitutional means and those who sought to break the English connection by force. As he suggests in the Lessons chapter, Parnell occupies a point between the constitutional Catholic reformer Daniel O'Connell and the 1916 revolutionary, James Connolly: 'This is brave Danny weeping his spache for the popers. This is cool Connolly wiping his hearth with brave Danny. And this, regard! how Chawleses Skewered parparaparnelligoes between brave Danny boy and the Connolly' (*FW* 303.8–12). The physical force movement in Ireland – as the Fenian rising of 1867 also serves to remind us –

posed a constant threat to constitutional reform. With the fall of Parnell in 1890, advanced nationalists in the Irish Republican Brotherhood embarked on a secret course which eventually led to Easter 1916. The encounter between Earwicker and the cad affords a breathtakingly telescoped view of Irish history, and behind the word 'pingping' can be heard the knock-out punch of the Easter Rising and the triumph of the physical force movement after the fall of Parnell. Joyce, meanwhile, 'unwishful as he felt of being hurled into eternity', watches from afar.

In *Time and Western Man* (1927), Wyndham Lewis attacked *Ulysses* for its 'suffocating, noetic expanse of objects, all of them lifeless, the sewage of a Past twenty years old, all neatly arranged in a meticulous sequence'.[12] In reply, Joyce mocks the upper-class English accent and at the same time effectively sums up Lewis's rather tedious argument in the book Joyce retitles '*Spice and Westend Woman* (utterly exhausted before publication, indiapepper edition shortly)' (*FW* 292.6–7): 'you must, how, in undivided reawlity draw the line somewhawre' (*FW* 292.31–2). In resisting those who sought to restrain his experiments with the English language, Joyce linked his fate with that of Parnell, who famously proclaimed that 'no man has the right to fix the boundary to the march of a nation'. With a slight shake of the kaleidoscope this slogan is transformed by Joyce into one of *Finnegans Wake*'s most quotable lines: 'no mouth has the might to set a mearbound to the march of a landsmaul' (*FW* 292.26–7).

The gestural and gentlemanly side of Joyce's politics has much in common with Parnell. Parnell sought Home Rule for Ireland but not complete separation, and this remained in essence Joyce's view. Joyce's mother tongue was English, he

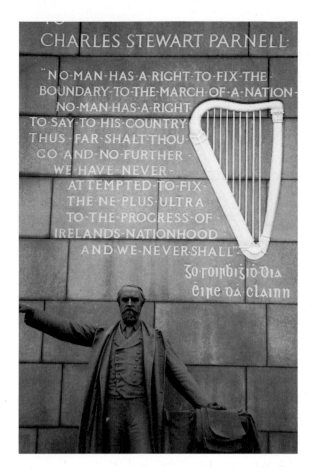

travelled with a British passport, was the recipient of a Civil List pension, and after his death Nora insisted his *Finnegans Wake* manuscripts went not to the National Library of Ireland but to the British Library in London. His experiments in *Finnegans Wake* with the English language convinced him that politics, like language, should not be governed by those who think might is right. Equally he realized, from his work on the history of language and on nationality, that boundaries can only be imposed artificially, that the language spoken in Dublin, for instance, is a mixture of Norse, Irish, and English etc. As for linguistic change in

the future, that resembles the 'march of a landsmaul', the march, that is, of 'New Norse', Ivar Aasen's belated attempt in the nineteenth century to make Landsmaal, a rural dialect, the standard language of Norway. But even as he proposes as much, Joyce knows it is faintly ridiculous; as he writes elsewhere in *Finnegans Wake*, 'this is nat language at any sinse of the world' (*FW* 83.12).

CHAPTER TWO
Joyce and Victorian Ireland
(2)

AFTER BEING WITHDRAWN FROM Clongowes, Joyce spent a short while at the Christian Brothers' school in Dublin, but then in April 1893, with his brother Stanislaus, he entered Belvedere College, Great Denmark Street (E3), as a day pupil. Belvedere was in some respects less impressive than Clongowes Wood, but to Joyce and his father it had the advantage of being run by the old firm of Jesuits, some of whom, such as Father Conmee, had taught at Clongowes. Belvedere had an immediate impact on Joyce and provided him with a new source of material for his fiction. In *A Portrait*, ten of Joyce's companions at Belvedere appear, including J. F. Byrne, the model for Cranly, Vincent Cosgrave, the model for Lynch, and Stephen's rival Vincent Heron, who is a composite of Cosgrave and Albrecht Connolly. The following year, 1893–4, Joyce's class included Richard Sheehy, James Lenehan (who later appears in 'Two Gallants' and in *Ulysses*), and David O'Connell (whose father has a small part in the 'Hades' episode of *Ulysses* as a caretaker at Glasnevin Cemetery).

Among the teachers at Belvedere, George Dempsey, the English master ('Mr Tate' in *A Portrait*) made a strong impression on Joyce. Every Tuesday the pupils turned in an English essay. Joyce enjoyed a reputation for essay-writing, and was frequently called upon to read his work to the class, and, while he did so, Dempsey, according to J. F. Byrne, 'would literally wriggle and chuckle with delight'.[1] In *A Portrait*, Mr Tate tackles Stephen about heresy in his essay:

> – Here. It's about the Creator and the soul. Rrm . . . rrm . . . rrm. . . . Ah! *without a possibility of ever approaching nearer.* That's heresy.
> Stephen murmured:
> – I meant *without a possibility of ever reaching.*
> It was a submission and Mr Tate, appeased, folded up the essay and passed it across to him, saying:
> – O . . . Ah! *ever reaching.* That's another story.
>
> (*P* 79)

There is nothing straightforward about Joyce's fictional use of his contemporaries and his masters at Belvedere and at university. As he says of the character of Shem in *Finnegans Wake*, he spent his time putting 'truth and untruth together' (*FW* 169.8–9). Sometimes he is attracted to the name; at other times he seems intent on creating an

1 George Dempsey, Joyce's English master at Belvedere ('Mr Tate' in *A Portrait*). *Courtesy of Fr. Bruce Bradley SJ.*

accurate portrait in fiction of the person he knew at school – though it would be wrong to assume that Joyce was ever a slave to his original model. On occasion, as in the case of the Sheehy brothers and Father Conmee, Joyce mixes historical fact and fiction in a way that is simultaneously untrue and revealing. To understand the conversation at the beginning of the 'Wandering Rocks', to keep to this example, Hugh Kenner suggests we need to know that the Sheehy boys were at Belvedere with Joyce and that they all left within a few years of 1898.[2] In the scene in *Ulysses*, Father Conmee has just descended the presbytery steps and is on his way to get Paddy Dignam's son accepted into the orphanage at Artane. Meeting Mrs Sheehy, the mother of the Sheehy boys and, more importantly, the wife of an MP, he stops to talk to her. Joyce deliberately omits

pieces of this conversation. 'Father Conmee was wonderfully well indeed. He would go to Buxton probably for the waters. And her boys, were they getting on well at Belvedere? Was that so?' (*U* 10.19–21) It is 1904, so the boys would have left Belvedere several years earlier. 'Was that so?' Suddenly, once we know the biographical details Joyce might be invoking, the conversation takes on a new dimension. 'Father Conmee was very glad indeed to hear that.' Reading Joyce is unfailingly demanding. In this passage, the impression is created that Father Conmee, for example, is a 'bland and courtly humanist' as Joyce later altered Herbert Gorman's description of him to read (*JJ* 29). In real life, according to another pupil at Clongowes, the priest was a 'prince among men, all kindliness and courtesy and with an exquisite literary gift that made his conversation a delight even to schoolboys'.[3] Joyce was also the recipient of Father Conmee's kindness: at Clongowes he took Joyce's side against Father Daly ('Father Dolan') (*JJ* 28–9), and probably played an active role in enabling Joyce to attend Belvedere as a free pupil.

In 1895 when James and Stanislaus were living in North Richmond Street they were invited on Sunday evenings to open house with the Sheehy family, who lived close by in a Georgian house on Belvedere Place (F2). According to Stanislaus, this was 'practically the only experience of what might be called social life that my brother had in Dublin' (*MBK* 72). They danced, sat in large armchairs, recited, sang, and took part in charades. The Sheehys breathed success. David Sheehy had been prominent in nationalist circles since his election as MP for Galway South in 1886; in 1903 he went on to defeat Parnell's brother for the seat of Meath South. Margaret was beginning to make a name for herself in amateur theatricals.

2 The Sheehy family, taken around 1902. At the back are Richard (Dick) and Eugene; in the middle Hanna, David Sheehy MP, Margaret, and Mary; in the front Father Eugene Sheehy, Kathleen (kneeling), and Mrs Sheehy (Bessie McCoy). *Courtesy of Judge David Sheehy and Fritz Senn, James Joyce Foundation, Zurich.*

Eugene, a year behind Joyce at Belvedere, was later to become a judge. In 1913, Richard was appointed Professor of Law at University College Galway. Kathleen took up the cause of Gaelic Ireland, and, on returning from a visit to the Aran Islands, decided her parents were insufficiently Irish.[4] Hanna, a pacifist, socialist, and a key figure in the women's suffrage movement in Ireland, married Francis Skeffington, who later became registrar at the Royal University. Perhaps not surprisingly, Mrs Sheehy, the MP's wife, believed she was presiding 'over the birth of a new ruling class: those who would run the country when Home Rule was won'.[5] The Sheehy family was confident, middle-class, and Catholic. It was in its own way outward-looking, capable of producing a critique of its own position – hence the radicalism of Kathleen and Hanna – and quite different from the Joyce household. But Joyce 'never lost his poise' (*MBK* 73) among them. Indeed he was, according to Eugene Sheehy, 'the star turn' and sang with gusto 'The Man Who Broke the Bank at Monte Carlo'.[6]

Joyce was particularly fond of Mary Sheehy, but she was emotionally attached to Thomas Kettle, whom she later married in September 1909. Kettle was a friend of

now but he felt that even that warm ample body could hardly compensate him for her distressing pertness and middle-class affectations' (*SH* 67). Stephen writes her poems, his feelings for her become public knowledge, and towards the end of *A Portrait*, Lynch whispers: '– Your beloved is here' (*P* 215).

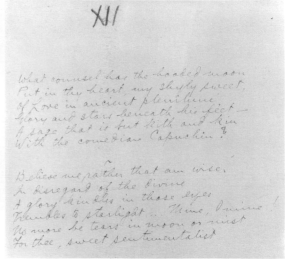

Ms 1.   *Courtesy of the Beinecke Rare Book and Manuscript Library, Yale University.*

Joyce's at university, where they were prominent members of the Literary and Historical Society, and in 1909 he supported Joyce in his attempt to secure a lectureship at his old university. Though Joyce was in Dublin in 1909, he was unable to attend the Sheehy–Kettle wedding. Instead, he sent them a copy of *Chamber Music* and invited them to visit Trieste on their honeymoon. According to Stanislaus, two poems in *Chamber Music*, 'What counsel has the hooded moon' and 'Lightly come and lightly go', were inspired by Mary Sheehy (*MBK* 150). Mary is also the model for Emma Clery in *Stephen Hero* and *A Portrait*. In *Stephen Hero*, Stephen 'would have liked nothing so well as an adventure with her

Joyce's interest in Mary possibly surfaces again in his play *Exiles*, the material for which derived in part from his 1909 visit to Dublin. Kettle (along with Oliver St John Gogarty, Vincent Cosgrave and Roberto Prezioso) is a model for Robert Hand in *Exiles*; Joyce is in Richard Rowan (and also Robert), Nora is in Bertha and Mary Sheehy possibly in Beatrice. *Exiles* articulates Joyce's complex male psychology – his fascination with triangular relationships and a repetition-compulsion to project on to others his own guilty, pleasurable, vicarious thoughts and desires. Richard has returned to Dublin with his wife Bertha seeking an academic appointment. Robert, as did Kettle in real life, has kindly agreed to support his candidature. Richard is attracted to Beatrice Justice, a cousin of Robert; Robert is in love with Bertha; Richard does not want to stand in Bertha's way since as he tells Robert he 'longed to be betrayed by you and by her' (E 87). At one point we learn that Richard has been writing long letters to Beatrice. According to Bertha, who is conscious of her inferior class position, it is Beatrice, with her 'fine and high character' (E 132), 'who brought my husband back to Ireland' (E 122).

Ellmann reports that in later life Mrs Kettle was 'surprised to learn that Joyce had a liking for her, and she can remember no signs of it' (Letters II. 238 n. 4). Indeed, when Joyce sent her a letter of condolence on the death of her husband in action in France in 1916, he betrays no sign of his earlier attachment to her:

> I have read this morning, with deep regret in the *Times* that my old school fellow and fellow student Lieutenant Kettle has been killed in action. I hope you will not deem it a stranger's intrusion on your grief to accept from me a word of sincere condolence. I remember very gratefully his benevolent and courteous friendliness to me when I was in Ireland seven years ago.
>
> (Letters I. 96)

Given that most of *Exiles* draws on people and events in Joyce's life or memory, it is curious that the biographical parallels to Richard's relationship with Beatrice remain relatively obscure.[7] Beatrice is obviously a foil for the more fully human Bertha; indeed, in his notes to the play Joyce refers to the 'abandoned cold temple' of Beatrice's mind (E 152). Perhaps while in Trieste Joyce harboured a lingering attachment to Mary

4 Thomas Kettle. The day before he was killed at the battle of the Somme in September 1916, he wrote: 'If I live, I mean to spend the rest of my life working for perpetual peace. I have seen war and faced artillery and know what an outrage it is against simple men.' (From T. M. Kettle, *Poems and Parodies*, Dublin: The Talbot Press, 1916.)

Sheehy. Less likely still, perhaps it was she who brought him back to Ireland in 1909. *Exiles* is a psychologically intense, strange play, whose meaning drifts beyond its biographical undertow, but when Richard insists that Bertha must 'know me as I am' (E 83), Joyce seems to be saying something about his own impossible, guilty feelings for idealized middle-class women like Mary Sheehy.

Joyce's adolescent awakening to sexuality took place while he was at Belvedere. This was a traumatic time for him, made more so by his religious upbringing in a country where Jansenist ideas were still in the ascendancy. The body was essentially a site of danger, a taboo area, there to be controlled like a subject people. At home, where there were repeated additions to the family (Mrs Joyce bore ten children), it would be strange if it did not occur to Joyce that copulation meant not pleasure but population. Whatever the case, by the age of fourteen Joyce was frequenting brothels and associating sexual pleasure, therefore, with something illicit and sinful. Inside the family, the issue of sexuality was too obvious, too painful, or perhaps too much surrounded by religious taboo. Like most young Irish men, Joyce had no one in the family or at school with whom to discuss his sexual drives. He was, however, troubled by his conscience. At the annual retreat in November 1896, contrary to Stanislaus's claim above, Joyce seems to have undergone a profound spiritual experience, well captured in *A Portrait* when Stephen determines to make a good confession:

> His eyes were dimmed with tears and, looking humbly up to heaven, he wept for the innocence he had lost. . . . It was not enough to lull the conscience with a tear and a prayer. He had to kneel before the minister of the Holy Ghost and tell over his hidden sins truly and repentantly.
>
> (*P* 139)

Padraic Colum recalls a conversation with Joyce in Paris in the 1930s that confirms this impression:

> For all his railing against the Church, Catholic philosophy was the only system that meant anything to Joyce, and I often wondered whether there had not been a real question of his entering the Jesuit order. . . . He spoke to me once of his decision in this matter, as if he really wanted me to know the truth. . . . He

mentioned . . . his early religious crisis and its negative outcome. 'Mind you,' he said, 'it was not a question of belief. It was the question of celibacy. I knew I could not live the life of a celibate.'[8]

In September 1897, Joyce was the un-official head boy at Belvedere, and he was re-elected prefect of the Sodality of the Blessed Virgin Mary. To his Jesuit masters he was a model pupil, member of a select group of boys chosen to set an example of piety to the others. They even suggested he might have a vocation for the priesthood, an idea that Joyce rejected only after a certain delay – contrary, that is, to the impression created in *A Portrait*. This period of his life witnessed the high-water mark of his involvement with Catholicism; thereafter came disengagement. By the end of the academic year 1897–8 his examination results, with the exception of English, were the lowest of any recorded in his four years at Belvedere. The self was in turmoil again, but this time the unrest could not be resolved by a return to piety or by 'Earwicker' thoughts that 'the rowmish devowtion known as the howly rowsary might reeform ihm' (*FW* 72.24–5). One of the essay titles set for the English examination that summer was 'Men may rise on stepping-stones / Of their dead selves, to higher things' – a title which chimes well with the idea of the sequential self that features so prominently in *A Portrait*. The shift from the eternal soul to the idea of a self that changes through time signalled an important moment of liberation for Joyce; human nature, as Cranly argues in *Stephen Hero*, is not 'a constant quantity', but is subject to change (*SH* 175).

The battle for his soul commenced in earnest. Mapping out Joyce's internal spiritual struggle can only be conjecture, gleaned for the most part from his fictional accounts. On the one side stood the Church and authority; on the other his wayward self. One way to reclaim his soul was by wholesale rejection or defiance of religion. When Stephen declares in *A Portrait* that he will not serve, he is consciously invoking the *non serviam* of Lucifer. But his self and his soul, largely formed by the Jesuits, could not be so easily appeased; neither would Stephen have been satisfied with becoming one of the Devil's cohorts. Significantly, Joyce supplemented his rejection of belief by attempting to reverse art and religion, to make religion serve art. When he began an enquiry into aesthetics, his intellect and vocabulary were steeped in Catholic theology, his conceptual framework largely governed by the thirteenth-century theologian St Thomas Aquinas. Joyce's idea of an 'epiphany', a 'sudden spiritual manifestation' as he describes it in *Stephen Hero* (*SH* 211), his aesthetic theory of beauty, summed up in the three Latin words *integritas*, *consonantia*, *claritas* (integrity or wholeness, symmetry, radiance) (*SH* 96), and his formulation of the 'priesthood of art', are all attempts at incorporating religion into the new self. Joyce's task is no less than to make sacred everyday reality, to show the 'significance of trivial events', affirm 'the spirit of man' (*SH* 80), to demonstrate how art and not religion is 'the very central expression of life' (*SH* 86). In *A Portrait*, he even risks comparing the artist to the God of Creation, 'refined out of existence, indifferent, paring his fingernails', and, not to be outdone, he includes an Annunciation scene where in 'the virgin womb of the imagination the word was made flesh' (*P* 215, 217). As he remarked to Stanislaus around 1900:

> – Don't you think, said he reflectively, choosing his words without haste, there is a certain resemblance between the mystery of the Mass and what I am trying to do? I mean that I am trying in my poems to give people some kind of intellectual pleasure or spiritual enjoyment by converting the bread of everyday life into something that has a permanent artistic life of its own . . . for their mental, moral, and spiritual uplift, he concluded glibly.
>
> (*MBK* 103–4)

'His Esthetic was in the main "applied Aquinas"', we are told in *Stephen Hero* (*SH* 77). In one respect, Joyce does to Aquinas what Aquinas had done to Aristotle, that is transpose the earlier system of ideas to a

6 Joyce among the Jesuits. 'You allude to me as a Catholic,' Joyce once remarked to Frank Budgen. 'Now for the sake of precision and to get the correct contour on me, you ought to allude to me as a Jesuit' (*JJ* 27). This photo was taken about 1900 when Joyce was a student at University College, Dublin. Joyce, hands in pockets, with 'jesuit bark and bitter bite' (*FW* 182.36), is second from left in the back row, his lifelong friend Constantine Curran at the front on the right. Leaning against the tree on the right is Robert Kenahan, the model for Moynihan in *A Portrait*. George Clancy ('Davin') is seated in front of Joyce. (Joyce presumably got this name from Maurice Davin, one of the founder-members with Michael Cusack of the Gaelic Athletic Association.) *Courtesy of the Beinecke Rare Book and Manuscript Library, Yale University.*

different order of reality. Aristotle provided Aquinas with a philosophical system that could be adapted to Christian theology. Joyce's relationship with Aquinas, however, is more problematic. Aquinas built on the work of Aristotle and assimilated his ideas into the 'higher' plane of Christianity, but Joyce was involved in a different kind of project, unsanctioned by any religious order or ecclesiastical tradition. For Joyce was competing with a religious view of the world and his only defence was the self, the demands of the body, and personal conviction – or, in the words of the famous triplet in *A Portrait*, 'silence, exile, and cunning' (*P* 247). Such a response illustrates the dilemma that confronted Joyce. This particular triplet echoes the less well-known *silentium, patientiam et preces* – silence, patience and prayer – of Lorenzo Ricci, an eighteenth-century leader of the Jesuits, who was later imprisoned and silenced by the papacy. Even Joyce's rebellion, then, as the *non serviam* also reminds us, is couched in the language of the dominant power. In *A Portrait*, Stephen says to Davin: 'When the soul of a man is born in this country there are nets flung at it to hold it back from flight. You talk to me of nationality, language, religion. I shall try to fly by those nets' (*P* 203). But what Joyce underestimated was the unity of form and content, that the two could not be so neatly separated, that talk of 'the soul', for example, implied a religious

1914 until his death in 1941. What the unfinished *Stephen Hero* and *A Portrait* demonstrate is that Joyce's real interests and intellectual ability lay not in aesthetics or in abstract philosophizing but in imaginative writing and in bringing together heterogeneous material. This brought in its wake its own series of problems, for, as the villanelle in *A Portrait* suggests, Joyce could not wholly convince himself of the Promethean course. There was always a suspicion that he was merely a penman and not, like Yeats, a poet, and that possibly all he was capable of was imitation and not creation from nothing. In *Finnegans Wake*, the Joyce figure Shem goes further and wonders if his work is not like Pigott's, a forgery, for he has a 'pelagiarist pen' (*FW* 182.3) and has possibly written the 'last word in stolentelling' (*FW* 424.35).

view of the world. Joyce rejected his Catholic upbringing and he never returned to the fold, but his exaggerated gestures of defiance suggested that vestigial attitudes remained to be incorporated or expunged.

Joyce was involved not only in making religion serve art but increasingly in a struggle to redirect his energies towards the secular world. *A Portrait* embodies the Daedalus-like movement upwards out of his city and country, out of the 'maze of narrow and dirty streets' (*P* 100); *Ulysses* and *Finnegans Wake* signal Joyce's return, a reassessment of life in terms not of departure but of *nostos* or return. Having broken the power of religion, Joyce embarked on a course of reorientation towards the human world, a task that was to occupy him from

31

MOORE'S *MELODIES* AND A *NATION* BALLAD

Tom Moore's *Irish Melodies*, which were composed between 1808 and 1834, became for Victorians on both sides of the Irish Sea a recognized source of comfort and entertainment, and Moore (1779–1852) quickly established himself as the Irish Burns. When Joyce as a child in the 1880s heard his father singing these melodies, he was absorbing an essential strand of Irish cultural life. Moore is an abiding presence in Joyce's work: according to Matthew Hodgart and Mabel Worthington (1959), *Finnegans Wake* contains references to 122 of the 124 *Irish Melodies*, and the other 2, they reckon, are probably also in there somewhere.[9] Joyce invoked Moore throughout his life and career as a writer, both at intense lyrical moments and during times of hardship. There is a touching scene in *A Portrait* when Stephen's parents leave the children gathered round the kitchen table for their meagre tea and go off in search of cheaper lodgings (*P* 162–4). The youngest child starts singing Moore's 'Oft in the Stilly Night', and the other children join in. The scene, rendered by Joyce without sentimentality or cynicism, stayed with him and many years later it is recalled again in *Finnegans Wake*, this time in even starker terms: 'the light of other days, dire dreary darkness; our awful dad, Timour of Tortur; puzzling, startling, shocking, nay, perturbing' (*FW* 136.20–2).[10]

Contemporary British audiences probably never detected the strength of Moore's patriotism, preferring instead a more prettified version of Ireland as reflected in such songs as 'The Meeting of the Waters' or 'Erin, the Tear and the Smile in Thine Eyes'.[11] In this way Moore was able to express his hidden feelings without setting at

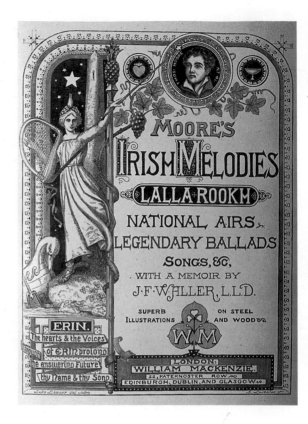

risk the financial support of his British patrons. But Irish audiences – especially among the Catholic middle class, whose power base expanded significantly in Victorian Ireland – relished the words of his songs. They knew, for example, that the subject of 'Oh! Breathe Not His Name' was Robert Emmet, the Irish revolutionary, who in 1803 led an abortive rising against the English; that Moore and Emmet were close friends as undergraduates in the 1790s at Trinity College, Dublin, and that in several of his songs, such as 'She Is Far From the Land' – another coded song, this time on the plight of Emmet's lover, Sarah Curran – Moore movingly commemorates that friendship.

Moore's songs nourished the dreams of

Victorian Ireland, and no evening's entertainment in a middle-class drawing-room would have been complete without *Irish Melodies*. But what gives the songs a special interest for the student of Joyce is that they are open to interpretation, and therefore to misinterpretation. Depending on your viewpoint, they are either sentimental or serious; they are designed to soften or to harden nationalist sensibilities; they either play to an English gallery or secretly harbour Gaelic resentment. When Joyce chooses to employ a song by Moore in his work, it takes on yet another aspect, for he never reproduces a Moore song quite as it should be; he invariably alters the complexion, the sense, the context.

11 Moore's 'Dear Harp of My Country' in the 1815 edition of *Melodies*.

34

With its nationalist associations, the harp was a favourite symbol for Moore in *Irish Melodies*. English Romantic poets of his time frequently linked the Aeolian harp with the Muse of inspiration, but for Moore the primary association of the harp was Ireland. 'Dear Harp of My Country', 'My Gentle Harp, Once More I Waken', 'Shall the Harp Then Be Silent?', 'The Harp That Once Through Tara's Halls' – the titles alone evoke Moore's kind of patriotism. His imagination worked best with the symbolic representation of his country. Joyce, on the other hand, knew that the traditional images of Ireland lacked freshness and could for the most part be deployed only ironically. In 'Aeolus', for example, the episode in *Ulysses* which is laid out with subheadings like a newspaper, Myles Crawford, the editor of the *Freeman's Journal*, sets about flossing his teeth:

> O, HARP EOLIAN!
> He took a reel of dental floss from his waistcoat pocket and, breaking off a piece, twanged it smartly between two and two of his resonant unwashed teeth.
> – Bingbang, bangbang.
>
> (U 7.370–4)

This is perhaps the first occasion in fiction when a person is described in the act of flossing – it must be the first and only time dental floss speaks or makes a noise. In the deliberate confusing of registers, in which low life and traditional art are equally mocked, the passage is true to form, a typical piece of Joycean humour that would have been completely foreign to Moore.

In 'Lestrygonians', Bloom, on his way to lunch, passes the old Irish house of parliament (F4):

> He crossed under Tommy Moore's roguish finger. They did right to put him

12 A 'teatimestained' (*FW* 114.29) Edwardian song postcard reproducing Moore's song.

13 An Edwardian postcard with lines from Moore's 'Come, Rest in this Bosom', sung with 'melancholy feeling, but not too slow'.

up over a urinal: meeting of the waters. Ought to be places for women. Running into cakeshops. Settle my hat straight. *There is not in this wide world a vallee.* Great song of Julia Morkan's. Kept her voice up to the very last. Pupil of Michael Balfe's, wasn't she?

(*U* 8.414–18)

Most Dubliners with a cursory knowledge of the works of Joyce and Moore are familiar with this joke about the 'meeting of the waters': today a plaque on the pavement in front of Moore's statue opposite the Bank of Ireland is there to remind them. Moore's song, which Julia Morkan, Gabriel Conroy's aunt in 'The Dead', used to sing, celebrates the meeting of the Avoca and the Avon.

In *A Portrait*, Stephen Dedalus thinks of Moore's statue as 'the droll statue of the national poet':

He looked at it without anger: for, though sloth of the body and of the soul crept over it like unseen vermin, over the

35

14 Michael Balfe, born in Dublin in 1808, wrote several popular operas including *The Bohemian Girl* (1843), often referred to in both *Ulysses* and *Finnegans Wake*, and *The Rose of Castille* (1857), the title of which recurs in 'Sirens' – earlier in the day, Bloom, his mind less anxious, manages a pun on it: 'Rows of cast steel' (*U* 7.591). (From John Boyle O'Reilly, *The Poetry and Song of Ireland*, New York: Gay Brothers, 1887.)

15 'The Meeting of the Waters' under the statue of Tom Moore (F4) in Dublin. The statue itself has probably done Moore as much harm as its position above a public urinal. With his 'roguish' finger and his dark cloak, he looks more like a Roman senator than the warm-hearted advocate of Ireland in the drawing-rooms of England. When the statue was first unveiled in 1857 someone wrote, 'Botch'd at first in pedestal and base, / Botch'd again to fit him in his place'. *Photograph Dan Harper.*

shuffling feet and up the folds of the cloak and around the servile head, it seemed humbly conscious of its indignity. It was a Firbolg in the borrowed cloak of a Milesian. . . .

(*P* 180)

The Firbolgs (*fir* is Gaelic for 'men', *bolg* for 'belly', 'bag', or 'bulge') ruled Ireland under their chief Bolgius, but in 271 BC, defeated at the Battle of Moytura by the Tuatha de Danaan, they were driven to islands off the west coast. The Tuatha de Danaan were in turn conquered by the Milesians from Spain. Stephen also alludes to Moore's servile attitude towards the British aristocracy, for, as Byron once quipped, 'Do but give Tom a good dinner, and a lord . . . and he is at the top of his happiness. Oh . . . TOMMY *loves* a Lord!'[12] The implication Joyce seems to be drawing is that, in spite of English patronage, in spite of the borrowed cloak of the later invader, Moore remained humbly Irish, one of the primitive bag men, and it is for this reason that

36

Stephen can look at his statue without anger.

From earliest childhood, Joyce was surrounded by the words and music of Moore. In later life, when encouraging his son Giorgio to take up singing as a profession, Joyce told him, 'Buy Moore's *Irish Melodies* and learn the following:

a) Fly not yet
b) O, ye dead
3) Quick we have but a second (this needs a lot of breath)
4) The time I lost in wooing
5) Silent, O Moyle
(this is a lovely air but G. should study the legend of Lir's daughters).'

(*Letters* III. 342)

Joyce had a thorough knowledge of the *Melodies*, the words, the music, how the songs were to be sung, their hidden meaning, the Irish myths and legends to which

IRISH MELODIES.   45

Fly not yet, the fount that play'd
In times of old through Ammon's shade,
Though icy cold by day it run,
Yet still, like souls of mirth, begun
To burn when night was near.
And thus, should woman's heart and looks
At noon be cold as winter brooks,
Nor kindle till the night, returning,
Brings their genial hour for burning.
    Oh! stay,—Oh! stay,—
    When did morning ever break,
    And find such beaming eyes awake
    As those that sparkle here?

FROM THIS HOUR THE PLEDGE IS GIVEN.

From this hour the pledge is given,
    From this hour my soul is thine:
Come what will, from earth or heaven,
    Weal or woe, thy fate be mine.
When the proud and great stood by thee,
    None dar'd thy rights to spurn;
And if now they're false and fly thee,
    Shall I, too, basely turn?
No;—whate'er the fires that try thee,
    In the same this heart shall burn.

Though the sea, where thou embarkest,
    Offers now a friendly shore,
Light may come where all looks darkest,
    Hope hath life, when life seems o'er.
And, of those past ages dreaming,
    When glory deck'd thy brow,
Of I fondly think, though seeming
    So fall'n and clouded now,
Thou'lt again break forth, all beaming,—
    None so bright, so blest as thou!

FLY NOT YET.

Fly not yet, 'tis just the hour,
When pleasure, like the midnight flower
That scorns the eye of vulgar light,
Begins to bloom for sons of night,
    And maids who love the moon.
'Twas but to bless these hours of shade
That beauty and the moon were made;
'Tis then their soft attractions glowing
Set the tides and goblets flowing.
    Oh! stay,—Oh! stay,—
    Joy so seldom weaves a chain
    Like this to-night, that oh! 'tis pain
    To break its links so soon.

they refer. But there is another aspect. Joyce inherited from his father a fine singing voice, and in his youth seriously entertained the thought of a career as a singer – Nora was convinced he should abandon writing and take up singing. In 1902, Joyce's name appeared on a concert programme along with that of John McCormack, the most gifted Irish singer of his generation, who delighted audiences with his rendering of Moore's songs. For Joyce, music was rarely a matter of passive appreciation but was primarily to do with performance, and in this sense whenever a Moore song appears in Joyce we should try to hear the music; for a Joyce text demands 'activating', demands that is to be treated as a score for performance.

To illustrate the way Joyce uses Moore, we can concentrate on 'Two Gallants', a story that depends for part of its meaning on a knowledge of one of the *Melodies*. In his schema for *Dubliners* Joyce assigns this story, with 'Eveline', 'After the Race', and 'The Boarding House', to 'Adolescence'. The story begins with Corley and Lenehan making for the centre of Dublin from Rutland Square (E3), north of the river. Absorbed in a conversation about picking up women, they pass the railings of Trinity College (F4), at which point Lenehan skips out into the road to catch the time by the clock above the college entrance. They follow the road round, past the bottom of Grafton Street and along Nassau Street until they come to Kildare Street (F5), where they turn right.

37

John M⁰ Cormack

Copyright by Bond Street Studios

The notes of the air throbbed deep and full. (*D* 54)

The song – the one Joyce recommended to Giorgio – concerns Ireland's exile from itself. In Irish legend, Fionnuala, one of Lir's three daughters, is transformed into a swan and condemned to wander over the waters of Ireland until the coming of Christianity. The Moyle, that part of the Irish Sea now called St George's Channel (or perhaps the Waters of Moyle off the Antrim coast), is silent, awaiting Fionnuala's return from exile. Kept in the background, with only the title given, the song is not so much heard as overheard. Joyce thereby avoids the charge of sentimentality, a charge he might not have escaped if he had quoted directly any of the languid lines:

Sadly, O Moyle! to thy winter-wave weeping,
Fate bids me languish long ages away:
Yet still in her darkness doth Erin lie sleeping,
Still doth the pure light its dawning delay!
When will that day-star, mildly springing,
Warm our Isle with peace and love?
When will Heaven, its sweet bell ringing,
Call my spirit to the fields above?

Not far from the porch of the club a harpist stood in the roadway, playing to a little ring of listeners. He plucked at the wires heedlessly, glancing quickly from time to time at the face of each new-comer and from time to time, wearily also, at the sky. His harp too, heedless that her coverings had fallen about her knees, seemed weary alike of the eyes of strangers and of her master's hands. One hand played in the bass the melody of *Silent, O Moyle*, while the other hand careered in the treble after each group of notes.

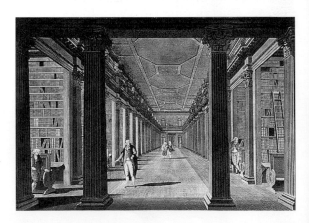

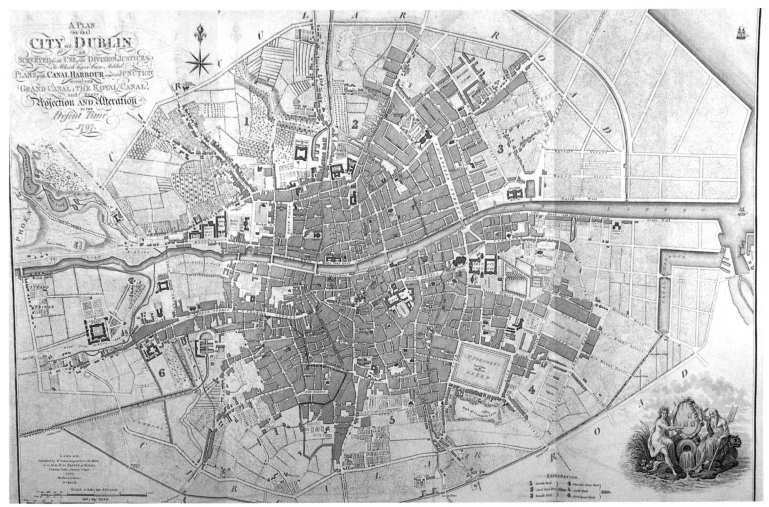

19 James Malton's map of Dublin, executed in the 1790s. Corley and Lenehan 'betray' no consciousness of history, yet their path takes them along routes made elegant by their Georgian ancestors.

20 The Kildare Street Club (F5), where English officers used to meet. In *Ulysses* Mr Kernan conjectures that the coat he is wearing, for which he paid half a sovereign second-hand, might once have belonged to 'some Kildare street club toff' (*U* 10.745). *Photograph Dan Harper*.

The club referred to in the story is the Kildare Street Club, in Joyce's time an exclusive Anglo-Irish social club which was also frequented by British army officers. As if to insist on a symbolic reading of his story, Joyce positions outside the club the Irish harp and an Irish harpist busking for money. The club represents British rule, and the harpist the fate of Ireland, condemned to poverty, careless of her appearance, living on sufferance, awaiting her release from the British yoke. Irish culture has been reduced to a 'little ring of listeners', and the Irish themselves alienated as it were by the eyes of 'strangers'. Ireland's sons, like Corley and Lenehan, seem indifferent to her plight. Oblivious of history, even the history of their oppression, the two gallants, as Donald Torchiana (1986) points out, wander through streets laid out by the Ascendancy

21 After passing the Kildare Street Club the two gallants march along to St Stephen's Green (F5). 'Here the noise of trams, the lights and the crowd released them from their silence' (*D* 54). St Stephen's Green, Malton tells us in his remarks accompanying this plate in *A Picturesque and Descriptive View of the City of Dublin*, was 'the place of muster for the Leinster division of the memorable Volunteers of Ireland, previous to their display of martial discipline in the Phoenix Park'. Joyce was learning in *Dubliners* how to condense and make use of the history of his native city.

in the eighteenth century, condemned to re-enact the betrayal of former generations. Their minds have become coarsened, their conversation crude and one-dimensional; their city has become empty, and they themselves victims of the 'pursuit'.

'The Croppy Boy'

In 1798, the United Irishmen under a Dublin-born Protestant Theobald Wolfe Tone (1763–98), attempted to shake off British rule in Ireland by force of arms. A number of risings took place throughout Ireland, the most significant being in County Wexford and in County Mayo. Sometimes known to historians as 'the Year of the French', on account of the French military force under General Humbert which landed in County Mayo to aid the rebels, the risings were quickly suppressed by Lord Cornwallis, and the leaders executed. The spirit of resistance, however, continued, and in 1803 Emmet led another rising, though this proved equally unsuccessful. But, as is often the case in modern Irish history, subsequent events were as decisive: 1798 and 1803 converted British victims into Irish heroes and secured the rapid development of Irish nationalism in the nineteenth century – Emmet's 'Speech from the Dock', for example, soon became part of nationalist rhetoric. 'Let no man write my epitaph. . . . When my country takes her place among the nations of the earth, then, and not till then, let my epitaph be written.'

The 1798 Rising produced not just martyrs but also a rich harvest of folk-songs and ballads, and one of these is especially relevant to an understanding of 'Sirens', the episode in *Ulysses* most associated with music. Carroll Malone's sentimental version of 'The Croppy Boy' first appeared in Thomas Davis's weekly newspaper the *Nation* in January 1845.[13] The song tells the story of a United Irishman from Wexford who goes to confession and tells the 'priest' that his father and his brothers have died in the struggle and now 'I alone am left of my name and race, I will go to Wexford and take their place'. Listening to his sins is not a priest but a yeoman captain, who suddenly reveals his true identity, arrests the croppy boy for being a member of a proscribed organization (a cropped head of hair indicating support for Jacobin ideas), and has him executed. The fate of Emmet and 'The Croppy Boy' are incorporated by Joyce into 'Sirens', along with several Moore songs to corroborate Bloom's Irishness. In 'Cyclops', the episode following 'Sirens', Bloom is scorned by the Citizen on account of his Jewishness and for not being Irish enough; but here in 'Sirens' the focus is on the Jewish victim's links with Irish nationalism. By deliberately forcing the comparison, Joyce never allows the tone to become maudlin. Bloom, too, is betrayed, suffers guilt about the affair he is conducting by correspondence with Martha Clifford, feels vulnerable that he will be exposed to ridicule, and even asks people to pray for him.

The Croppy Boy
A Ballad of '98
'Good men and true in this house who
  dwell,
To a stranger *bouchal* I pray you tell,

Is the priest at home, or may he be seen?
I would speak a word with Father Green'

'The priest's at home, boy, and may be
  seen;
'Tis easy speaking with Father Green;
But you must wait till I go and see
If the holy father alone may be.'

The youth has entered an empty hall –
What a lonely sound has his light footfall!
And the gloomy chamber's chill and bare,
With a vested priest in a lonely chair.

The youth has knelt to tell his sins.
'Nomine Dei,' the youth begins;
At 'Mea culpa' he beats his breast
And in broken murmurs he speaks the
  rest.

'At the siege of Ross did my father fall,
And at Gorey my loving brothers all,
I alone am left of my name and race,
I will go to Wexford and take their place.

'I cursed three times since last Easter Day –
At Mass-time once I went to play;
I passed the churchyard one day in haste
And forgot to pray for my mother's rest.

'I bear no hate against living thing,
But I love my country above the King.
Now, Father, bless me and let me go,
To die if God has ordained it so.'

The priest said naught, but a rustling
  noise
Made the youth look up in wild surprise:
The robes were off, and in scarlet there
Sat a yeoman captain with fiery glare.

With fiery glare and with fury hoarse,
Instead of blessing he breathed a curse:
''Twas a good thought, boy, to come

here and shrive
For one short hour is your time to live.

'Upon yon river three tenders float,
The priest's in one – if he isn't shot –
We hold this house for our lord the King,
And, Amen, say I, may all traitors swing!'

At Geneva Barracks that young man died,
And at Passage they have his body laid.
Good people, who live in peace and joy,
Breathe a prayer, shed a tear for the
    Croppy Boy![14]

The first 63 lines of 'Sirens' form the overture to the episode, a condensed version of what is to come, and through it all can be heard the words of 'The Croppy Boy'. But, as the hour when he is to be cuckolded by 'Blazes' Boylan approaches, Bloom discovers the words speaking to his own situation:

A moonlit nightcall: far, far.
I feel so sad. P.S. So lonely blooming.
Listen!
. . . .
Wait while you wait. Hee hee. Wait while
    you hee.
But wait!
. . . .
Naminedamine. Preacher is he.
All gone. All fallen.
. . . .
Amen! He gnashed in fury.
. . . .
Pray for him! Pray, good people!
                                (*U* 11.31–51)

When Ben Dollard sings the song in the Ormond Hotel, Bloom remembers he too is the last of his 'name and race' (*U* 11.1064–5), a Jewish cuckold without a male heir. The humour is never far away. Joyce smiles at the way singer, song and audience are sometimes confused – at one point '*Bless me,*

father, Dollard the croppy cried. *Bless me and let me go*' (*U* 11.1074). He also gently mocks the confusion of (a) syllable and word, as when Bloom asks, 'How will you pun? You punish me?' (*U* 11.890–1), and (b) character and author, as when Bloom takes over Joyce's thoughts about his own collection of verse, 'Chamber music. Could make a kind of pun on that. It is a kind of music I often thought when she' (*U* 11.979–80). When the song ends, Bloom's personality has been disseminated into a string of words and sounds:

Scaring eavesdropping boots croppy bootsboy Bloom in the Ormond hallway heard the growls and roars of bravo, fat backslapping, their boots all treading, boots not the boots the boy. General chorus off for a swill to wash it down. Glad I avoided.

                                (*U* 11.1142–5)

43

23 'Bronze by Gold'. Richard Hamilton's delightful rendering of Miss Kennedy and Miss Douce, barmaids in the Ormond Hotel. 'Sirens' begins inauspiciously for the reader with a profoundly enigmatic statement: 'Bronze by gold heard the hoofirons, steely-ringing' (*U* 11.1). Written thus, without regard for syntactical, 'spatial' relationships, it has the shock of a futurist sound poem, but in fact the two barmaids are but listening to the sounds of the viceregal calvacade passing in the street outside. *Courtesy Richard Hamilton and Waddington Graphics, London.*

The irony of that last sentence is that Bloom is unable to avoid external reality mirroring his own internal plight.

Bloom attempts to listen to the songs, but he is distracted by the contents of Martha Clifford's letter and by thoughts of being cuckolded. In a frenzy of uncontrollable reductionism, everything in this episode begins to devolve into its constituent parts: language, music, Bloom's personality. Bloom's name loses its final 'm', and suffers other forms of indignity. It is transformed, as in 'Blue bloom is on the', into a noun without upper case, and made to rhyme with 'blew'. It becomes an adjective, 'blooming', a genitive 'Bloowhose', and at one point his first name loses its status as a pronoun and is downgraded to an adjective – 'Bloom bent leopold ear' (*U* 11.637). 'Sirens' is narrated from Bloom's perspective, and consequently the distinction between external reality and inner consciousness is under special strain here. Moore's song ''Tis the Last Rose of Summer,' (Left blooming alone), which is confused by Bloom with 'The Rose of Castille', reminds him of his own 'lonely blooming' and of Molly's Spanish upbringing in Gibraltar. There seems no escape from his torment. 'The Harp that Once Through Tara's Halls' recalls Bloom's courting days among the rhododendrons on Howth Head with Molly, but it is accompanied by the 'jingle jaunty jaunty' of Boylan's jaunting car: 'The harp that once or twice. Cool hands. Ben Howth, the rhododendrons. We are their harps. I. He. Old. Young' (*U* 11.581–3).

In 'Sirens', Moore's *Melodies* and other well-known nineteenth-century Irish songs are often the butt of Joyce's levelling humour. 'The Minstrel Boy' can be heard inside the phrase 'that minstrel boy of the wild wet west' (*U* 11.268–9), 'The Moun-tains of Mourne' inside 'faraway mourning mountain eye' (*U* 11.273), 'The Last Rose of Summer' inside 'one last, one lonely, last sardine of summer' (*U* 11.1220–1). 'Sirens' makes more general, often humorous, use of the 1798/1803 episode in Irish history. Emmet's speech from the dock becomes Bloom's 'eppripfftaph' (*U* 11.61), an epitaph that contains the initials RIP surrounded in this case by a series of plosives – by the end of the episode the vowel has disappeared and we are left with a sequence of fifteen consonants which capture the noise of Bloom farting, from double p to quadruple f: 'Pprrpffrrppffff' (*U* 11.1293).

Occasionally, the serio-comic nature of 'Sirens' leaves the reader unsure of how to respond. The opening line, for example, of John Kells Ingram's *Nation* ballad, 'The Memory of the Dead' – 'Who fears to speak of Ninety-Eight?' – is converted by Bloom into 'Who fears to speak of nineteen four?' (*U* 11.1072–3). This is initially humorous – a 'Bloomer', an observation that is not quite right. Bloom is worried that 1904 might be permanently associated in his mind with being cuckolded; he might also be thinking of 'ninety-four', that is, 1894, the year his son Rudy died, leaving him the last of his name and race. If so, Joyce is perhaps poking fun at Bloom's sentimentalism and the special place accorded the eldest son in Jewish culture.

Moore provided Joyce with a useful protective shield or banner – or, we might say, invoking Yeats, a mask. Moore's sense of Irish identity was uncomplicated, and citing a line or phrase from his *Melodies* enabled Joyce to create a resonance against his text, a point of reference which was not only accepted as quintessentially Irish but which could also be deployed to probe the narrow definitions of Irishness. Joyce sub-merged his feelings beneath an avant-garde

QUEEN VICTORIA'S LAST VISIT TO IRELAND: HER MAJESTY IN HER DONKEY CARRIAGE

In the spring of 1900, Queen Victoria gave up a much-needed holiday in the warm, soft air of the Riviera in order to show, by a long and busy stay in Dublin, her grateful admiration for the splendid bravery of the Irish soldiers in South Africa.   The above photograph, probably the last ever taken of her Majesty, shows her during that memorable visit.

24   A Victorian valedictory. (From *Edward VII: His Life and Times*, ed. Richard Holmes, London, n.d. ?1910.)

episode, the oxymoron 'silent roar' (*U* 11.35), for example, which appears in the overture, gathers new meaning. Bloom compares Miss Kennedy's ear to a shell: the 'ear too is a shell' (*U* 11.938), and the sea-shell image is continued in 'The sea they think they hear. Singing. A roar' (*U* 11.945). More emotionally, inside the phrase can also be heard Moore's song of exile, 'Silent, O Moyle! Be the Roar of Thy Water'. This is a different form of exile from Stephen Dedalus's 'silence, exile, and cunning', but Joyce knew both states, and if the Jesuits brought out his youthful defiance, Moore – and to some extent the 1840s *Nation* ballad-writers – helped him stay in touch with the authentic Ireland of his childhood.

25 César Abin's caricature of Joyce, executed under Joyce's direction, first appeared in *transition* in 1932. Designed to stress the unheroic side of Joyce's life, it shows him escaping from the cobwebs of his native Dublin, leaving in the process a large black hole. His body is turned into a question-mark, his black hat carries an unlucky number, his dark glasses suggest his near-blindness, his clothes are patched, and in his pocket can be discerned the title of the song mentioned in 'The Dead', 'Let Me Like a Soldier Fall' – a reference to his ill health and to his attachment to sentimental songs both Italian and Irish.

'invisible' exterior, as if he feared exposing his vulnerable self: as his sister Eileen put it, 'He hated people finding out what he was really like'.[15] It says much, for example, of Joyce's Victorian sensibility that he thought Carroll Malone's version of 'The Croppy Boy' 'un nobile e semplice poema musicale, profondamente sincero e dramatico' ['a pure and noble musical poem, profoundly sincere and dramatic'] (*Letters* III. 335 and n. 2). 'Sirens' is a virtuoso performance on Joyce's part, full of 'crashing chords', of the yoking together by force of jarring sounds and calls to the heart. It is in such moments that the lyrical Joyce is present. Throughout the

CHAPTER THREE
Joyce, Nora and the West of Ireland

1 Berenice Abbott's photograph of Nora Joyce, taken in Paris *c.* 1928. Nora was fashion-conscious and, when she could afford to, patronized the best couturiers: Paris in the 1920s suited her admirably. *Courtesy of the Beinecke Rare Book and Manuscript Library, Yale University.*

NORA BARNACLE

BEFORE HE MET HIS future wife, the Galway-born Nora Barnacle, Joyce's idea of the west of Ireland was probably not unlike Stephen Dedalus's on the eve of his departure for Paris. Stephen is momentarily detained by Mulrennan's account of an old man he encountered in the west:

He told us he met an old man there in a mountain cabin. Old man had red eyes and short pipe. Old man spoke Irish. Mulrennan spoke Irish. Then old man and Mulrennan spoke English. Mulrennan spoke to him about universe and stars. Old man sat, listened, smoked, spat. Then said:

– Ah, there must be terrible queer creatures at the latter end of the world.

I fear him. I fear his redrimmed horny eyes. It is with him I must struggle all through this night till day come, till he or I lie dead, gripping him by the sinewy throat till . . . Till what? Till he yield to me? No. I mean him no harm.

(*P* 251–2)

After falling in love with Nora Barnacle, Joyce's understanding of the west entered a new phase. Nora's life, the subject of a recent biography by Brenda Maddox,[1] significantly reshaped his view of Ireland. The west could no longer be banished to a remote corner of his mind, but had somehow to be incorporated into his overall judgement of the world. Nora helped Joyce remain faithful to his imagination, deepened his understanding of the west, and recalled, especially through her broad Galway accent, an Ireland beyond the Pale. In the context of the final word of 'Penelope' she taught him to say yes, to accept Ireland, and to find a home for his rebellious spirit. Indeed, perhaps she did more, for as Bertha proudly boasts to Beatrice in *Exiles*, 'I made him a man' (*E* 128).

Nora and Joyce first met on Nassau Street (F4) in Dublin on 10 June 1904. Ironically – but this is also in keeping – the most momentous meeting of his life was a chance encounter: Joyce stopped Nora in the street and asked her out. It was an unlikely match, a woman from the west of Ireland, who was not especially intellectual or artistic, and the rather remote, thin-faced, intense, slightly dandyish Dubliner, who had lived in Paris but who had never once visited the west of his own country. In his dirty canvas shoes and yachting cap, Nora mistook him for a sailor, and from his blue eyes she thought he might be Swedish. Having graduated from university in 1902 and being without regular

2   In *A Portrait*, Stephen
Dedalus imagines going
home from Clongowes. 'Through
Clane they drove, cheering and
cheered. The peasant women
stood at the halfdoors, the men
stood here and there' (*P* 20).
Later in the novel, Stephen
recalls the incident in
conversation with Davin.
Davin tells him how one night
in the Ballyhoura hills he was
invited into a cottage by a half-
undressed woman. The figure
of the sexually aroused but
frustrated peasant woman
becomes for Stephen 'a type of
her race and his own, a batlike
soul waking to the consciousness of itself in darkness and
secrecy and loneliness and,
through the eyes and voice and
gesture of a woman without
guile, calling the stranger to
her bed' (*P* 183). This is
perhaps the closest Joyce comes
to a primitivist view of the
Irish country people (the use of
the word 'peasant' betrays his
Dublin background). *Photograph Dan Harper. Courtesy of
Bunratty Folk Park and Shannon
Heritage Ltd, County Clare.*

3 'I fear his redrimmed horny eyes' (*P* 251). The old man in Mulrennan's story reminds Stephen as he embarks for the continent that his struggle with the world cannot ignore ancient Ireland. Joyce's world seems so different from life in the west. This photograph shows Joseph McHugh, the Liscannor publican who, until his death in December 1989, was among the most famous 'curates' in the west of Ireland. If Joyce had engaged him in conversation, which pose would he have adopted – the Dubliner's view of the primitive west, or the 'bullockbefriending bard' (*U* 2.431) approach with which Stephen thinks Mulligan will taunt him in *Ulysses*? Perhaps Joyce would have been struck dumb with fear, an occupant of the same island as his compatriot on the Atlantic seaboard. Whatever the case, it is difficult to see Joyce talking about the price of yearlings or the state of hare-coursing in the country. *Photograph Dan Harper.*

employment, Joyce entertained the hope of becoming a singer or possibly a writer. When the young Yeats first encountered the old Fenian John O'Leary, he realized he was 'in the presence of his theme';[2] in similar fashion, Joyce, on meeting Nora, unknowingly arrived at the source of significant new material and the vital focus for a writing career. Until 1904 he was a would-be writer; after that date much of the material of his fiction – namely the first twenty-two years of his life – was ready to be *forged*.

Nora Barnacle was born on 21 or 22 March 1884, the second daughter of a seamstress and of an alcoholic baker who, as Joyce eloquently put it, 'drank all the buns and loaves like a man' (*Letters* II. 72). Her mother's family, the Healys, were not without status or pretensions, and Michael Healy, Nora's uncle, eventually became Inspector of Custom and Receiver of Wrecks in Galway. Nora spent much of her childhood at her grandmother's, away from her drunken father; he was eventually thrown out of the house when Nora was about twelve.[3] Around the same time, Nora left school, and was taken on as a helper in the local Presentation Convent. An attractive girl, she took to going out, liked dances, practical jokes, cross-dressing, and boys. With her father gone, another of her mother's brothers, Tommy, assumed control. Uncle Tommy was extremely protective of Nora and was angry, for example, to learn she had been seeing a Protestant boy named Willie Mulvagh (spelt 'Mulvey' in *Ulysses*), who was three years her senior.

4 Nassau Street (F4), where on 10 June 1904 Joyce made a pass at Nora. Notice the various modes of transport, the beautifully laid-out tramway, the bicycles, the horse and carriage, all under the watchful eye of the traffic policeman. Notice also the adverts for Amstel Lager Beers, Jeyes, and Canada Life (above Morton's shop), the man halfway up the ladder painting the Empire Billiard Room, the 'cheap sale now proceeding' at Racine, and the shop at the corner, Yeates and Son. In *Ulysses* Leopold Bloom is struck by the German fieldglasses in this shop and thinks of Germans 'making their way everywhere. Sell on easy terms to capture trade' (*U* 8.555). The time is 4.45 p.m., the number 129 tram is on its way to Nelson's Pillar in Sackville Street, and not one person is bare-headed. *Courtesy of the National Library of Ireland.*

Nora had many admirers – that is unexceptional. More remarkable is the fact that two of them died young. The first was Michael Feeney, who contracted typhoid and pneumonia and died aged sixteen in 1897. The other was Michael Bodkin, who, on hearing that Nora was leaving Galway for Dublin, rose from his sickbed, set off through the rain, and, according to Gretta Conroy's account in 'The Dead', attracted her attention by throwing a stone up against the window. '– I implored of him to go home at once and told him he would get his death in the rain. But he said he did not want to live' (*D* 221). Not long afterwards he died of tuberculosis.

Nora grew up in a small-town, provincial atmosphere. There were no bright lights, and dances were held not in glittering ballrooms but at crossroads where town and country met. When her biographer writes that Nora was 'irretrievably urban' or that she would 'explore the streets of Galway and Eyre Square',[4] she forgets that Galway, with a population of less than 14,000 in 1891, was a city only in name, and was more like a county town serving a rural hinterland than a thriving metropolis. Gretta captures it precisely in her description of Michael Furey and herself: 'We used to go out together, walking, you know, Gabriel, like the way they do in the country' (*D* 221). Not that Galway was without interest. The city's historical association with Spain is evident in the Spanish Arch and the Spanish Parade, where Spanish merchants and their families used to promenade. There is also a self-contained fishing quarter known as the Claddagh (Gaelic for 'beach'), where in former times the men and women of the tribes of Galway lived, refusing to mix with neighbouring clans. The Claddagh was Galway's 'Irishtown', the home of Claddagh rings, where the fisherwomen

wore a traditional costume of blue cloak, red petticoat and handkerchief.

Notwithstanding Galway's charm, at the earliest opportunity Nora escaped to Dublin. There she found work as a domestic in Finn's Hotel on Leinster Street (F4). After meeting Joyce, she spent her free evenings with him, much to the annoyance of Joyce's brother Stanislaus and of his friends at the time, Oliver St John Gogarty and Vincent Cosgrave. Joyce and Nora exchanged numerous letters – turn-of-the-century Dublin had five postal deliveries a day – and were soon professing love for each other. Joyce's other commitments that summer – to singing and to writing – were all profoundly affected by this new relationship. At the end of August 1904, he again appeared on a concert platform with John McCormack. 'Mr James A. Joyce,' wrote

the music correspondent of the *Freeman's Journal*, 'the possessor of a sweet tenor voice, sang charmingly "The Salley Gardens", and gave a pathetic rendering of "The Croppy Boy"' (*JJ* 168 n.). A week before, on 22 August 1904, in the Antient Concert Rooms on Great Brunswick Street (F4 unmarked), Joyce sang about an Irish girl who preferred the 'Coulin' (an Irish boy with flowing locks) to the English stranger.

It was the first occasion on which Nora heard Joyce perform in public. Moore's song of exile, 'Though the Last Glimpse of Erin', seems particularly appropriate given that Joyce and Nora were, within ten weeks, to leave Ireland effectively for ever:

In exile thy bosom shall still be my home,
And thine eyes make my climate wherever we roam.

Nora was ever associated in Joyce's mind with exile: as Richard says of Bertha at the end of *Exiles*, she was his 'bride in exile' (*E* 143). Exile gave to their relationship, as well as to Joyce's writing about Ireland, an intensity and a purpose that might otherwise have been missing.

The same August of 1904 witnessed the publication of 'The Sisters' – signed 'Stephen Daedalus' – in George Russell's *Irish Homestead* and the composition of the emigration story 'Eveline', which was published in the same magazine on 10 September. Significant changes were also under way in Joyce's other relationships. In early September, Gogarty invited him to share his accommodation in the Martello Tower at Sandycove. Joyce stayed only some five nights, and left after an incident which marked the final break with his erstwhile drinking companion.

Nora Joyce was a capable woman. She was not like Eveline, sitting at the window 'watching the evening invade the avenue' (*D* 36), but more like her own mother, independent and strong-willed. She was also intelligent as her later fluency in French, German, and Italian suggests. In spite of Joyce's many promptings, however, Nora seems to have kept a portion of her life hidden from him. Joyce never quite got the measure of Nora, or – to express it somewhat differently – he never exhausted converting her life into literature. For her part, she never idolized him, even after he became famous in Paris in the 1920s. When Joyce was at home writing, he often wore a white coat so as to maximize the light for his poor eyesight. But if he ever emerged to welcome guests dressed in this way, he would be censured by Nora. 'For God's sake, Jim, take that coat off you!' She referred to *Ulysses* as 'Oolissays', *Finnegans Wake* as 'that chop suey', and would shout in to him in the room where he was working, 'Now, Jim, stop writing or stop laughing'.[5] Of her life in Paris she once complained to her sister, 'There's one thing I hate – going out to dinner and sitting with artists till 1:00 in the morning. They'd bore you stiff, Kathleen' (*JJ* 639).

Few women would have had the courage in 1904 to elope with a man to an uncertain destination in continental Europe without the protection of marriage. Nora also had the composure not to be troubled by the snobbery of Joyce's friends and family, especially his father. It took John Joyce several years to come round to approving of Nora as a fit partner for the boy whom he had sent to the best school in Ireland. On learning of Nora Barnacle's surname, he remarked somewhat caustically that, with a name like that, 'she'll never leave him'.[6] When Nora and Joyce were saying their separate goodbyes to friends and relations at the North Wall (G4) in October 1904, John Joyce was the only person there who did not know his son had a travelling companion. Bertha may not have been, as Robert in *Exiles* suavely tells Richard, his 'equal', but she was determined that neither Richard nor any of Beatrice's 'clan' would ever 'humble' her (*E* 45, 67, 128). Joyce must have been particularly struck by Nora's defiance.

NORA THE FEMALE CHARACTER

Nora occupies such a large space in Joyce's writing that it is impossible to imagine his work without her. Gretta Conroy in 'The Dead', Bertha in *Exiles*, Molly Bloom in *Ulysses*, and Anna Livia Plurabelle in *Finnegans Wake* – all have their source in the person of Nora. Indeed, the moment Joyce met Nora, he started writing about her or about his feelings for her – witness the

8 'What a time you were, she said.' Bloom and Molly in the less anxious earlier episode of 'Calypso'. Pen and wash drawing by the Leeds artist John Jones. *Courtesy of John Jones.*

What a time you were, she said.

summer 1904 letters and the elopement story· 'Eveline', written in August 1904. The dominant female character in the novel begun before June 1904 is at once out of reach, an object of desire, and the Muse of inspiration; after June 1904, the characters who are biographically linked with Nora are more complex; they are married, in possession of a past, and refuse to be put on a pedestal. There is a complexity also in Joyce's identification with Nora. A relatively uncomplicated sympathy soon gives way to a more problematic relationship, which often betrays the intensity of his anxiety.

56

Molly Bloom represents Joyce's most complete identification with Nora, and the association is in the first instance carried in the voice. Molly's soliloquy – both like and unlike a letter the reader has an opportunity of secretly reading – is wholly engrossing, a welcome return to the initial style of the first half of *Ulysses*. Molly's voice is unsentimental, gossipy, never coarse, full of Irish cadences; its pitch is always unmistakable, self-authenticating. Reading Nora's letters Joyce must have been impressed with their intimacy, their chattiness, and their disregard for the difference between writing and speech. Molly's thoughts, everywhere accompanied by the simultaneous absence of punctuation and the profusion of 'speech-markers', constantly surprise us by their sudden shifts of mood and comic juxtapositions:

> he never can explain a thing simply the way a body can understand then he goes and burns the bottom out of the pan all for his kidney this one not so much there's the mark of his teeth still where he tried to bite the nipple I had to scream out aren't they fearful trying to hurt you I had a great breast of milk with Milly enough for two he said I could have got a pound a week as a wet nurse from the Belladonna all swelled out the morning that delicate looking student that stopped in no. 28 with the Citrons Penrose nearly caught me washing through the window what was his studenting only for I snapped up the towel to my face hurt me they used to weaning her till he got doctor Brady to give me the Belladonna prescription I had to get him to suck them they were so hard he said it was sweeter and thicker than cows then he wanted to milk me into the tea well he's beyond everything I declare somebody ought to put him in the budget if I only could remember one half of the things and write a book out of it the works of Master Poldy yes

Ms 1. *Courtesy of The Huntington Library.*

he never can explain a thing simply the way a body can understand then he goes and burns the bottom out of the pan all for his Kidney this one not so much theres the mark of his teeth still where he tried to bite the nipple I had to scream out arent they fearful trying to hurt you I had a great breast of milk with Milly enough for two what was the reason of that he said I could have got a pound a week as a wet nurse all swelled out the morning that delicate looking student that stopped in no 28 with the Citrons Penrose nearly caught me washing through the window only for I snapped up the towel to my face that was his studenting hurt me they used to weaning her till he got doctor Brady to give me the belladonna prescription I had to get him to suck them they were so hard he said it was sweeter and thicker than cows then he wanted to milk me into the tea well hes beyond everything I declare somebody ought to put him in the budget if I only could remember the 1 half of the things and write a book out of it the works of Master Poldy yes

(*U* 18.566–80)

Molly's thoughts move rapidly from a general observation arising from Bloom's attempt in 'Calypso' to define metamorphosis – 'he came out with some jawbreakers about the incarnation' – to memories of Bloom biting her nipple after the birth of Milly. The passage is tied to the physical world with a close-up picture of Molly attending to her body – 'theres the mark of his teeth'. Molly remembers the pain but she also enjoys the memory: Bloom sucking her and comparing her milk to a cow's; Bloom's suggestion that he milk her into the tea; her own humorous way of defending herself and returning her body to the human world of language – 'I declare somebody ought to put him in the budget'. In Homeric terms Molly is both Calypso and Penelope, both

the alluring object of desire, namely the body, and the weaver of memories.

The voice is so distinctive here that we almost forget that the words are *written* – even the upper-case 'Kidney' in the printed version we assume is a typographical error rather than a cue for reading. Similarly, with the form: Molly's soliloquy is oral, private, an 'interior monologue' – not like a letter, for a letter is addressed to someone. And yet, as the process of composition reminds us, Molly's thoughts *were* composed, with Joyce constantly adding to and refining what he had written. Dropping the apostrophe before s came later in that process; although it reads as if it were there from the start, the phrase 'well he's beyond everything' is a later addition; and Joyce still had not settled on how to write '1' in the phrase 'the 1 half of the things' (a phrase which echoes the remark in Joyce's letter to Stanislaus of November 1906: 'I forget half the things I wanted to do'). Or take words like 'body' and 'metamorphosis', which Molly uses unconsciously. These trigger for the reader echoes from their association with Bloom and Stephen. In 'Lotus Eaters', Bloom is addressed by McCoy with the remark '– How's the body?' (*U* 5.86), while Stephen in 'Proteus' wrestles with the philosophical issue of change. Molly's soliloquy represents Joyce's return, the figure who encloses, who includes the opposition of the citizen and the artist, the body and mind, father and son, Bloom and Stephen.

Joyce's celebration of the female body combines a similar embracing of the close-up and the distanced view, both the unconscious physical detail and a consciously worked structuring of the material. We glimpse in Molly's soliloquy Joyce's delight in putting into words the female experience of breast-feeding, menstruation, passing water, masturbation, making love and having an orgasm. The link is there with Nora. In the early years of their relationship, Joyce enjoyed listening to Nora use the chamber pot, an activity that suggested a title for his first collection of poems – *Chamber Music*, or 'Shamebred Music' as he calls it in *Finnegans Wake* (164.15–16). Throughout Molly's soliloquy, Nora is present, ceaselessly criss-crossing the border between life and art, between the body and language. Molly is a woman in her thirties, as was Nora when 'Penelope' was being written in 1921. But Molly is not Nora; she is Joyce's imagination of the absent Nora. Once again the inconsequential private experience becomes part of a larger patterning: Molly's chamber pot in 'Penelope' is 'orangekeyed' and thus is linked to Mr Deasy's Northern political sympathies, the House of Keyes, and the wider symbolism of keys:

```
                                          I better not make
an allnight sitting on this affair they ought to make them a bit
bigger so that a woman could sit on it properly he kneels down to
do it I suppose there isn't in all creation another man with the
habits he has look at the way he's sleeping at the foot of the bed
it's well he doesn't kick or he might knock out all my teeth
```

Ms 2.   *Courtesy of the State University of New York at Buffalo.*

I better not make an alnight sitting on this affair they ought to make chambers a natural size so that a woman could sit on it properly he kneels down to do it I suppose there isnt in all creation another man with the habits he has look at the way hes sleeping at the foot of the bed how can he without a hard bolster its well he doesnt kick or he might knock out all my teeth

(*U* 18.1195–200)

The changes in the process of composition

here underline Joyce's inventiveness. The phrase 'a bit bigger' becomes 'a natural size'; 'allnight' is shortened to the less educated 'alnight'; 'how can he without a hard bolster' is a later insertion, another detail added to the 'flow' of Molly's thoughts.

Joyce relishes imagining what it must be like to be a woman. Molly looks at her breasts and her nipples, the cultural meanings they possess, and the beauty of the female form compared with the male nude:

2 the same in case of twins theyre supposed to represent beauty placed up there like those statues in the museum one of them pretending to hide it with her hand are they so beautiful of course compared with what a man looks like with his two bags full and his other thing hanging down out of him or sticking up at you like a hatrack no wonder they hide it with a cabbageleaf [see *Ms 3*]

(*U* 18.539–44)

What does a woman think about the female body? What does she think about the male body? What does she think a man thinks about the female body? What does a man think about a woman thinking about the female body? Joyce celebrates the female form but he does so by restraining a lingering lyrical impulse. To Molly, the body is both endlessly fascinating and absurd. Joyce does not scoff but allows Molly's folk medicine to stand on its own – 'cabbageleaf' and all. The changes here between typescript and final version show how some of the best moments in 'Penelope' were written 'between the lines' as it were.

From language and the body to desire. Molly is not just a body composed of physical organs; nor is she simply an object of desire; she also possesses a body that desires. In his portrayal of Molly, Joyce attends to all these aspects. In this regard,

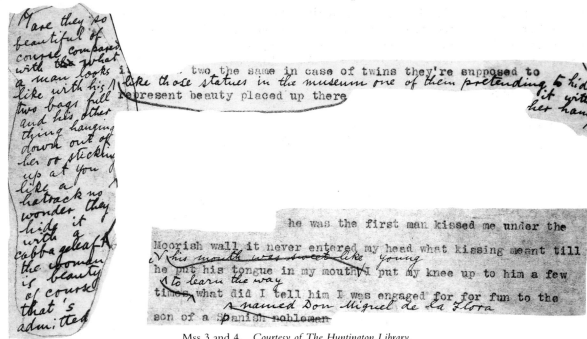

two the same in case of twins they're supposed to *like those statues in the museum one of them* represent beauty placed up there *pretending to hide it with her hand*

are they so beautiful of course compared with the what a man looks like with his two bags full and his other thing hanging down out of her or sticking up at you like a hatrack no wonder they hide it with a cabbageleaf the woman is beauty of course that's admitted

he was the first man kissed me under the Moorish wall it never entered my head what kissing meant till *his mouth was sweet like young* he put his tongue in my mouth *I* put my knee up to him a few *to learn the way* times what did I tell him I was engaged for for fun to the *named Don Miguel de la Flora* son of a Spanish nobleman

Mss 3 and 4. *Courtesy of The Huntington Library.*

Joyce shows us how Molly is a creature of her past, and in particular how her sexual imagination is coloured by her Gibraltar childhood and adolescence. Joyce evokes Molly's childhood in Gibraltar as if it were Nora's childhood in the Gibraltar of Ireland, namely the 'Spanish' city of Galway. Molly inherited from her Spanish mother, Lunita Laredo, dark eyes and an attractive figure. She is proud of her body and she loves the image of darkness and what it signifies for her: 'a lot of that touching must go on in theatres in the crush in the dark' (*U* 18.1039–40). Governing her sexual imagination are memories of sexual arousal on Gibraltar 'under the Moorish wall':

> he was the first man kissed me under the Moorish wall my sweetheart when a boy it never entered my head what kissing meant till he put his tongue in my mouth his mouth was sweetlike young I put my

knee up to him a few times to learn the way what did I tell him I was engaged for for fun to the son of a Spanish nobleman named Don Miguel de la Flora and he believed me that I was to be married to him in 3 years time theres many a true word spoken in jest there is a flower that bloometh a few things I told him true about myself just for him to be imagining the Spanish girls he didnt like [see Ms 4] (*U* 18.769–77)

Later in the episode, Molly recalls kissing Bloom on Howth Head, 'the day I got him to propose to me yes first I gave him the bit of seedcake out of my mouth' (*U* 18.1573–4), and this, too, is accompanied by memories of sexual encounters amid a culture which Molly makes exotic and erotic. The following lines from the earliest stage of composition mark the final sequence of 'Penelope'.

59

one true thing he said in his life and the sun shining for you today yes that was why I liked him because I saw he understood or felt what a woman is and I knew I could always get round him and I gave him all the pleasure I could leading him on till he asked me to say yes and I wouldn't answer first only looked out over the sea and the sky I was thinking of so many things he didn't know of Mulvey and Mr Stanhope and Hester and father and old captain Groves and the sailors playing all birds fly and I say stoop and washing up dishes they called it on the pier and the sentry in front of the governors house with the thing round his white helmet poor devil half roasted and the Spanish girls laughing in their shawls and their tall combs and the auctions in the morning the Greeks and the jews and the Arabs and the devil knows who else from all the ends of Europe and Duke street and the fowl market all clucking outside Larby Sharons and the poor donkeys slipping half asleep and the vague fellows in the cloaks asleep in the shade on the steps and the big wheels of the carts of the bulls and the old castle thousands of years old yes and those handsome Moors all in white and turbans like kings asking you to sit down in their little bit of a shop and Ronda with the old windows of the posadas glancing eyes a lattice hid for her lover to kiss the iron and the wineshops half open at night and the castanets and the night we missed the boat at Algeciras the watchman going about serene with his lamp and O that awful deepdown torrent O and the sea the sea crimson sometimes like fire and the glorious sunsets and the figtrees in the Alameda gardens and Gibraltar as a girl where I was a flower of the mountain and how he kissed me under the Moorish wall and I thought well as well him as another and then I asked him with my eyes to ask again and then he asked me would I to say yes my mountain flower and first I put my arms around him and drew him down to me so he could feel my breasts all perfume and I said I will yes.

Trieste — Zurich — Paris
1914 — 1921

Ms 5. *Courtesy of the State University of New York at Buffalo.*

one true thing he said in his life and the sun shining for you today yes that was why I liked him because I saw he understood or felt what a woman is and I knew I could always get round him and I gave him all the pleasure I could leading him on till he asked me to say yes and I wouldn't answer first only looked out over the sea and the sky I was thinking of so many things he didn't know of Mulvey and Mr Stanhope and Hester and father and old captain Groves and the Alameda gardens and Gibraltar as a girl where I was a flower of the mountain and how he kissed me under the Moorish wall and I thought well as well him as another and then I asked him with my eyes to ask again and then he asked me would I to say yes my mountain flower and first I put my arms around him and drew him down to me so he could feel my breasts all perfume and I said I will yes.

Trieste — Zurich — Paris
1914 — 1921

Ms 5. *Courtesy of the State University of New York at Buffalo.*

9 (*facing page*) Windmill Hill Road in Gibraltar. In 'Penelope' Molly remembers walking up this hill: 'I went up Windmill hill to the flats that Sunday morning with captain Rubios that was dead spyglass like the sentry had he said hed have one or two from on board I wore that frock from the B Marche paris and the coral necklace the straits shining I could see over to Morocco almost the bay of Tangier white and the Atlas mountain with snow on it and the straits like a river so clear Harry Molly darling I was thinking of him on the sea all the time after at mass when my petticoat began to slip down at the elevation weeks and weeks I kept the handkerchief under my pillow for the smell of him' (*U* 18.856–64). When Joyce was composing this episode, as Card (1984) reminds us, he had in front of him *A History of Gibraltar and Its Sieges* (1870) by Frederick Stephens, Henry Field's *Gibraltar* (1889), and the *Gibraltar Directory* of 1902, all of which he put to good use. (From *Picturesque Europe*, 1876–9.)

60

It was at this point that Joyce drew a line and added the names of his continental cities and the dates within which the work had been composed. But 'Penelope' was still some way from being completed, as can be seen from the way he expanded these few lines into some thirty in the final version. In September 1921 – less than five months away from the date of publication – Joyce, 'the last word in stolentelling' (*FW* 424.35), wrote to Budgen seeking more material for 'Penelope'; he wanted for example the words to the song 'In Old Madrid'.

The more closely we examine Molly Bloom's soliloquy, the more perhaps it discloses Joyce's anxiety in his identification

10 An Edwardian colour postcard. 'Bosom I saw, both full, throat warbling. First I saw. She thanked me. Why did she me? Fate. Spanishy eyes. Under a peartree alone patio this hour in old Madrid one side in shadow Dolores shedolores' (*U* 11.731–4). These are among Bloom's earliest memories of 'Spanishy' Molly. In 'Penelope', after recalling Boylan's dull love letters, Molly romantically imagines singing 'In Old Madrid' to Stephen: 'will I ever go back there again all new faces two glancing eyes a lattice hid Ill sing that for him theyre my eyes if hes anything of a poet two eyes as darkly bright as loves own star arent those beautiful words' (*U* 18.1338–40).

with Nora. Often this comes in momentary asides, as for example in the reference to the Claddagh ring, possibly given Molly by a former lover (*U* 18.866), or in her thought that 'Mulveys was the first' (*U* 18.748), or as in the final passage of 'so many things he didnt know of Mulvey' (*U* 18.1582). Joyce may be doing no more than play with the idea of being an outsider, a cuckold. The beguiling frankness of 'Penelope' – the 'clou' of the book, as Joyce once called it (*Letters* I. 170), the topper, the star turn – seems all-enveloping. But given his obsession with Nora's previous sexual partners, such asides carry an autobiographical trace. During

61

> A few light taps upon the pane made him turn to the window. It had begun to snow again. He watched sleepily the flakes, silver and dark, falling obliquely against the lamplight. The time had come for him to set out on his journey westward. Yes, the newspapers were right: snow was general all over Ireland. It was falling on every part of the dark central plain, on the treeless hills, falling softly upon the Bog of Allen, and, farther westward, softly falling into the dark mutinous Shannon waves. It was falling, too, upon every part of the lonely churchyard on the hill where Michael Furey lay buried. It lay thickly drifted on the crooked crosses and headstones, on the spears of the little gate, on the barren thorns. His soul swooned slowly as he heard the snow falling faintly through the universe, and faintly falling, like the descent of their last end, upon all the living and the dead.

She Weeps over Rahoon

Rain on Rahoon falls softly, softly falling,
Where my dark lover lies.
Sad is his voice that calls me, sadly calling,
At grey moonrise.

Love, hear thou
How soft, how sad his voice is ever calling,
Ever unanswered and the dark rain falling
Then as now.

Dark too our hearts, O love, shall lie and cold
As his sad heart has lain
Under the moongrey nettles, the black mould
And muttering rain.

three periods Joyce's anxiety about Nora deserves special notice – Nora's sexual life before June 1904, during Joyce's stay in Dublin in 1909, and in the writing of *Exiles* in 1913–15.

Part of Joyce's aim when he began composing 'The Dead' in September 1906 was to capture something of the 'ingenuous insularity and hospitality' of his city and country. To the widely travelled Joyce, Ireland was 'more beautiful naturally in my opinion than what I have seen of England, Switzerland, France, Austria or Italy' (*Letters* II. 166). Only in Dublin and Paris did he feel at his ease. 'The Dead' was to compensate for the one-sidedness of the other stories of *Dubliners*. But in the process of writing the story, or composing it in his mind, Joyce's doubts about Nora's past lovers were rekindled. Or at least this is what we gather from the end of the story. Gretta and Gabriel return to the Gresham Hotel (F3); Gretta falls asleep, while Gabriel stares out of a window, reflecting on the image of snow falling all over Ireland. In his mind he follows the snow westward, back towards the source of the story and the graveyard at Rahoon (see *Ms 6*).

'The Dead' closes with Gabriel's reverie, but the train of thought leading back to Rahoon continued to disturb Joyce. In 1912, five years after completing the story, Joyce returned to Ireland and visited the cemetery at Oughterard, where he imagined 'Michael Furey' was buried. There he found a headstone with 'J. Joyce' on it, 'an occult verification', as Ellmann puts it, 'of the journey westward of Gabriel in "The Dead"' (*JJ* 325). 'The Dead' was still fresh in Joyce's mind or revived by his journey west, for a similar highly charged mood, this time viewed initially from Nora's perspective, is evoked in 'She Weeps Over Rahoon', a poem written in August 1912:

11 'He used to sing that song, *The Lass of Aughrim*. He was very delicate. . . . I can see him so plainly. . . . Such eyes as he had: big dark eyes! And such an expression in them – an expression! . . . He died when he was only seventeen. Isn't it a terrible thing to die so young as that?' (*D* 219). Anjelica Huston as Gretta Conroy in John Huston's film of *The Dead*. Donal McCann looks on anxiously amid the shadows. *Courtesy of Zenith Productions and Liffey Films Inc.*

'She Weeps Over Rahoon' is Joyce's attempt to capture Nora's 'Other', his vain hope of renewing his power over her and exorcizing the ghost of Michael Bodkin. The first stanza is spoken from Nora's viewpoint; the second stanza addresses her present 'Love', presumably Joyce; the final stanza is perhaps the same person or Joyce himself sympathizing with the first speaker. Identifying with Nora, seeing the world from her viewpoint, is Joyce's characteristic mode as she emerges in the composite figure of Gretta-Bertha-Molly-Anna Livia. But such identification is under particular strain in this poem, as if Joyce sensed a resistance to his encroachments on Nora's memories. The 'too' of the last stanza rings false, while the rain that falls in the first stanza has been uncertainly transformed into 'muttering rain'. In spite of the trance-like rhythms, there is no stilling of Joyce's anxiety.

'The Dead', then, did not expunge Joyce's feelings of jealousy but seems further to have complicated the relationship between experience and writing: his writing now no longer simply trailed behind experience but circled anxiously round an already established pattern of experience in writing. Three years earlier, in the autumn of 1909, as noted in Chapter 2, Joyce returned to Ireland from Trieste without Nora to explore the prospects of work in his native city. This was a distressing time for him, since Vincent Cosgrave suggested – falsely – that during the summer of 1904 he too had been intimate with Nora. Joyce demanded that Nora tell him the truth. A heated correspondence ensued, during which Nora asked him to forget the ignorant Galway girl who had come across his life. This provoked a reply, in a letter dated 19 November 1909, as moving as any passage in Joyce's fiction, a measure both of his distraught state and of

his absolute dependence on Nora. He had returned to Finn's Hotel, trying to recapture something of her presence, her 'mysterious beauty.' He begins the letter without a salutation, addresses Nora in the third person, and ends the letter without signing it.

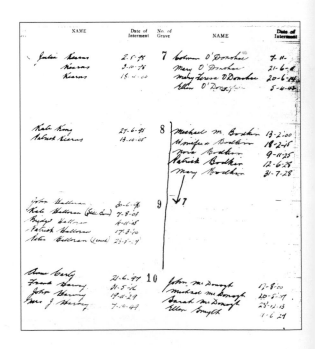

12 Michael Maria Bodkin's grave in Rahoon Cemetery, Galway. A student at University College, Galway, he died when he was twenty. Nora was then fifteen. *Photograph the author.*

13 Michael Bodkin's name in the Rahoon Cemetery Register. *Photograph the author. Courtesy of Galway Corporation.*

64

Ms 8. (The rest of this beautiful letter can be found in pages 266–7 of *Letters* II). *Courtesy of the Library of Cornell University.*

Joyce's Victorian sensibility shines through such lines, and though it is slightly overdone there is genuine hurt here. 'A strange land this is to me though I was born in it and bear one of its old names', in a strange house, with a strange girl, who has strange beautiful blue eyes. A 'stranger' in Irish culture is often associated with the foreigner and especially with the English: the harp in 'Two Gallants' seems weary of the eyes of 'strangers' (*D* 54); 'we want no more strangers in our house', the Citizen warns in 'Cyclops' (*U* 12.1150–1). Joyce, however, feels an outsider for a different reason. The Irish, he notices, 'stare at me in the street though I was born among them' (*Letters* II. 255). He even admits to loathing Ireland and the Irish.

All this material, overlaid with other experiences from Trieste and from his subsequent visit to Dublin in 1912, surfaces, painfully and at times embarrassingly, in Joyce's only extant play. The themes of *Exiles* – suspicion, guilt, betrayal, loyalty, the male view of women – revolve around sexual jealousy, with the interest of the play shifting from Richard to Bertha. Richard is full of contradictory feelings. He desires Bertha entirely for himself, but he also wants her to have complete liberty. '[I]n the very core of my ignoble heart', he tells Robert, 'I longed to be betrayed by you and by her – in the dark, in the night – secretly, meanly, craftily'. Bertha 'has spoken always of her innocence, as I have spoken always of my guilt, humbling me' (*E* 87). When alone with his wife, Richard confesses, 'I have a wild delight in my soul, Bertha, as I look at you. I see you as you are yourself.' But her relationship with Robert has unbalanced him: 'That I came first in your life or before him then – that may be nothing to you. You may be his more than mine' (*E* 94). When Bertha is on her own with Robert she tells him, 'You know the kind he is. He asks about everything. The ins and outs' (*E* 102). At the end of the play Bertha tries to re-assure her husband of her love, but Richard

65

speaks of the 'deep wound of doubt in my soul'.

I have wounded my soul for you — a deep wound of doubt which can never be healed. I can never know, never in this world. I do not wish to know or to believe. I do not care. It is not in the darkness of belief that I desire you. But in restless living wounding doubt. To hold you by no bonds, even of love, to be united with you in body and soul in utter nakedness.

Ms 9 (*E* 144). *Courtesy of the Beinecke Rare Book and Manuscript Library, Yale University.*

Fittingly, however, Bertha is allowed the final speech, and she pleads for renewal and a return to the early days of their courtship: 'Forget me and love me again as you did the first time. . . . O, my strange wild lover, come back to me again!' (*E* 145).

The case against *Exiles* can seem over-powering. Propelled almost entirely by Joyce's deep-rooted psychological fears about Nora's unfaithfulness, the play lacks the Joycean lightness of touch and the re-assuring Irish voice. Normally, Joyce is his own master, but *Exiles* seems weighed down by one of its models, *When We Dead Awaken* (1899) – Ibsen's last play, which Joyce had championed as an undergraduate. In the themes, imagery, tone, and content of the play and in its references to Bertha being Richard's 'work', in that he has given her new life and then killed her, Joyce's debt to Ibsen is discernible throughout. In *Exiles*, the transmutation of life into art is both too direct and not direct enough. The dialogue

66

seems modelled on actual conversations between Joyce and Nora – or what we assume took place between them – and, by comparison with the letter quoted above, it is often awkward and self-conscious. Indeed, although she is Irish, Bertha sug-gests an Ibsen heroine returning to her town amid the fjords.

Without *Exiles*, however, Joyce's œuvre would be significantly diminished. The play is an honest and, some would argue, profound, meditation on 'marriage'[7] on the way love is 'so unnatural a phenomenon that it can scarcely repeat itself' (*E* 147), and on the transgressive nature of human sexuality as seen through a man's eyes. Ensnared in Richard's sexual fantasies, the unmarried Bertha is involved in a struggle to retain her independence. She has to separate the language of freedom that Richard employs on her behalf (which is actually another form of oppression) from his psychological warfare that threatens her freedom. What is impressive is the way she stands her ground and battles through. To Beatrice she declares somewhat bitterly:

(bitterly) Ideas and ideas! But the people in this world have other ideas or pretend to. They have to put up with him in spite of his ideas because he is able to do something. Me no. I am nothing.

Ms 10 (*E* 127). *Courtesy of the Beinecke Rare Book and Manuscript Library, Yale University.*

And for Richard she invokes a vocabulary similar to the one Joyce used in his 1909 letter:

14 Roberto Prezioso was editor of *Il Piccolo della Sera*, the Triestine daily newspaper to which Joyce contributed several important articles on Irish culture and politics. Joyce's jealousy was aroused when in 1911–12 Prezioso began making advances to Nora. This photograph was taken on 13 March 1913 outside the Hotel de Ville in Trieste. From left to right: Silvio Benco, Sabatino Lopez, Sem Benelli, Dr Attilio Tamaro, Preziozo, Arturo Ziffer, and Marino de Szombathely. Benco worked for *Il Piccolo* and took a long-term interest in Joyce's work. Tamaro was one of Joyce's pupils and in 1907 invited him to give three public lectures on Ireland at the Università del Popolo. Szombathely appears in *Ulysses* as Bloom's Hungarian grandfather: 'Szombathely begat Virag and Virag begat Bloom' (*U* 15.1868). *Courtesy of Civici Musei di Storia ed Arte, Trieste.*

Ms 11 (*E* 133). *Courtesy of the Beinecke Rare Book and Manuscript Library, Yale University.*

This is Joyce mixing voices and identities. In one respect, the play is not unlike an act of reparation to Nora for having taken her into exile. In another respect, so pervasive is the psychological displacement at work here that it is hard to disentangle Joyce's voice either from Nora's or from his relationship with Nora. Through suffering, for example, through being tempted to sin with Robert,

Bertha rediscovers her virgin soul again: 'Forget me and love me again as you did the first time' (*E* 145). But it is unclear if this is Joyce speaking on behalf of Nora, on his own behalf, or on behalf of Nora for his own sake.

The pursuit of Nora in Joyce's writings is shadowed by another fraught relationship. Gabriel Conroy's thoughts drift westward over the Bog of Allen towards the 'mutinous Shannon waves' (*D* 223). When the wider context of Irish history is recalled, Joyce's use of the word 'mutinous' is especially suggestive; mutinous links Gabriel's inability to rule either his wife's or his own emotions with the hidden Ireland driven underground in the eighteenth century by the Protestant Ascendancy. Perhaps the autobiographical pressure is most in evidence at this point, for Nora's origins, like

Gretta's, lay on the other side of the dark mutinous Shannon waves.

A pattern suggests itself here between Dublin versus the West, male versus female, husband versus wife. Joyce is a Dubliner, and part of the strangeness he experienced in 1909 in his own country stemmed from the strangeness of the male Dubliner *vis-à-vis* the 'female' west of Ireland. He calls Nora 'you dear strange little girl', 'the little curious Galway girl', and 'my little Galway bride' (*Letters* II. 254, 249, 242). He loves in Nora 'the beauty and doom of the race of whom I am a child' (*Letters* II. 267). He tries singing 'your song *The Lass of Aughrim*' only to find his voice trembling 'with emotion' (*Letters* II. 242). Paradoxically – and this time unlike Gabriel Conroy – it is through Nora's strangeness that Joyce overcomes his estrangement, re-establishes his purity, and renews his feelings for his city and country.

Nora helped Joyce come to terms with his guilt as a Dubliner, and in this regard we might read 'Penelope', with its deliberately prosaic and domestic attitude to life, as a celebration not only of Nora but also of the hidden Ireland too often seen in masculinist heroic terms. Molly knows, as does Joyce, that woman is the assuager of male guilt and the Comforter – more impressive, more relevant, and more comic than the tragic Cathleen ni Houlihan or the Poor Old Woman: men are 'so weak and puling when theyre sick they want a woman to get well if his nose bleeds youd think it was O tragic' (*U*: 18.23–4).

EN/GENDERING JOYCE

In recent years Joyce and gender has been the subject of considerable, often lively, critical disagreement among feminists. To Marilyn French, 'Joyce's approach to sexuality [is]

primarily one of exposure'. 'By making Bloom the most extreme and ridiculous exemplar of human sexuality in the novel – perhaps in any novel – he insists that we accept also that part of Bloom, and consequently that part of ourselves.'[8] In *Joyce and Feminism* (1984), Bonnie Kime Scott stresses 'the female strands of Joyce's experience', and at one point engagingly confesses that Joyce 'gets at my vulnerable places': 'I feel mocked for the feminine wiles I have occasionally practised and the consumerist vanities I have indulged in, as did Adrienne Monnier in reading "Nausicaa".'[9] Julia Kristeva, on the other hand, admires Joyce not for expressing the female but for writing the feminine.[10] To Kristeva, Joyce is 'unreadable', his texts impossible to 'be reduced to representation', part of a revolution in poetic language centring on what she refers to as 'the semiotic *chora*'.[11]

Other feminists have taken their cue from different sources and emerged with different emphases. Christine van Boheemen provides a Lacanian reading of *Ulysses* and shows how the text 'rests upon the strategy of using the successful inscription of the "other" (in Joyce, woman) as legitimation for the new signifying practice'.[12] Frances Restuccia, deploying Deleuze's anti-Oedipal theory of masochism, argues that Joyce, in the movement from realism to textuality in *Ulysses*, transforms the stick into the pen.[13]

The issue of female language has received special attention. Sandra Gilbert and Susan Gubar take Joyce to task for transforming the *materna lingua* (mother tongue) into a *patrius sermo* (a father speech), for silencing 'precisely the chaos which seemed to refuse to be silenced – what Julia Kristeva sees as the uncontrollable "*semiotique*" of non-sense – into a cosmos of controllable common sense(s)'.[14] The interest in female language issues naturally in concern with the female

17 Henry Sharpe's drawing prompts the question: How much did Joyce's imagination owe to Nora? Who engendered whom? (From Mairéad Byrne and Henry J. Sharpe, *Joyce – A Clew*, Dublin: Bluett and Co., 1981.) *Courtesy of Henry Sharpe.*

18 'The dark mutinous Shannon waves' (*D* 223). The river Shannon at Limerick looking towards Sarsfield Bridge. In 1690 Patrick Sarsfield led one of the last attempts to prevent Ireland falling to William of Orange, skilfully defending the walls of Limerick against him. The following year the Dutch general managed to cross the Shannon, and at the Battle of Aughrim he inflicted the final defeat on the Jacobite cause in Ireland. *Photograph Dan Harper*.

voices in Joyce. In this respect, Shari Benstock, following Derrida, links the difficulty of reading the *Wake* with the 'riddle of femininity in the woman's body':

When man has tried to read the riddle, he has stripped woman of her complexity, emptied her of significance. By privileging the 'telling' of the *Wake*, the giving of priority to its spoken language, critics have silenced whole portions of *Wake* language in the denial of the link between woman and writing. The reader's effort is similar to Earwicker's: to possess knowledge (of his sin) by limiting that knowledge; to put a stop to the dissemination of the letter through the postal system; to deny desire and its effects; to censure the fear of castration that desire brings in its wake.[15]

The critical debate indicates how difficult it is to pin down Joyce.[16] The gulf between text and interpretation remains. Though his texts are grounded in so many specific details, they lend themselves to all kinds of abstract system-building. Some feminist critics assert that the Molly Bloom soliloquy represents Joyce's attack on the Law of the Father or that the flow of Molly's thoughts affords an example of 'feminine writing', or that this episode constitutes a paean to her body. I am tempted to make some large-scale interpretation of its meaning in the novel as a whole – about it marking the end of a journey, the passage from Stephen's no to Molly's yes. In any interpretation the reader is concerned with Joyce's position in this episode. Is he positioned as a man or as a woman? What attracts me about the Joycean text is its indeterminacy, its lack of certainty, the continuity and discontinuity between word and world; that what is being described could be described otherwise; the text's ability simultaneously to deride and

uphold. In other words I am more persuaded by the sheer volume of unfinished business Joyce has produced, by the cautionary sign hanging over his work: 'Don't jump to conclusions.'

Joyce's contexts

Joyce is a scandal, not only because he is the author of a 'blue' book but – perhaps more importantly today – because his texts resist interpretation. A tactical way of negotiating this difficulty or impasse – at least initially – is to attend to the contexts that contributed to Joyce's understanding of gender: the general ideas current at the time, his cultural milieu and literary heritage, his reading, the Irish context, his family background, his sexual relationships. In 1897, for example, there appeared an article in the *Illustrated English Magazine* entitled 'What It Must Be Like To Be Beautiful':

If a beautiful woman should set down, with unaffected frankness, her actual sensations and impressions on realising the effects of her beauty as she goes her way through life, what a clamour of envious spite would be provoked! Yet what a book it would be!... But no woman would ever write such a book. And, after all, is it not better so? If we knew all, idealism would be impossible, and without ideals what would life be worth?[17]

In 1896 *The Book of Beauty* was published, consisting of a series of articles by upper-class women interspersed with their portraits. One writer complains:

The bloodhound Realism is tracking Mystery to her secret places, and, as she flies, from every haunt where of old she loved to linger, some grace has vanished, some delicate delusion dies. Our so-called *fin-de-siècle* poets, painters, and novelists, care more for the interpretation than for the substance, and seek by weird combinations and unconventional treatment to express the inexpressible, their meaning being, so to speak, intentional, self-conscious mystery writ large in abnormal language.[18]

These passages act as sharp reminders of a climate of ideas that reached (down) even to Joyce. In the November 1909 letter to Nora, cited above, he writes: 'What a mysterious beauty clothes every place where she has lived!' (*Letters* II. 267). In the notes to *Exiles*, Nora is 'the earth, dark, formless, mother, made beautiful by the moonlit night, darkly conscious of her instincts' (*E* 151). Molly is Joyce's attempt to 'set down, with unaffected frankness, [a woman's] actual sensations and impressions on realising the effects of her beauty as she goes her way through life'. On the other hand, there is little that is mysterious about Molly, and her body is to her a source of interest rather than mystery. Joyce is a bloodhound realist, 'tracking Mystery to her secret places', but his intention is in part sacramental: to convert 'the bread of everyday life into something that has a permanent artistic life of its own' (*MBK* 104).

Joyce's understanding of gender also owes something to his literary predecessors, to his distaste for the prudery in much English Victorian fiction, and to his admiration for Flaubert. Molly Bloom can be seen as Joyce's intertextual 'reply' to Madame Bovary. There is a striking moment in 'Wandering Rocks' when 'a plump bare generous arm' (*U* 10.251) is observed throwing down a coin to the one-legged sailor in Eccles Street. For a moment we could be reading the *fiacre* scene in *Madame Bovary*, when Emma tears up the letter severing her adulterous contact with Léon and throws the pieces out of the carriage window. Like Emma, Molly has embarked on an adulterous course, but she accepts her sensuous nature, and, unlike Emma, will not be destroyed by her extramarital affair. Joyce's ability to 'answer' Flaubert is not always so decisive, for Flaubert's legacy was ambivalent – the gender-ambiguous nature of writing, the detachment of '*le style*' from '*l'homme*', and the temptation for the writer to substitute writing for experience.

What part did Joyce's education in Ireland play in his understanding of gender? What part did Jansenist attitudes towards sexuality and the specific male indifference or hostility to women play in Joyce's construction of gender in his writing? What did his being Irish contribute to his understanding of sexuality? Did it make any difference that he was a Dubliner and married to a woman from the west of Ireland? Is there something specifically Irish about the essentially private Joyce, who insisted elsewhere on 'silence, exile and cunning' (*P* 247), revealing so much about his own life? Ironically, perhaps Joyce found his feminine voice – if that is what it is – not through the development of inwardness but through the more external method of classical rhetoric: *imitatio*. Through practising a given style of writing, the pupil consciously took on styles not his own. The Jesuit-educated Joyce extended this method and applied it with characteristic determination and thoroughness to his representation of women.

In a suggestive passage, Stanislaus recalls his brother referring to 'the asexual intellect of the Irish':

He did not mean that Irishmen are less virile than others (families are rather larger in Ireland than elsewhere), but that

19   Harriet Shaw Weaver in September 1919. Photograph by Hilda Ward. *Courtesy of Jane Lidderdale, OBE.*

sexual motives have little influence on their lives. Sexuality is in their lives a thing apart which rarely 'gets entangled with reality'. This indifference or concealed hostility of Irishmen to women is reflected in the character of their women. It would be interesting to determine whether the coldness, bigotry, and absolute lack of romanticism of Irish women are innate or unconsciously desired by the males of the race; for, in the last analysis, women are always blamed by men for being just what men themselves have made them.

(*MBK* 158)

If this view of sexual relations in Ireland is correct, Joyce, who ensured that his sexuality did get entangled with reality, is unlike the average Irishman. The Jesuits imparted to Joyce a model of the intellect as a separate entity, celibate in its dealings with the body and life. Perhaps in developing a sexual intellect, Joyce was consciously attempting to overcome his background, to think through his senses – 'thought through my eyes' (*U* 3.1–2), as the Blakean Stephen puts it at the beginning of 'Proteus'.

All his life Joyce was, to adopt the title of John McGahern's recent novel (itself a quotation from the 'Hail Mary'), 'amongst women'. In childhood there was his mother, his six sisters (Margaret, May, Eileen, Eva, Florence and Mabel), Mrs Conway, his aunts (especially Aunt Josephine, his favourite). In adolescence there was Mary Sheehy and the Sodality of the Blessed Virgin Mary; in early manhood, Nora.[19] In Trieste he recreated this female environment, first with the addition of Lucia, his daughter, then by inviting his sisters Eva and Eileen to live with him. In Paris in the 1920s, his 'extended' family included Harriet Shaw Weaver, his English patroness, and women

of the Left Bank, especially Sylvia Beach and Adrienne Monnier, who were largely responsible for the publication of *Ulysses*. Later came Helen Kastor Fleischman, who married his son Giorgio, and Maria Jolas, who gave him valuable support from 1928 onwards, especially in advising on Lucia's mental illness. Apart from his schooldays – and even at Clongowes he formed an attachment to a nurse in the infirmary – there was never a time when women were absent from his life.

In this sense the central place accorded to female experience in Joyce's writing is but a reflection of his own immediate cir-

20 Joyce amongst women at Feldkirch in 1932. Nora and Lucia are in the back, Joyce and Lucia's nurse in the front. According to Eugene Jolas in Dachy (1990), Lucia was always accompanied by her nurse at this period. *Courtesy of the Beinecke Rare Book and Manuscript Library, Yale University.*

cumstances. Consider the range of female characters in his work: aunts in 'The Sisters' and in 'The Dead'; sisters such as Dilly Dedalus in 'Wandering Rocks'; daughters such as Eveline, Polly and Kathleen in *Dubliners* or Issy in *Finnegans Wake*; mothers such as Mrs Mooney or Mrs Kearney in *Dubliners*, or Mina Purefoy in *Ulysses*, or Anna Livia in *Finnegans Wake*; wives such as Mrs Kernan or Gretta Conroy in *Dubliners*, or Bertha in *Exiles*, or Molly Bloom and Anna Livia; washerwomen as in 'Clay' and *Finnegans Wake*. Most of the female characters in his writings are defined by their family role and in general they are not objects of desire. On the other hand, working women scarcely exist, and when they do they occupy lowly places as domestics (Lily in 'The Dead' or the 'slavey' in 'Two Gallants'), kitchen helpers (Maria in 'Clay'), a typist (Miss Dunne in *Ulysses*), a shop assistant (the blonde girl in Thornton's), prostitutes (in *A Portrait* and 'Circe'), washerwomen (in *Finnegans Wake*), someone who delivers milk (the 'poor old woman' in 'Telemachus'). Molly is a professional singer but we only see her at home. However, it is also true to say that Joyce betrays an anxiety about the limited roles assigned to women and about their hidden feelings. In 'Scylla and Charybdis', Stephen reflects on the part Anne Hathaway played in Shakespeare's development; in 'Oxen of the Sun', Mina Purefoy struggles in labour offstage, her voice silenced by rowdy male medical students; in 'Wandering Rocks', Dilly Dedalus, 'loitering by the curbstone' outside Dillon's auctionrooms (*U* 10.644), suffers the indignity of being forced to plead with her father for housekeeping money; in 'The Dead', Gabriel Conroy is stung by the legitimate complaints and feelings of three women – Lily, Miss Ivors and Gretta.

At this point a number of conclusions

suggest themselves. Firstly, Joyce is attentive to the voice of female suffering. Secondly, it is through women that he writes some of his most striking passages. Thirdly, Joyce seems intent on capturing in the Irish voices of Molly and Anna Livia an inclusive female voice, not unlike the Chorus in Greek drama, ever responding in the wings to the damage men are effecting on the stage of history. And fourthly, like the women on the banks of the Liffey washing their menfolk's clothes, Joyce uses his writing, as the opening to 'Anna Livia Plurabelle' suggests, both to expose and to cleanse his own shame (see *Ms 12*). With the

Ms 12. The opening passage of 'Anna Livia Plurabelle' with Joyce compounding the problem for printer and reader alike. *Courtesy of the Beinecke Rare Book and Manuscript Library, Yale University.*

F Ask Lictor Hackett or Lector
Reade on Garda Growley
on the Boy with
the Billyclub.

by dredgerous layds and
devious delts, playin catched
and mythed with the gleam
of her shadda, 61

R And his derry's
own drawl and
his corkscrew blather
and his doubling stutter
and his gullaway swank.

Huges Caput Earlyfouler?

O tell me all about Anna Livia! I want to hear all
about Anna Livia. Well, you know Anna Livia? Yes,
of course, we all know Anna Livia. Tell me all. Tell me
now. You'll die when you hear. Well, you know, when
the old chap went futt and did what you know. Yes,
I know, go on. Wash away and don't be dabbling. Tuck up
your sleeves and loosen your talktapes. Or whatever it was
they try to make out he tried to do in the Fiendish park. He's
an awful old rep. Look at the shirt of him! Look at the dirt
of it! He has all my water black on me. And it steeping
and stuping since this time last week. How many times is
it I wonder I washed it? I know by heart the places he likes
to soil. Scorching my hand and starving my famine to make
his private linen public. Wallop it well with your battle
and clean it. My wrists are rusty rubbing the mouldaw
stains. And the dneepers of wet and the gangres of sin in it!
What was it he did a tail at all on Animal Sunday? And how
long was he under lough and neagh. It was put in the papers
what he did, illysus distilling and all. But time will tell. I
know it will. Time and tide will wash for no man. O, the old
old rep! And the cut of him! And the strut of him! How he
used to hold his head as high as a howeth, the famous old
duke alien, with a hump of grandeur on him like a walking
rat. What age is he at all at all? Or where was he born or
how was he found. And were him and her ever spliced? I
heard he dug good tin with his doll when he brought her home,
Sabine asthore, in a parakeet's cage, the quaggy way for
stumbling. Who sold you that jackalantern's tale? In a
gabbard he landed, the boat of life, and he loosed two croa-
kers from under his tilt, the old Phenician rover. By the

R fears for
a happy
isthmass.

Flowey and
Mount on
the brink of
time with
wishes and R

Don Dom

O pass
me that
and oxus!
axcother
Domb domb
and his
wee follyo.

Was her banns never loosened in Adam
and Eve's and

nicies and priers,
the King fierceas Humphrey, with

from the
harbourless
Ivernikan
Okean!

77

exception of his volumes of verse, it is difficult to see how any of Joyce's texts could have been written by someone with a clear conscience.

Joyce's positioning

There is a curious mixture in Joyce of surplus and unreconstructed material. The surplus makes for difficulty in interpretation, the unreconstructed makes the author only too familiar. Joyce remains the uncertain celebrator of female experience. Take the following passage from Molly's soliloquy:

have we too much blood up in us or what
O patience above it's pouring out of me like the sea anyhow he didn't
make me pregnant as big as he is I don't want to ruin the clean sheets
∧the clean
linen I wore brought it on too damn it damn it and they always want
to see a stain on the bed to know you're a virgin for them all that's
troubling them they're such fools too you could be a widow or divorced
forty times over a daub of red ink would do or blackberry juice no
that's too purply O let me up out of this pooh sweets of sin

Ms 13.   *Courtesy of the State University of New York at Buffalo.*

have we too much blood up in us or what O patience above its pouring out of me like the sea anyhow he didnt make me pregnant as big as he is I dont want to ruin the clean sheets I just put on I suppose the clean linen I wore brought it on too damn it damn it and they always want to see a stain on the bed to know youre a virgin for them all thats troubling them theyre such fools too you could be a widow or divorced 40 times over a daub of red ink would do or blackberry juice no that's too purply O Jamesy let me up out of this pooh sweets of sin

(*U* 18.1122–9)

This is a striking attempt by a man to render what it must be like to be a woman experiencing menstruation; that Molly relies on folk medicine rather than on medical fact

78

adds to the interest. It reads effortlessly, but in fact it has been thoroughly worked at by Joyce. Consider, for example, the different types of utterance in such a short passage:

An interrogative: Have we too much blood in us or what?
An invocation: O, patience above, it's pouring out of me like the sea!
An expression of relief: Anyhow he didn't make me pregnant as big as he is.
A wish: I don't want to ruin the clean sheets I just put on.
A supposition: I suppose the clean linen I wore brought it on too.
An exclamation: Damn it! Damn it!
An observation: And they always want to see a stain on the bed to know you're a virgin for them.
A deduction: All that's troubling them.
A judgement: They're such fools too.
An example: You could be a widow and divorced 40 times over.
Possible advice: A daub of red ink would do or blackberry juice.
A qualification: No that's too purply.
A plea (to the author?): O Jamesy let me up out of this.
An expression of disdain: Pooh.
A title of a book: Sweets of Sin.

If the passage were set out this way, it would of course lose its force, and something similar would happen if we sought to paraphrase it:

Molly begins with a general, scientific-sounding question about the amount of menstrual blood in her. This is followed by the thought that Boylan didn't make her pregnant. She is anxious about spilling blood on the sheet and imagines her period has been brought on by wearing clean linen. A momentary outburst of anger about her period is quickly superseded by thoughts about men wanting proof of a woman's virginity and how foolish they are if this is all that troubles them . . .

At stake is the way Joyce naturalizes the ever-changing focus. Ironically, in a passage that flows so readily, the conjunction 'and' is used only once – and then it is to suggest a different train of thought.

Part of our interest in such a passage resides in it being written by a man and not by a woman. At one level we read it as the thoughts of a woman, at another as if it *were* the thoughts of a woman. There is a constant shifting back and forth between *as* and *as if*. But it is more than this, for the humour in such a passage seems almost designed to hide the male author behind his female character. The fluctuation allows Joyce scope to explore the illusions each sex has of the other. Molly's odd beliefs have a wider provenance, and every schoolboy learns about blood on the sheet. Karen Lawrence argues that Molly is beyond Joyce's control: 'Molly represents the problem of woman represented by the male pen, a staging of alterity that reveals itself as masquerade.'[20] But, in part at least, Joyce seems to get away with it – the collusion, the errors, the prejudices. Indeed, if he were alive today, he would not be short of other masks to hide behind – the suspicious deconstructionist ('Only the free play of the text counts'); the French feminist ('I am the finest example of "feminine writing" in modern literature'); the post-1989 unattached Marxist ('As far as subversion is concerned, my work knows no bounds').

Joyce's position *vis-à-vis* Molly owes part of its indeterminacy to her position in language. Molly's voice, which seems on the surface highly distinctive, is pieced together from common phrases and clichés.

Take the following phrases from passages cited above:

> arent they fearful
> hes beyond everything
> I declare
> I better not
> I suppose there isnt in all creation
> look at the way
> how can he
> its well he doesnt
> of course
> no wonder they [hide it]
> it never entered my head
> what did I tell him

Such phrases are constantly heard in ordinary speech, especially in Ireland. 'I declare' initiates an expression of some force (here used ironically by Molly), while 'there isnt in all creation' reminds us perhaps of Synge and the language of Irish country people. Molly's speech is so full and varied that it is best approached via pragmatics and conversational analysis rather than via traditional grammar; only a method sensitive to implicature, sequencing, presupposition, overlap, and discourse deixis could do justice to her soliloquy and to our role as non-addressed participants. Through Molly, Joyce celebrates not so much the distinctive individual voice as the common tongue. Her speech is peppered with popular phrases, which acquire a humorous quality by their unusual context:

> I could have got a pound a week
> alnight sitting
> a natural size
> he kneels down [to do it]
> knock out all my teeth
> in case of twins
> placed up there
> pretending to hide it
> two bags full
> sticking up at you

22 'Blazes Boylan and Molly' from an original embossed colour engraving by Saul Field. (From Saul Field and Morton P. Levitt, *Bloomsday: An Interpretation of James Joyce's 'Ulysses'*, Greenwich, Conn: New York Graphic Society, 1972.) *Courtesy of Jean Townsend-Field.*

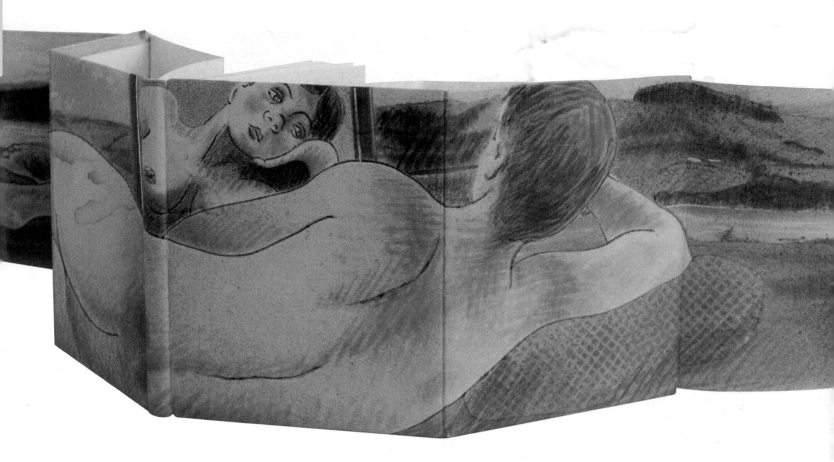

Joyce is an expert at investing ordinary phrases with significance. Molly's soliloquy is assembled from all kinds of fragments: the language of advertising (a natural size), parliamentary procedure (an all-night sitting), aggressive encounters (knock out all my teeth), the language of rational enquiry (in case of), the language of mockery and perhaps mocking servility (two bags full – the catch-phrase is 'three bags full' – a phrase that can be read from Molly's point of view or perhaps with Bloom's 'all-present-and-correct' attitude in mind). But Joyce manages

a lot of touching
for fun
(40) times over

to bring together all this material into what is sometimes misleadingly interpreted as a single voice. 'Penelope' is a triumph of weaving and concealment both in linguistic terms and in terms of gender; the concealment, however, questions the seemingly 'natural' flow of Molly's thoughts as well as Joyce's putative absence.[21]

Joyce is a blackguard, a 'hybrid', a 'sham' as he calls Shem (*FW* 169.9, 170.25). Was there ever heard of such low blackguardism? Positively it woolies one to think over it?' (*FW* 180.31–2) Even worse: 'every honest to goodness man in the land of the space of today knows that his back life will not stand being written about in black and white' (*FW* 169.6–8). At times Joyce is on the side of the

23 Cover for *Pomes Penyeach* designed and executed in 1991 by Trevor Jones. The binding has double boards, hinged at the fore-edges. *Design and photograph © Trevor Jones 1991. Reproduced with permission.*

angels, having 'fallen from a higher world' (*E* 50–1); at other times, he is a reprobate, who needs to have his soul built up 'out of the ruins of its shame' (*E* 87). In spite of his brassy claim in *Finnegans Wake* that 'I can psoakoonaloose myself any time I want' (*FW* 522:34–5), Joyce never ceases to betray contradictory forces at work, some conscious, some unconscious, some positive, others negative. Fascinated by the construction of gender differences and how these were separately experienced by men and women, he sought an impossible knowledge. In this regard, 'Penelope' mixes in fairly equal measure distortion and desire.

Take Molly's remark that 'I thought well as well him as another' (*U* 18.1604–5). The possessive Joyce would have been upset by such a thought if it were Nora's, but the male fantasizer Joyce can admit to a vicarious – perhaps homosexual – pleasure at being relegated to but one of a male series. Alternatively, through writing he can find a 'writing cure', a way of dealing with his anxious (dis)possession of Nora through imagining, in writing, the worst. By contrast, 'Nausicaa' stems more directly from a prurient interest and a preoccupation with the lingering male gaze.

CHAPTER FOUR
Dubliners, *Topography, and Social Class*

WE ARE ACCUSTOMED TO considering the verbal and aural qualities of Joyce's work, but his imagination was also intensely visual – never more so than in his use of maps and in his reconstruction of the streets of Dublin. Indeed, *Dubliners* is not unlike a commentary, an *ekphrasis*, on a visual representation – in this case a map of his native city. The experience of reading *Dubliners* is greatly enriched when accompanied by such a map, and for our purposes here we can make good use of Bartholomew's 1900 map of Dublin, which includes Joyce's beloved tram routes and the place-names with which he was familiar.

The stories of *Dubliners* were written in 1904–7, when Joyce was close enough to his own memory of Dublin not to have to rely on a map. There was something reassuring and comforting – especially after October 1904, when he was in exile abroad – in retracing familiar routes in his mind. Maps in Joyce – the maps he evokes in his texts, that is – are a visual reconstruction of scenes of his childhood and youth, and indelibly scored therefore with attachment and feeling. As the twelfth-century Gaelic word *dinnseanchas*, a compilatory text that records lists of place-names, reminds us, the affection for a local habitation has a long history in Ireland. Joyce belongs to this Irish tradition of paying homage to one's place of origin, but, as in everything else, he consciously transforms his lineage – often beyond recognition. To Joyce in 1905, writing to Grant Richards in support of his stories, Dublin was a European capital: 'I do not think that any writer has yet presented Dublin to the world. It has been a capital of Europe for thousands of years, it is supposed to be the second city of the British Empire and it is nearly three times as big as Venice' (*Letters* II. 122). *Dubliners* is a book of advocacy, and one of its underlying messages is: 'Look, Dublin is an important capital and deserves to be taken seriously.' Joyce does not rest there, for he refuses to preach: he *assumes* the importance of his native city and in doing so manages to exorcize any provincialism attaching to the concept of *dinnseanchas*.

Joyce is fastidious about the immediate details that surround our lives. He makes much of tram routes, the names of the streets, the 'street furniture', the hotels and bars, the realistic texture of turn-of-the-century Dublin. Such devotion might initially appear as obsessive, but it is in this way that the city is recuperated and made familiar. Once, while walking down

Universitätstrasse in Zurich with his artist friend Frank Budgen, Joyce indicated his intention in *Ulysses* of providing a picture of Dublin so complete 'that if the city one day suddenly disappeared from the earth it could be reconstructed out of my book'.[1] Joyce's attention to detail has been rewarded.

Indeed, we have all become a little more Joycean, and are less disturbed than Cyril Connolly evidently was when Joyce remarked to him: 'I am afraid I am more interested, Mr Connolly, in the Dublin street names than in the riddle of the universe'.[2]

84

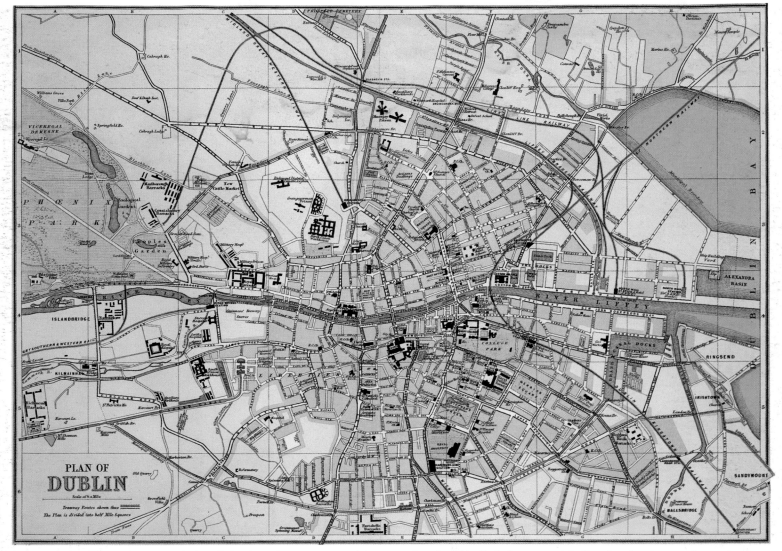

2 Bartholomew's map of Dublin, which includes the tramway routes, so important a feature of Joyce's fiction, was originally printed on 5 September 1900. Some place-names have changed since Irish independence, most notably the following: Sackville Street (E3, F4: now O'Connell Street), Great Brunswick Street (now Pearse Street), Rutland Square (E3: now Parnell Square), Royal University (E5, F5: now University College and no longer on St Stephen's Green), Westland Row Station (F4: now Pearse Station), Amiens Street Station (F3: now Connolly Station), Kings Bridge Station (C4: now Heuston Station). Nelson's Pillar (F3) on Sackville Street was blown up 1966, the fiftieth anniversary of the Easter Rising. Some locations, such as the National Maternity Hospital in Holles Street (G5), scene of 'Oxen of the Sun', are missing from this map. One or two changes can be observed between this map and the one reproduced in Bartholomew's *Gazetteer of the British Isles* (1904): Leinster Hall (F4) becomes the Theatre Royal, the Royal Dublin Society (F5) becomes Leinster Lawn, and the Queen's Inns (E3) becomes the King's Inns. *Copyright* © *Bartholomew, 1990. Reproduced with permission.*

1 'So This Is Dyoublong? Hush! Caution! Echoland!' (*FW* 13.4–5).
M. J. MacManus in *So This Is Dublin* (1927) facetiously remarked: 'Mr James Joyce has been paying a visit to Dublin in search of local colour for the new book which he has planned, to be called An Irish Odyssey. He spent a considerable time visiting the Corporation Sewage Farm, the Wicklow manure factory, and the sloblands at Fairview. Before returning to Paris he stated that he had derived keen satisfaction from his visit to his native city.' In *Finnegans Wake* Joyce answers venom with humour, and plays with the idea that the word 'Dublin' contains within it a question: 'do you belong?': 'So This Is Dyoublong?' *Photograph Dan Harper.*

Joyce's method is particularly suited to our environmentally conscious age: lose nothing, retrieve everything, and always recycle. Joyce not only presses the same streets into service in different texts, he also deploys the same characters. Nosey Flynn, whom Farrington finds 'sitting up in his usual corner of Davy Byrne's' (*D* 93), is still there in his 'nook' when Bloom (too) seeks a refuge, this time from the Lestrygonians (*U* 8.737). Martin Cunningham, last seen in 'Grace', pokes 'his silkhatted head into the creaking carriage' (*U* 6.1–2) of the funeral cortège in 'Hades'. But something else is at work. For Joyce's fiction is of a piece, an extraordinary ceaseless return to the storehouse of his childhood and youth in Dublin. *Dubliners* rehearses the themes that are more systematically explored in *Ulysses*; *Finnegans Wake* mines ground first excavated in *Dubliners*. Not unreasonably, Margot Norris has recently suggested that the figure being waked in Joyce's last work is none other than Father Flynn himself, and that the women washing dirty clothes in 'Anna Livia Plurabelle' are reincarnations of the women from Maria's laundry in 'Clay'.[3]

Bartholomew's map, useful for general orientation purposes, brings out several features: Phoenix Park on the left, the North and South Circular Roads, the railway lines with their terminals, the tram routes, the river Liffey bisecting the city, the rivers Tolka and Dodder, the Grand Canal and the Royal Canal: it also shows the density of streets in the central area inside the circular roads, the sparseness in areas adjoining the four corners of the map. In 1904 the city of Dublin had a population of some 290,000, most of whom lived in the area inside the nine-mile perimeter drawn by the two circular roads. These people worked in brewing and distilling, shipbuilding, and in the manufacture of poplin, hats, and agri-

cultural implements. Dublin was an important trading centre, and the Liffey was lined with ships and docks for some two and a half miles in from the sea. The city was also the terminus of a network of privately owned railways dating from 1844 when the Dublin and Kingstown Railway was established.

Other features on Bartholomew's map also stand out when listed:

Station terminals: Harcourt Street (E6), Westland Row (F4), Tara Street (F4), North Wall (G4), Amiens Street (F3), Broadstone (D3), and Kings Bridge (C4).

Prisons: Mountjoy (E2), Kilmainham (A5), Grangegorman (D3).

Barracks: Linen Hall (E3), Beggar's Bush (H5), Royal (C4), Richmond (A5), Marlborough (B3), Portobello (E6), Wellington (D6), Aldborough (G3).

Churches: St Patrick's (E5) and Christ Church (E4), which are cathedrals; St George's (E2); the Roman Catholic Church in Upper Gardiner Street (F2).

Hospitals: Kilmainham Royal (B4), Swifts (C4), Steevens (C4), Sir Patrick Duns (G5), Mater Misericordiae (E2), Whitworth (F2), Meath (E5).

Charitable institutions: Blind Asylum (F6), Old Man's Asylum (F6), Female Orphan House (C2), Widows Retreat (F2), Deaf and Dumb Institute (B2), St Vincent de Paul Orphanage (D1).

Hotels: Jury's (E4), Gresham's (F3), The Shelbourne (F5).

Theatres: Theatre Royal (F4) (marked 'Leinster Hall' on map), Queen's (F4), Gaiety (E5), Rotunda (E3), the Empire Palace (E4). (The Mechanics Institute in Lower Abbey Street (F4) became in 1904 the Abbey Theatre.)

Universities: Royal (F5), Trinity (F4).

Municipal land and buildings: Gas Works (H5), Richmond District Lunatic Asylum (D3), South Union Workhouse (C5), North Union Workhouse (D3), Phoenix Park (A3), Prospect Cemetery at Glasnevin (D1), Public Library in Capel Street (E3).

National Buildings: the Custom House (F4), the Four Courts (D4), the Bank of Ireland (F4), National Library (F5), Museum and Gallery (F5), the Viceregal Demesne (A2), the General Post Office (E4).

In addition, we might notice the number of artisan dwellings, the fish and vegetable market and the cattle market, the various statues and monuments round the city: O'Connell and Nelson in Sackville Street (F4); the Wellington Monument and the Gough statue in the Phoenix Park (B4, B5); the Wolfe Tone statue at the corner of St Stephen's Green (E5); Tom Moore's statue outside Trinity College (F4); and that most famous landmark of all – Guinness's Brewery (C4).

Throughout *Dubliners* Joyce enlists these topographical features for his own artistic purposes. 'The Sisters' is set in a house in

4 The Provost's House (F4) as seen by Malton in the 1790s. In *Ulysses*, Bloom on his way to lunch passes this point and thinks of Dr Salmon: 'Provost's house. The reverend Dr Salmon: tinned salmon. Well tinned in there. Like a mortuary chapel. Wouldn't live in it if they paid me' (*U* 8.496–7). (From *A Picturesque and Descriptive View of Dublin*, 1792–9.)

Great Britain Street (E3); 'The Boarding House' in Hardwicke Street (E3); 'A Mother' in the Antient Concert Rooms in Great Brunswick Street (F4); 'Ivy Day in the Committee Room' in Wicklow Street (E4); 'The Dead' in a house on Ushers Quay (D4). In 'After the Race' the four young men draw up – significantly, in a story about money – near the Bank of Ireland (F4); less significantly, in 'An Encounter', we learn that Joe Dillon's parents go to eight o'clock Mass every morning at the Jesuit church in Gardiner Street (F2), the same church where in 'Grace' Father Purdon adapts the Christian message for the business community; 'Eveline' closes with Frank's departure from the North Wall station (G4). Farrington in 'Counterparts', after a night drinking in Davy Byrne's in Duke Street (F4/5), the Scotch House on Burgh Quay (F4) and Mulligans in Poolbeg Street (F4), catches the Sandymount tram home; on alighting at Shelbourne Road (H5), he 'steered his great body along in the shadow of the wall of the barracks' (*D* 97), that is, the Beggar's Bush barracks in Ballsbridge (H5). In 'Araby' the boy catches the train for the bazaar at Amiens Street Station (F3); Gabriel and Gretta Conroy in 'The Dead' are booked into Greshams' Hotel in Sackville Street (F3). Bartholomew's map also allows

5   Malton's view of the
Rotunda and New Rooms
adjoining (E3). The Rotunda,
designed by John Ensor, was
built in 1757, the New Rooms,
designed by Richard Johnston,
added in 1785. In Joyce's story
'A Painful Case', Mr Duffy
first meets Mrs Sinico at a
concert held in the Rotunda. In
Ulysses, Bloom in the funeral
cortège passes by the Rotunda;
a little later Boylan, on his way
for his rendezvous with Molly,
finds the mare going too slow
up the hill by the Rotunda:
'Too slow for Boylan,
blazes Boylan, impatience
Boylan, joggled the mare'
(*U* 11.765–6). (From *A
Picturesque and Descriptive View
of Dublin*, 1792–9.)

6   View from Capel Street
looking towards Essex Bridge
(E4) (now Grattan Bridge),
which, according to Malton,
'exhibits one of the most
striking scenes which Dublin in
its internal effects furnishes'.
Malton's sketch is busy with
information: notice the
Military State Lottery Office
on the left, the woman with the
baby in the first-floor room,
the man cleaning the lamps on
the bridge, the use of gestures,
the presence of children and
dogs, the *human* perspective.
(From *A Picturesque and
Descriptive View of Dublin*,
1792–9.)

us to reconstruct tram routes. Maria, in
'Clay', in her journey to see her brother
catches two trams, one from Ballsbridge
(H6) to Nelson's Pillar (F3) ('twenty
minutes') and one from the Pillar to
Drumcondra (F2) (also 'twenty minutes').

More significantly, what also emerges
from a consideration of such details is that
in *Dubliners* Joyce is still learning how to
handle the map of his city for fictional purposes. The layering of his stories with
factual content not only provides the reader
with a naturalistic slice of life, but also
establishes certain limits within which the
author's imagination can work. Joyce
thought George Moore's *The Untilled Field*
(1903), a collection of short stories, 'damned
stupid':

A lady who has been living for three years
on the line between Bray and Dublin is
told by her husband that there is a meeting
in Dublin at which he must be present.
She looks up the table to see the hours of
the trains. This on DW and WR [Dublin,
Wicklow and Wexford Railway] where
the trains go regularly: this after three
years. Isn't it rather stupid of Moore. And
the punctuation! Madonna!

(*Letters* II. 71)

Joyce requires us to become familiar with
the city's contours, thus ensuring that
Dublin is never relegated to pictorial background. Equally, he prompts us into
asking questions. Is it significant that Little
Chandler's route from his place of work at
King's Inns (Queen's Inns on the 1900 map:
E3) to Corless's in St Andrew Street (E4)
takes him over Grattan's Bridge (E4) and
past the Castle (E4)? Grattan, we may
recall, was leader of the short-lived Irish
Parliament established in 1782, which was
abolished by the Act of Union in 1801; the
Castle was the headquarters of the British
administration in Ireland. On the other
hand, it takes Maria twenty minutes to
travel from Ballsbridge to the centre of
Dublin, and twenty minutes from there to
the Canal Bridge at Drumcondra (F2) –
which leaves 'twenty minutes to buy the
things' (*D* 100). Such information is deployed by Joyce for more conventional
fictional purposes: Maria's wordiness reflects
her interior consciousness and is appropriate therefore in a story about concealed,
deluded, romantic expectations.

Bartholomew's map of Dublin is drawn
from above: it sets out without discrimi-
nation a bird's-eye view of the city, street
by street. Joyce combines a topographical

impression of the city with an interior human landscape. The effect of this is to provide the city with a realistic texture while allowing rapid shifts in perspective from detachment to involvement, from third to first person, from the person as object to the person as subject. Such a technique reaches its apotheosis (and the point beyond which it can only dissolve into parody) in 'Wandering Rocks'. But in *Dubliners* Joyce's use of the technique is invariably delightful, especially when it is associated with indirect free speech, as in the case of Maria. Joyce's work exists between interior consciousness and the complex network that makes up the city. A comparison suggests itself between Joyce's Dublin and the evocation of London in the work of, say, Charles Dickens or Virginia Woolf. Take the opening sequence of Chapter 3 of *Little Dorrit* (1857):

> It was a Sunday evening in London, gloomy, close, and stale. Maddening church bells . . . . Melancholy streets, in a penitential garb of soot, steeped the souls of the people who were condemned to look at them out of windows, in dire despondency. . . . Nothing to see but streets, streets, streets.

Dickens's broad brush, combining as it does a moral sensibility with a consciousness of symbolic significance, is deployed here to show connections between the material and the social. Joyce, on the other hand, uses a particularizing pen stroke that focuses on the specific, leaving the reader to make the connections. 'Let us leave theories there and return to here's here' (*FW* 76.10). Joyce's city invariably precedes him and when he names a street he is naming something already there. But in the process Joyce alters the relationship between signified and signifier and reveals a city simultaneously dependent on and independent of his pen. He also insists on geographical accuracy, but here too, while his city may be in the grip of paralysis it is never anonymous or indeed immobile. On the other hand, in contrast with the portrait of London streets in *Mrs Dalloway* (1925), Joyce's streets are 'democratic', often without the trappings or the associations of power, and never the site of some metaphysical or existential void. If there is a void in Joyce's work – and I am not convinced there is – it resides perhaps in the moment at which we sense that the realistic texture has been composed, frozen of necessity in time, the technique possibly applicable to any city, simultaneously constructed and deconstructed.

In early stories such as 'An Encounter' and 'Araby', the events take place at the edge of the city. In the first the boys set off from North Strand (G2), walk along East Wall (G2–H2–H3–H4), cross the river near North Wall goods station (H4), and proceed down York Road into Ringsend (H4). In 'Araby', the boy's journey takes him from his home in North Richmond Street (F2) down to Amiens Street Station (F3), where he boards the special train which comes to a halt after Westland Row Station (F4). In 'After the Race', as is apparent from tracing their route – by car, on foot, by train, by yacht – the foreigners (with the Irishman Doyle in tow) treat the city with a certain contempt. They speed into the city along the Naas Road (A5), draw up outside the Bank (F4), stroll through the centre of Dublin

where that night 'the city wore the mask of a capital' (*D* 46), and head off to Kingstown via Westland Row Station (F4), to join the American's yacht anchored in Dublin Bay. In 'A Painful Case', Mr Duffy and Mrs Sinico live just outside the area described by Bartholomew's map, Mr Duffy at Chapelizod (west of A4), Mrs Sinico 'outside Dublin' (*D* 111) in Sydney Parade (south-west of I6). Part of Mr Duffy's elusiveness – his suburban, intellectual distaste for the 'body' of the city – comes from the way he seems to pop up in different parts of the city: at the Rotunda (E3), the concert at Earlsfort Terrace (F5), the bank where he works in Lower Baggot Street (F5), the eating house in George's Street (E4). Only when he is outside the city do we see him walking, and then it is to survey the city from Magazine Hill in the Phoenix Park (A4).

Crossing the river Liffey also plays its part in the stories, though not in any systematic way. In 'An Encounter' the river acts as a rite of passage, a transition from innocence to experience. When Little Chandler crosses Grattan Bridge, 'he looked down the river towards the lower quays and pitied the poor stunted houses' (*D* 73). When the Conroys and their party cross O'Connell Bridge (F4), Miss O'Callaghan comments that one always sees a white horse when crossing that bridge. Similarly with east–west and north–south relations: Maria embarks on a long journey from Ballsbridge to Drumcondra; Mr Kernan is rescued from the bar in Grafton Street (F4) and taken north across the river to his home in Glasnevin Road (E1); the feckless Farrington works for a boss from the North of Ireland; Gabriel Conroy's imagination drifts with the falling snow westward across Ireland. The map of the city suggests to Joyce a range of possibilities, some symbolic

and biographical, others social and political.

Joyce employs so much of the city's topography that the landmarks he omits, or deploys in a cursory manner, become significant. The Viceregal Demesne (A2) and the British presence, for example, are either missing or played down. Mr Power is a member of the Royal Irish Constabulary, but 'Grace' is not about secular 'power'; Lenehan's route takes him along streets laid out or improved during the Ascendancy, but such an interpretation is apparent only to an experienced eye; the sisters live on 'Great Britain Street', but it is unclear what, if anything, Joyce intended by this. If we invoke Marx's distinction between the State and Civil Society, it becomes apparent that *Dubliners* is primarily concerned with Civil Society – with culture, communications, Catholicism, shopping. The State – the legislature, the executive, the judiciary – is a given, but is not the primary focus of Joyce's attention. The number of barracks shown in Bartholomew's map suggests that Dublin was no ordinary city but heavily garrisoned – as if the British authorities were expecting trouble. Even Catholicism in *Dubliners* is seen in terms of Civil Society – fallen priests, sermons for the laity, types of religious school – rather than as twinned with the State. *Dubliners* is not 'Wandering

Rocks', therefore, that 'systematising' episode in *Ulysses* which shows Dublin caught in the vice of Church and State, 'framed' by Father Conmee and the Earl of Dudley's procession. But the stories do point in that direction, towards 'Telemachus' and the theme of Ireland's dispossession by England.

JOYCE'S CLASS CONSCIOUSNESS

Dubliners is an enormously rich source-book for the study of social class. Indeed, take away the class aspects and *Dubliners*

The Royal Irish.

8 Malton's view of the Four Courts (D4) from the river. In *The Young Painter's Maulstick: Being a Practical Treatise on Perspective* (1800), Malton writes: 'Everything we see is seen perspectively; whether it be a house, a man, or beast, or tree, or ship, or plains, or hills, or water, or all together . . . no object appears as it is.' Joyce, too, invariably sees things 'perspectively'. He even grounds his aesthetics in mathematical concepts such as parallax, and to illustrate his theory of epiphany makes use of the Ballast Office clock on Westmoreland Street (F4) and the different positions from which it can be observed. (From *A Picturesque and Descriptive View of Dublin*, 1792–9.)

9 Hugh Thomson's humorous sketch of two members of the Royal Irish Constabulary in Stephen Gwynn's *Highways and Byways in Donegal and Antrim* (London: Macmillan 1899 new ed. 1928). In 'Grace', Mr Kernan, finally indignant that a policeman was involved in the pub incident, 'resented any affront put upon him by those whom he called country bumpkins. '– Is this what we pay rates for? he asked. To feed and clothe these ignorant bostoons' (*D* 160).

is a surprisingly thin text. Unfortunately, many critics, preoccupied with myth or symbolism or other less threatening textual matters, have tended either to ignore the class issue altogether or to rest content with the general observation that in *Dubliners* Joyce deals with the lower middle class. But Joyce is a profoundly class-conscious writer, and few writers have captured the nuances of social class better than Joyce. He is an expert at rendering class differences in terms of dress, accent, money, behaviour, and he also recognizes that class is a matter of relationships, of perception, of slippages between class aspiration and actual class identity, between family and work, family and neighbours.

It is only, for example, when Mr Power in 'Grace' accompanies Mr Kernan home and notices the accents of Mr Kernan's children that he realizes the extent of his friend's social decline. Mrs Kernan, embarrassed by having no drink in the house to offer Mr Power, feels acutely her own (inferior) class position. All the time Joyce attends to details which convey a whole world-view. In 'Counterparts', Farrington is broke; it is just past the middle of the month, and he is dependent on an employer he thinks his inferior – the story is not unlike a miniature version of the conflict between the feckless Catholic South and the industrious Protestant North. Farrington's dark mood intensifies; alcohol beckons; he pawns his watch. Joyce then adds that with money in his pocket Farrington can stare 'masterfully at the office-girls' (*D* 93) in the street. Such power, however, is temporary, for in the Scotch House he has to guard his money from spongers like the Englishman Weathers, who 'much to Farrington's relief . . . drank a glass of bitter this time' (*D* 95).

From his own background on the edge of the middle class, Joyce was alive to the part that class plays in people's lives, and in *Dubliners* he inclines towards the border area between classes. A comparison with George Orwell suggests itself at this point. Class in Orwell, as Raymond Williams reminds us, 'is described mainly in terms of differences and snobberies in accent, clothes, tastes, furnishing, food'. In consequence, 'another set of facts, in which class is a powerful and continuing economic relationship – as between the owners of property and capital and the owners only of labour and skill – is effectively masked.'[4] Joyce in this regard is not unlike Orwell, but, equally, important differences between the workings of class in Britain and Ireland need to be registered. Firstly, Orwell's preoccupation with class belongs to a long history that includes Cobbett, Carlyle, Disraeli, and Lawrence. Joyce, on the other hand, is at the beginning of a process, for, in delineating the presence of social class in the capital of Ireland he is providing an important critique of the emerging nationalism which paid (and still pays) scant regard to such differences. Secondly, the attitude Joyce adopts in *Dubliners* towards social class is not aimed at exposure or one of crusading zeal – 'look what life is like among the downtrodden of the earth'. Neither is it patronizing or deferential – 'look how interesting life is among those people'. These are the people of his city and he is down there among them. Thirdly, while Orwell described England as 'a family with the wrong members in control',[5] the colonial encounter ruled out such leniency in Ireland. Joyce knew that class could not be wished away: the only occasion in *Dubliners* when a toast is raised to that classless entity, 'Humanity', is in 'After the Race', just before the Irishman Jimmy Doyle suffers a humiliating defeat at the hands of two wealthy French entrepreneurs.

To invoke Lukács's distinction in his essay 'Narrate or Describe?', we might be tempted to argue that Joyce narrates and Orwell describes.[6] Joyce understood from inside the nature of Irish social class; he had no need to journey to the borders of his experience – no need, therefore, to travel to Wigan Pier, or Barcelona, or to live among down-and-outs in Paris or London. Orwell's position is that of an external observer, Joyce's that of someone with first-hand knowledge of the social group he is describing. It is more complicated than this, however, for Orwell stresses his position as an outsider; furthermore, he transfers to other borderline groupings his own border-line experience. Like Orwell, Joyce reminds us that knowledge of the context of people's lives is the first step on the road to sympathy. In the first decade of his life Joyce was waited on by servants; thereafter, his family's social decline enabled the young artist to experience at first hand the life-style of the poor, and in particular to observe those in humble jobs – servants, shop workers, caretakers, and, in 'Clay', washer-women. Orwell, too, was sensitized to the plight of the dispossessed, but in a way such experience disfranchised him. Maria in 'Clay' would be relegated by Orwell to a social statistic, perhaps like the woman he sees from a train in *The Road to Wigan Pier* (1936), poking a stick into a drainpipe. But in Joyce the character exists within the recuperative framework of a narrative, laden with family and romantic delusions.

Maria could hardly have a more lowly occupation; she is a helper in the kitchens at the Dublin by Lamplight laundry, which is attached to a house for fallen women. Maria's life comes complete in this one story: long hours at work, riding crowded trams, hurried moments shopping, short family visits on special occasions such as

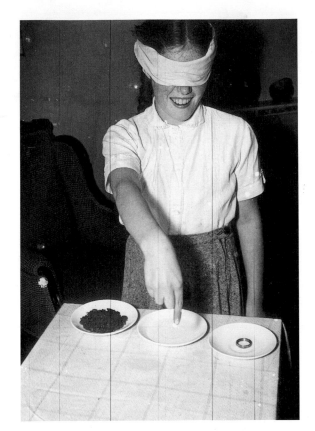

10 Maurice Curtin's photograph of a Hallowe'en Divination Game taken in 1935. In 'Clay', Maria, blindfold, stands in front of a table on which there are three saucers, one containing a prayer-book, a second water, and a third a ring. One of the 'next-door girls' mischievously places some clay from the garden in another saucer and it is this one on which Maria's hand unfortunately alights. Not for her the ring of marriage or the religious life, but death. Joyce's Ireland was highly stratified, but, as this story suggests, he had available to him an oral tradition that continued to surface in the modern capital. *Courtesy of the Department of Irish Folklore, University College, Dublin.*

Hallowe'en, and accompanying it all the (deluded) hope of marriage. With two half-crowns and some coppers in her purse (with silver clasps), taking her old brown rain cloak with her, she sets off from the Laundry in Ballsbridge (H5). The tram drops her at Nelson's Pillar (F3). She buys a dozen mixed penny cakes at Downes's, goes round to Henry Street (E3) in search of a plum cake with more almond icing on top, and annoys an assistant by her slowness in deciding. Eventually, she sees what she wants and parts with two shillings and fourpence. By the time she arrives at her brother's house, the plum cake is gone and she 'nearly cried outright' (D 104) at the money thrown away. Joyce's problem is not insufficient but excessive knowledge.

The child's view of social class

If the first three stories of *Dubliners* reflect his childhood, then Joyce was learning all the time about class. In the opening story, 'The Sisters', the boy notices Nannie's worn heels and how clumsily her skirt is hooked at the back (*D* 14). In an earlier version of the story the sisters are described as not very intelligent; in the final version, Eliza mistakenly refers to the *Freeman's General*, not *Journal*, and to 'rheumatic' and not 'pneumatic' wheels. Joyce also stresses the sisters' disappointment: how, presumably, they once had high expectations of their brother who had been educated in Rome for the priesthood, how their economic fortunes are tied to his. But with his failure as a priest, the tables are turned, and, 'poor as we are' (*D* 16), the sisters are obliged to look after him in their 'unassuming shop, registered under the vague name of *Drapery*' (*D* 11). In Joyce's world people decline slowly rather than suddenly, and they bear their disappointment quietly through time. The boy, on the other hand, is – at least in his own mind – not of the sisters' social class and he takes care to distinguish himself from them, refusing the sherry they offer him. They assume their brother was resigned in death – 'quite resigned' (*D* 15) – but what the boy sees is a 'very truculent' face (*D* 14). Significantly, this adjective is repeated in the closing moments of the story: Eliza hears only silence in the house, but the boy hears his friend lying in his coffin 'solemn and truculent in death' (*D* 18). The boy's identification with the priest – intensified by Cotter's remarks and by Eliza's suggestion that it was the boy who was responsible for her brother's decline – suggests a class pressure at work, the need on the part of the

boy to raise himself above the distillery talk of his home and the limited perceptions of his aunts.

This sense of being different is carried into the next story, 'An Encounter', where we read of Father Butler's disparaging remarks about National School boys. Later, the narrator is keen to disclose to the 'queer old josser' that he and his friend Mahony are not National School boys (*D* 20, 26, 27). It is at first odd – though less so after reading 'The Sisters' – that in the midst of such an encounter the boy should be so particular and seek to differentiate himself from poorer children. But we need to remember that with his 'frail canvas shoes' (*D* 21) – which he notices that morning while waiting for Mahony and watching the horse-drawn tram pull business people into the city – his physical appearance is an incomplete reflection of his inner state. The boy knows he is superior to others, including his friend Mahony, who 'used slang freely' (*D* 22). His identity as a person derives in part from his perception of being different, and he wants this strange adult, whose 'accent was good' (*D* 26), to recognize his true worth. He is shouted at by drivers of groaning carts, notices a crowd of ragged girls and the squalid streets where families of fishermen live (*D* 23, 22, 24), and is called 'Swaddler' by other children, who assume from the cricket club badge in Mahony's cap that he and Mahony are Protestants. Through it all can be heard again Joyce's father referring to the Jesuits as the gentlemen of Catholic education and insisting that his eldest son be educated by them:

– Christian brothers be damned! said Mr Dedalus. Is it with Paddy Stink and Micky Mud? No, let him stick to the jesuits in God's name since he began with them. They'll be of service to him in after years. Those are the fellows that can get you a position.

(P 71)

'Araby', the third story of childhood, begins with a reference to the noisy children from the Christian Brothers' school in North Richmond Street (F2). The street itself is carefully defined in terms of social class: its occupants are concerned to maintain standards against the 'rough tribes from the cottages' behind the houses (D 30). The boy's house has a 'front parlour' with a blind pulled down to within an inch of the bottom – through which space the boy peers out at Mangan's sister opposite. There is also a back drawing-room with a tea table where visitors, such as Mrs Mercer, a pawnbroker's widow, are entertained (though in this household the phrase would be more like 'make yourself at home'). In the hall is a hat stand and a hat brush; upstairs the rooms have high ceilings. Again, the boy feels himself to be different, a feeling this time expressed through the language of chivalry: 'I imagined that I bore my chalice safely through a throng of foes' (D 31). On Father Flynn's breast the boy sees 'an idle chalice' (D 18); here in 'Araby' the boy has taken up that chalice and pushes on through the crowd at the railway station and on to his goal – the bazaar. Once there, he passes two men 'counting money on a salver' (D 35), an image that recalls Jesus' attack on the money-lenders in the Temple. The boy has come to a holy place to exchange the money in his hand for a token of his affection for a girl, but discovers he is unable to escape from a world of gross material concerns. He is struck by the English accents of assistants who show no interest in him. His high ideals founder and he comes to realize 'gazing up into the darkness' (D 35) that such emotions are nothing more than 'vanity'.

Gender and social class

'Eveline' is an emigration story deliberately complicated by gender and social class. 'She sat at the window watching the evening invade the avenue' (D 36). The opening sentence contains an essential clue to what is to follow, for this is a story about being invaded. Instead of drawn blinds, we are in a world where the curtains give off 'the odour of dusty cretonne' (D 36). In this working-class home the defences against the world are undermined. A man from Belfast bought a near-by field and built houses in it; inside the home, the harmonium is broken, and in spite of her weekly dusting Eveline wonders 'where on earth all the dust came from' (D 37); her mother, after a 'life of commonplace sacrifices closing in final craziness' (D 40), is dead, and Eveline is left with constant squabbles with her father over her wages from the Stores. Frank offers her escape, takes her to see *The Bohemian Girl*, where they sit in 'an unaccustomed part of the theatre' (D 39), and he regales her with stories of far-away places. The balance of the story would be tipped, one suspects, against Eveline if Frank were a wholly sympathetic person, but there is something less than 'frank' about him. 'Frank was very kind, manly, open-hearted' (D 38), she thinks to herself, but even as she does so there is a suggestion that she feels the need to justify something. Eveline's predicament is delicately captured by Joyce. A victim of patriarchal society, she is caught between the demands of her father, commitment to her dying mother, and the unknown future as represented by Frank. In spite of showing her fatalism, Joyce takes care not to condemn Eveline. He understands her plight, knows she has been so crushed by a series of 'invasions' that she is finally unable to voice how she feels. 'Her eyes gave him

95

no sign of love or farewell or recognition' (D 41).

'Two Gallants' is not only, as we have seen in Chapter 2, about political betrayal, it is also a tale of mean streets and the deformation of sexual relations in class society. It speaks plainly of not working, of living off others, informing, gambling, using women for sexual and economic favours, and – as we learn at the end of the story when the woman disappears into the house in Baggott Street (F5) and comes back with a small gold coin – possibly stealing from employers. The military association of the title is picked up throughout in the language of the story (stride, swing of burly body, boots of the conqueror) and particularly in the description of Corley, the son of a police inspector, possibly a police informer, who 'had inherited his father's frame and gait' (D 51). On his way to meet his 'slavey' near St Stephen's Green, Corley tells Lenehan that it's a 'mug's game' (D 52) spending money on women, especially when you can get a slavey or a tart to give you sex, money and tobacco. Corley sees his 'slavey' as inferior in both class and gender: she is a domestic servant, he the son of a police inspector. His previous attempts at gallantry with 'girls off the South Circular' (spending on tram fares, theatre, chocolate) did not pay off: '– And damn the thing I ever got out of it' (D 52). On the other hand, he tells Lenehan, 'there's nothing to touch a good slavey' (D 52).

Corley gains satisfaction not so much in seducing the woman as in getting her to pay for the sexual favours she is providing. What the woman gains Joyce leaves unrecorded – perhaps Corley represents romance for her or the possibility of escape from the drudgery of domestic service. Her date with him seems more than perfunctory. She is wearing a blue dress and white sailor hat, her 'Sunday finery' (D 55), and stands on the kerb, 'swinging a sunshade in one hand' (D 54). When they meet 'she swung her sunshade more quickly and executed half turns on her heels'. There is nothing coy about her: she has 'frank rude health' and 'unabashed blue eyes' and is wearing a big bunch of red flowers pinned in her bosom, 'stems upwards' (D 55). What happens after they catch the Donnybrook tram is left unrecorded. The gold coin at the end of the story suggests conquest on Corley's part, but we only have Corley's 'gesture' for that.

The meshing of the class and gender discourse of 'Two Gallants' is further underlined by Joyce's lengthy description of what seems to be a parallel scene in which Lenehan, after listlessly retracing his steps to Rutland Square (E3), enters a poor-looking shop seeking refreshment:

> He sat down at an uncovered wooden table opposite two work-girls and a mechanic. A slatternly girl waited on him.
> – How much is a plate of peas? he asked.
> – Three halfpence, sir, said the girl.
> – Bring me a plate of peas, he said, and a bottle of ginger beer.
>
> (D 57)

While Corley is perhaps 'pulling it off' with his 'slavey', Lenehan is waited on by a 'slatternly girl'. Inside the bar the girl is 'slatternly'; in the street the 'slavey' is transformed by her clothes and exudes an air of confidence. The two women occupy similar positions in the class structure, but in the first situation class acts as a barrier to keep people (together and) apart; in the second, class is there to be transgressed and exploited. To a person such as Lenehan (the same applies to those women like the 'slavey' who no longer live at home) the streets offer a sense of freedom, but inside the bar he is forced to confront a world more closely defined in class terms.

At this point in the story Joyce adds a remark which surprises readers who imagined Lenehan as simply working-class: 'He spoke roughly in order to belie his air of gentility for his entry had been followed by a pause of talk' (D 57). Joyce insists on Lenehan's class position even if 'No one knew how he achieved the stern task of living' (D 50). In the bar Lenehan feels uncomfortable and excluded: his accent and demeanour betray his superior class position; at the same time he is reduced to eating there because of his poverty. Joyce notices something else. At the beginning of the story Lenehan, in keeping with the image of a casual male predator, wears his yachting cap 'shoved far back from his forehead' (D 49); inside the bar, 'to appear natural he pushed his cap back on his head' (D 57).

How were women in Dublin society to better themselves given that they were held back by low-status occupations? For many women the only possibility was through marriage, but, as 'Two Gallants' reminds us, unskilled working-class women were threatened by male predators. 'The Boarding House' is a companion story, only this time the focus is on female predators – mothers preying on daughters, mothers and daughters preying on men. Joyce takes similar care to contextualize the story throughout by reference to social class. The lace curtains at the window signal propriety and prevent idle prying from passers-by; they also allow the female predator privacy in which to blackmail a respectable Catholic office-worker. Mrs Mooney is a butcher's daughter who married her father's foreman and herself ran a butcher's shop. Her husband was an alcoholic who abused her; after ejecting him, she opened a boarding house in Hardwicke Street (E3). Joyce gives us

enough information in this sketch of her life to suggest her psychological motivation. She had married beneath her, had married the wrong man, and she was determined her daughter would not repeat her mistakes.

The 'boardelhouse', as it is called in *Finnegans Wake* (FW 186.31), caters for a floating population of tourists from Liverpool and the Isle of Man, music-hall artistes, and a resident population of clerks from the city. Mrs Mooney charges fifteen shillings a week, which means that her clientele have to be careful white-collar workers or a rung above – Eveline earns seven shillings a week as a shop worker; Farrington works in an office but has to pawn his watch. Mrs Mooney, too, is careful with money: Mary the servant collects pieces of broken bread for Tuesday's bread pudding, and the sugar and butter are kept under lock and key (D 64). On Saturday nights she allows the residents to use the front drawing-room for reunions – and the nineteen-year-old Polly is given 'the run of the young men' (D 63). Never far away is Mrs Mooney, the procuress shrewdly aware that Polly's virginity is her only currency. Her son Jack and her daughter Polly have edged a little way up the social ladder, from shop to office work: Jack is employed as a clerk to a commission agent and Polly (briefly) as a typist. But neither has made a significant break into a different social class: Jack uses soldiers' obscenities and Polly is brought home from her office when Mrs Mooney learns that Mr Mooney, 'a disreputable sheriff's man' (D 63), had been calling to see her.

The class trap is set. Because of his long-standing employment at a Catholic wine merchant's office, Mr Doran is forced into marriage: if he does not accede to Mrs Mooney's demand, his employers will be informed of his disgraceful moral behaviour and he will be sacked. Mr Doran feels the situation intensely, the more so because he realizes his friends and family will look down on Polly, partly because of her 'disreputable' father, partly because the boarding house was 'beginning to get a certain fame', and partly because Polly was 'a little vulgar' in the way she spoke: 'she said *I seen* and *If I had've known*' (*D* 66).

Class superiority

In the Christmas dinner scene in *A Portrait*, Mr Dedalus complains bitterly that the Irish are a 'priestridden Godforsaken race' (*P* 37). After reading *Dubliners*, he might have added 'classridden'. Joyce's class-conscious eye ranges widely over his native city: in 'After the Race', he alights on the tension between aspiring middle-class Dubliner and confident European middle class; in 'A Little Cloud', the issue of class and colonialism; in 'A Mother', class and the petit-bourgeois Irish Literary Revival; in 'Ivy Day in the Committee Room', the state of Irish politics after the fall of Parnell, especially *vis-à-vis* the Dublin working class; in 'A Painful Case', the attitude of the suburban lower middle class towards the city centre; in 'Grace' the involvement of the Church in supporting lower-middle-class snobbery.

In 'After the Race', with its picture of the unequal terrain between the Irish lower middle class and the European middle class, Joyce underlines the way consciousness and human relations are determined by class and economics. The car speeds into Dublin along the Naas Road and 'through this channel of poverty and inaction the Continent sped its wealth and industry' (*D* 42). Ségouin, reputed to own some of the biggest hotels in France, is about to launch a motor establishment in Paris with Rivière as his manager. By contrast, the Nationalist views of Jimmy Doyle's father were modified, we are informed, as his butcher's business improved. 'After the Race' is about class insecurity. Doyle is sent to Cambridge for a term; his father is covertly proud of his son's spending beyond the family's means – but it cannot be sustained and Doyle is brought home. Ever 'conscious of the labour latent in money' (*D* 44), Doyle feels acutely the tension between the class aspirations of his parents and his own unease among the rich and famous. When his father looks at Jimmy's dress tie, he 'may have felt even commercially satisfied at having secured for his son qualities often unpurchasable' (*D* 45). In contrast, Jimmy ends the night losing at cards and suffers the final indignity of watching his companions 'calculate his I.O.U.'s for him' (*D* 48).

In 'A Little Cloud' we are told, even before his return from London, that Gallagher had 'got on' (*D* 70). Eight years previously as he waved goodbye to Gallagher from the North Wall (G4), Little Chandler was impressed by his friend's 'travelled air, his well-cut tweed suit and fearless accent' (*D* 70). By contrast, from his office window at the King's Inns (E3) where he works, 'the little cloud' observes the 'untidy nurses and decrepit old men who drowsed on the benches' (*D* 71) and thinks of the consolation of poetry. In this story Joyce rehearses the familiar theme of Dublin, formerly the second city of the Empire, now representing poverty and decline, while London, the imperial capital, means money and opportunity. On his way to meet Gallagher at Corless's Chandler passes a 'horde of grimy children', and picks his way deftly 'through all that minute vermin-like life and under the shadow of the gaunt spectral mansions in which the old nobility of Dublin had roistered' (*D* 71). Chandler's passage from the King's Inns through the streets of his native city is a recapitulation of Ireland's decline. In his 1907 history and guide to Dublin, D. A. Chart informs us that architecturally the King's Inns, where students were trained for the Bar, 'contemptuously turns its back on the departed grandeur of Henrietta Street'.[7] Chandler's route takes him past the spectral mansions of Georgian Dublin; past Grattan Bridge (E4), past the Castle (E4), and towards Trinity (F4), traditional home of British culture in Ireland. Chandler inhabits a city in decline: as he crosses Grattan's Bridge, he 'looked down the river towards the lower quays and pitied the poor stunted houses'. 'Every step brought him nearer to London, farther from his own sober inartistic life' (D 73). Chandler is allowed his dreams and his illusions, his contempt for his native city and country, his inflated view of London.

Disappointment properly awaits him. On meeting Gallagher, Chandler discovers he is estranged from his friend of eight years before. Gallagher speaks of Dublin in the breezy, patronizing language of the returned emigrant: 'I feel a ton better since I landed again in dear dirty Dublin' (D 75). He has seen life, 'knocked about' (D 76). 'There's no woman like the Parisienne – for style, for go' (D 77). Chandler is struck by his friend's 'new gaudy manner', by the crudeness of his accent and expression, but he is unable to gainsay him. Gallagher, on the other hand, relishes the triumph of his return and his material success. 'I mean to marry money' seems calculated to offend his stay-at-home friend, who has just invited him to dinner with his wife. Home is the direction of the story, and home for Chandler means furniture on hire purchase, no money to employ a servant, forgetting the tea and sugar, buying a blouse as a present for his wife which she thinks overpriced, and the sound of a child crying. The little cloud's 'tears of remorse' (D 85) end the story, but they are not, as might be expected, tears of regret but a sign that he has entertained thoughts beyond his station.

'A Mother' provides perhaps the most pointed class-based contemporary critique of the Irish Literary Revival, if for one sentence alone: 'When the Irish Revival began to be appreciable Mrs Kearney determined to take advantage of her daughter's name and brought an Irish teacher to the house' (D 137). The 'Mother' in this case is not the heroic figure of Cathleen ni Houlihan but a lower-middle-class snob educated at a high-class convent. When 'she drew near the limit', Mrs Kearney unromantically married a bootmaker, whose conversation 'took place at intervals in his great brown beard' (D 137). Thereafter, any romance in her life was channelled through her daughter Kathleen. The dispute in 'A Mother' does not hinge on the reduction in Kathleen's fee after the abandonment of the Friday evening concert. Mrs Kearney has money: the *charmeuse* from Brown Thomas's which she let into Kathleen's dress 'cost a pretty penny' (D 138) and she buys twelve two-shilling concert tickets for her friends. No, what concerns her is contact with people from a lower class. She uses the issue of the fee to distance herself from those involved in the concert and to wreak her revenge on those she considers beneath her. At the first night she notices that the men are not in evening dress, that Mr Fitzpatrick, the secretary of the Society organizing the concerts, 'wore his soft brown hat carelessly on the side of his head and that his accent was flat', that he chewed up one end of the programme while talking to her (D 139). On Thursday the audience behaved 'indecorously as if the concert were an informal dress rehearsal' (D 140). Her anger alights on the contract. She tackles Mr Fitzpatrick.

He plays for time and informs her he will bring the matter to his Committee. Mrs Kearney's reply hits the precise note: '– And who is the *Cometty*, pray?' (*D* 141).

'Ivy Day in the Committee Room', the first of the so-called stories of public life in *Dubliners*, hints at a class-based critique of post-Parnellite politics in Ireland. Joyce, as we saw in Chapter 1, dwells on the gulf between the rhetoric of politics and the material circumstances of people's lives. Mr O'Connor, 'a grey-haired young man' (*D* 118) and Mr Tierney's agent in the local municipal election, rolls his own cigarettes, wears a pair of leaky boots, and is worried about not being paid by Tierney. The conversation is appropriately desultory and drifts along accumulating images of humour and political sterility. Jack's son is a 'drunken bowsy' (*D* 120) and has been without regular employment since leaving school; Henchy imagines driving out of the Mansion House 'in all my vermin' (*D* 127); Jack relays his conversation with the Mansion House porter and how the Mayor sends out for a pound of chops for his dinner: '*what kind of people is going at all now?*' (*D* 128).

Joe Hynes's entry introduces a different political perspective, for not only is he a supporter of Parnell, he also endorses the socialist candidate Colgan. 'The working-man is not looking for fat jobs for his sons and nephews and cousins' (*D* 121). Hynes is the man of principle in an age of betrayal – and the Parnellite principle is here linked with the position of the working class (though even Hynes is accused of 'sponging' and lacking 'some spark of man-hood' [*D* 124]). Hynes's tribute to Parnell provides the only glimpse of integrity/intensity in politics, but even that is couched in sentimentality and nostalgia.

Underlying this story can be discerned the emergence of working-class politics in turn-of-the-century Dublin. James Connolly's Irish Socialist Republican Party was formed in 1897; mass trade unionism was about to expand with the formation in 1909 of Jim Larkin's Irish Transport and General Workers' Union. Joyce is no Sean O'Casey, the Dublin writer who best reflects these changes; the 'son of a Parnellite organiser', Joyce seems more intent on showing the decline of the old rather than the rise of new forces in Ireland. But he was clear-eyed enough to discern a link between the working-class candidate and the former uncrowned king of Ireland.

Through a series of homologous structures, 'A Painful Case' highlights the split between the suburbs and the city centre of Dublin, between the mind and the body, between public morality and private feeling. The story focuses on lower-middle-class detachment and its intermittent desire for contact with humanity, and it brings out Mr Duffy's *inability* to live 'as far as possible from the city of which he was a citizen' (*D* 107). Mr Duffy, who considers the other suburbs of Dublin 'mean, modern and pretentious', lives in Chapelizod in a room with lofty, bare walls and an outlook over a disused distillery and over the 'shallow river on which Dublin is built' (*D* 107). He has an interest in literature, in music, and in radical politics, at one time attending meetings of (Connolly's?) Irish Socialist Party. Mrs Sinico, the wife of a 'captain of a mercantile boat plying between Dublin and Holland' (*D* 110), also lives outside Dublin, in a 'little cottage' with a 'dark discreet room' in Sydney Parade. Mr Duffy is attracted to Mrs Sinico, the relationship blossoms, but Mr Duffy then retreats into the 'incurable loneliness' of the soul (*D* 111). Four years later, while eating in his customary restaurant in George's Street (E4), he reads a report in the newspaper of her suicide at Sydney Parade station, and suffers a mixture of emotions: lofty disdain for her action and self-righteousness that he is not responsible, followed by remorse and a realization as he surveys Dublin from Magazine Hill (A4) in the Phoenix Park that he is an 'outcast from life's feast' (D 117).

'Grace' is a further instance of Joyce's class-based critique of Irish society. Mr Kernan, a commercial traveller of the old school, wears a 'dinged silk hat'; the constable who attends the scene licks the lead of his pencil and speaks with a 'suspicious provincial accent' (D 151); Mr Power, as we have seen, is surprised at the Kernan children's accents; Mr Power, employed in the Royal Irish Constabulary in Dublin Castle, resents Mr McCoy, who is but a secretary in the City Coroner's office, addressing him by his first name; the secular priests are referred to at one point as 'ignorant, bumptious' (D 164), while the Jesuits are the 'boyos' with influence (D 163); and, to crown it all, Father Purdon 'came to speak to business men and he would speak to them in a businesslike way' (D 174). By means of such details, Joyce builds up a portrait of snobbery among lower-middle-class Dubliners – their disdain for Irish country people, their use of decorum to protect their class position, their concern with privilege and power (the pun on Mr Power's name). There is no escape in religion, for the Church mirrors the secular class-based world; at another level there is an escape, for the Jesuits are past masters at massaging the conscience of the business community. 'Grace' can be read as Joyce's reply to Pope Leo XIII's encyclical *Rerum Novarum* (1891), which laid the foundations for the Church's modern social teachings. Little chance of change in Ireland, Joyce seems to be saying, and even spiritual changes can be accommodated within existing class structures, attitudes, and behaviour.

'The Dead' widens the critique to include the middle class – or at least those on the fringes of it – and is a recapitulation of class attitudes found elsewhere in the collection. The Morkan sisters – the parallels with the opening story suggest themselves – rent the upper part of a house on Usher's Island (D4) from a corn factor who lives on the ground floor. 'Though their life was modest they believed in eating well; the best of everything: diamond-bone sirloins, three-shilling tea and the best bottled stout' (D 176). They have two servants, Bessie and Lily, a piano, a floor that glitters with beeswax, a heavy chandelier. They are anxious that Freddy Malins should not arrive 'screwed', especially with Mary Jane's pupils present, for their niece is a music teacher and her pupils are from 'better-class families on the Kingstown and Dalkey line' (D 176). When Mr Browne arrives he assumes a 'very low Dublin accent', but is ignored by Mary Jane's pupils (D 183). Gabriel, the sisters' nephew, is their (re)assurance. He is dependable, thoughtful, and caring, almost the patriarch of the family who continues the traditions – such as carving the goose at Christmas – and the one who deals with drunken guests.

'The Dead', a story in part about Irish generosity, is also concerned with anxieties about roots, initially sketched by Joyce in class terms, widened to include nationality, and then narrowed to a personal focus. When Gabriel arrives, he scrapes his goloshes on the mat and steps out in his patent-leather shoes. While outside the drawing-room he listens to the clacking of the men's heels and realizes that 'their grade of culture' differs from his (D 179). Joyce chooses his phrase with care. Gabriel has little sense of a common culture. He sees the world in terms

101

11 'I will not attempt to play to-night the part that Paris played on another occasion. . . For when I view them in turn, whether it be our chief hostess herself, whose good heart, whose too good heart, has become a byword with all who know her, or her sister, who seems to be gifted with perennial youth and whose singing must have been a surprise and a revelation to us all tonight, or, last but not least, when I consider our youngest hostess, talented, cheerful, hard-working and the best of nieces, I confess, Ladies and Gentlemen, that I do not know to which of them I should award the prize.' (D 204–5). Donal McCann as Gabriel Conroy in John Huston's film *The Dead*, extolling the praises of Aunt Julia, Aunt Kate, and Mary Jane. *Courtesy of Zenith Productions and Liffey Films Inc.*

of a social ladder, but he cannot escape the consequences of such a view, and throughout the evening he is constantly reminded of his roots. His mother, 'sensible of the dignity of family life' (D 186), named her sons Constantine and Gabriel, and she had opposed Gabriel's marriage to Gretta, Gretta being 'country cute' (D 187). Constantine is now senior curate at Balbriggan, and Gabriel writes a literary column for the Dublin *Daily Express*. They have come a long way from the starch mill which was owned by their grandfather, a 'glue-boiler' (D 207), as Gabriel cavalierly remarks, only to be immediately corrected by his aunt. Gabriel's other roots are in the west of Ireland, where his wife comes from. The nationalist Miss Ivors tackles him about holidaying in the west, but he replies that 'Irish is not my language' (D 189). 'The Dead' is about displacement, and it centres on the multiple displacement of Gabriel from his aunts, from his mother, from the younger generation, from his cultural roots, from women, from the servant Lily, from Miss Ivors, and finally from his wife.

Students often complain that nothing happens in *Dubliners*: they feel uninvolved, frustrated, often angry that the stories yield so little. Partly this is because these are 'inside stories'; partly because they deal relentlessly, so it seems, with the unattractive themes of paralysis and decline. Joyce's eye is so 'disillusioning' that even epiphanic moments – such as Gabriel's or Eveline's or that of the boy in 'Araby' – resemble an *anagnorisis* in Greek tragedy, a moment of recognition when the protagonist finally realizes his or her fate. The movement of *Dubliners* is ever downwards, towards the puncturing of illusions, and coming down to earth. Like the priest in 'The Sisters', Joyce is a disappointment. '–Ah, poor James!' 'He was too scrupulous always' (D 16, 17). And we are like the boy puzzling our heads to 'extract meaning from his unfinished sentences' (D 11). However, it would be wrong to leave it there, for if we attend to the detail of these stories we can uncover a powerful and entertaining critique of the role of social class in Edwardian Dublin.

CHAPTER FIVE
Joyce and Edwardian Dublin

DUBLIN: AN EDWARDIAN CITY

AFTER HIS CORONATION IN 1901, Edward VII made several visits to Ireland. According to one observer, writing in 1907, his 'unequalled tact and diplomacy has made a whole half-hostile nation his warm admirers. His Majesty is well-known to entertain a kindly feeling for both the country and the people.'[1] Edward's presence in Joyce's fiction tells a different story. In 'Ivy Day in the Committee Room', Mr Henchy is fulsome in his praise of the King of England. 'He's a man of the world, and he means well by us. He's a jolly fine decent fellow, if you ask me, and no damn nonsense about him. He just says to himself: *The old one never went to see these wild Irish. By Christ, I'll go myself and see what they're like*' (D 132). But then, Mr Henchy is a 'West Briton'. In 'Circe', the King is assigned a part to play, but he barely survives the mauling handed out to him by Joyce in the stage directions:

(*Edward the Seventh appears in an archway. He wears a white jersey on which an image of the Sacred Heart is stitched with the insignia of Garter and Thistle, Golden Fleece, Elephant of Denmark, Skinner's and Probyn's horse, Lincoln's Inn bencher and ancient and honourable artillery company of Massachusetts. He* sucks a red jujube. He is robed as a grand elect perfect and sublime mason with trowel and apron, marked made in Germany. *In his left hand he holds a plasterer's bucket on which is printed* Défense d'uriner. *A roar of welcome greets him.*)

(U 15.4449–57)

The plebeian Joyce took delight in associating the British Establishment with the urinal. In 'Wandering Rocks' the Earl of Dudley's cavalcade passes Simon Dedalus on Ormond Quay (E4): 'On Ormond quay Mr Simon Dedalus, steering his way from the greenhouse for the subsheriff's office, stood still in midstreet and brought his hat low. His Excellency graciously returned Mr Dedalus' greeting' (U 10.1199–202). In Ireland, as Hugh Kenner reminds us, a toilet is sometimes referred to as a 'greenhouse'.[2] Simon Dedalus, on his way from the toilet, has forgotten to button his trousers. In the middle of the street he suddenly remembers and covers himself. 'His Excellency', the Lord-Lieutenant of Ireland and the representative of the British Crown, assumes that one of his subjects is showing respect and returns the greeting. Across the colonial divide, even basic signs get misread. Just before this passage, the narrator informs us that 'from its sluice in Wood quay wall

105

2   Davy Stephens, the legendary King of the Newsboys, had his pitch at Kingstown Harbour (now Dun Laoghaire) where the main cross-channel steamer docked. In a working life of nearly half a century he met all the leading politicians and public figures of his day, including Edward VII when he was Prince of Wales and later King. In 'Circe', accompanied by a bevy of barefoot newsboys, he is heard shouting out: '*Messenger of the Sacred Heart* and *Evening Telegraph* with Saint Patrick's Day supplement. Containing the new addresses of all the cuckolds in Dublin' (*U* 15.1125–7). *Courtesy of the National Library of Ireland.*

DAVY STEPHENS. 8992. W.L.

under Tom Devan's office Poddle river hung out in fealty a tongue of liquid sewage' (*U* 10.1196–7), a grotesque image presumably designed to reveal the limits of imperialism. His family's declining social position increased Joyce's awareness of the discontinuity between officialdom and the private citizen. The public world had failed him – history, politics, religion, employment, a career, his family – but he still had the self, that territory which he was determined to protect by 'silence, exile, and cunning' (*P* 247) and from where he could launch attacks on those in power.

Edwardian Dublin was, as the subtitle of Joseph O'Brien's comprehensive survey reminds us, a 'city in distress'.[3] Certainly this is the overriding impression, but it should not obscure other more positive developments. The electric tramway system, for example, was laid between 1896 and 1901, and from Nelson's Pillar (F3) in Sackville Street trams, driven by electricity generated at the Ringsend power station, radiated out across fifty miles of the city. Dublin, which was backward in terms of town planning and social legislation, was in this regard deemed a model for other cities in the UK. Electricity for public lighting was installed at the turn of the century; the first public library on its own premises was opened on Charleville Mall (G2), North Strand, in 1900; and the conscience of Dublin Corporation began to be pricked by the plight of the city's poor, whose state was among the most abject in Europe. Slowly, a new civic sense was being revived. About this time also the motor car made its first appearance in Ireland. In 1902, the Irish Automobile Club was founded; in 1903, the Gordon Bennett Trophy race was held in Ireland; in 1905, there were 138 private cars and 9 commercial vehicles licensed in Dublin; by 1912 no Dublin firm with pre-

tensions was without at least one commercial delivery van.

Such developments brought about an inevitable change in people's consciousness. A new reading public, a new theatre and cinema audience all made their first appearance in Edwardian Dublin. At least seven daily newspapers, catering for different political tastes, were published in the city: the Unionist *Irish Times*, which had a circulation of around 45,000; the *Freeman's Journal* (40,000) and *Evening Telegraph* (26,000), which supported the Irish Parliamentary Party; the *Daily Express* (11,000) and the *Evening Herald*, which were Conservative; and the *Daily Independent* and *Evening Mail*, which adopted more independent positions. There were three leading theatres: the Theatre Royal (marked Leinster Hall, F4), the Gaiety (E5), and the Queen's (F4). In *Ulysses*, there are repeated references to the performance of *Leah* that night of 16 June 1904 at the Gaiety, while a poster draws our attention to Marie Kendall at the Empire music hall (E4). In 'Telemachus' we learn that Stephen's mother saw Edwin Hamilton's *Turko the Terrible* at the Gaiety, possibly the 1873 production that initiated the vogue for pantomime at Christmas. In fact, by 1909 all three theatres in Dublin had surrendered to the holiday demand for pantomime: for the rest of the year the programme consisted of visits from repertory companies, a Shakespeare play, appearances by artists such as Bernhardt, Melba, or Pavlova, a play by Boucicault such as *The Colleen Bawn*, or an opera performed by an English company such as the D'Oyly Carte.

Dublin boasted two concert halls – the Rotunda and the Antient Concert Rooms in Great Brunswick Street (F4) – and several music halls, including the Empire Palace in Dame Street (E4), the Tivoli, and the Bijou, into which audiences were enticed by artists

3 Edwardian Dublin was a different city from the one painted by Sheridan Le Fanu in his mid-Victorian novel *The House by the Churchyard* (1863) or by George Moore in his Land League novel *A Drama in Muslin* (1886). To Joyce it was both 'the centre of paralysis' and the city he could not stop writing about. This is a familiar view of the river Liffey looking towards Halfpenny Bridge

billed as 'The Wonder of the Age', 'The Most Powerful Man on Earth', 'The Beau Brummell of the Halls'. Once inside, they were entertained by acrobats, magicians, comedians and comediennes, ventriloquists, and artists in drag; they listened to songs such as 'Nellie Dean', 'Never Mind', 'I May Be Crazy But I Love You', 'At Trinity Church I Met My Doom', and 'The Man Who Broke the Bank at Monte Carlo'; they

witnessed acts such as the 'pedestal clog dancers', 'two real Hebrews', and 'nine real American negroes'.

Edwardian Dublin also saw the beginnings of the cinema, an initiative in which Joyce played an active, if short-lived, part. In October 1909, he visited Dublin for the second time that year to open the Volta in Mary Street (E4), the first cinema in the city; the project was financed by four Triestine businessmen who employed Joyce as their agent. In the *Evening Telegraph* on 21 December Joyce received special praise for the 'remarkably good' initial experiment and for 'the success of the inaugural exhibition'. He then returned to Trieste, but for various reasons, including possibly Joyce's neglect and the wrong choice of films, the enterprise began to collapse; in July 1910, to avoid further losses, the cinema was sold. Joyce's venture was a little premature. By 1914 Dublin, with its twenty-seven cinemas, had become a city of picture palaces, and the era of the music hall was over. In the meantime a new urban, mass-entertainment culture had been created.

Communications

Joyce was intrigued by all aspects of his native city, not least the rapidly developing system of communications, including transport, newspapers, and advertising, typewriters and telephones. His city was not like a mirror for reflecting subjective moods, but more like a network of interconnections, at the centre of which was an active human consciousness. Dublin was a commercial rather than an industrial city; it was small-scale and compact; it was the capital of a country essentially rural and traditional; it was a city full of talk. Joyce was not detained therefore by images of the city as 'coketown' or by doubts as to the value of modernization. The theme of industrialization and culture, which was central for nineteenth- and twentieth-century British writers from Dickens to Lawrence, passed him by. Perhaps for this reason he was quick to discern how city-dwellers, for the first time in history, were being transformed into office-workers and mass consumers. Joyce rarely lost an opportunity to be first in the field. 'After the Race', whose sustaining

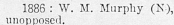

DUBLÍN—ST. PATRICK'S.
*Mr. W. Field (N) ....Unopposed.
Electorate : 9,691.

1886 : W. M. Murphy (N), unopposed.
1892 poll : W. Field (P), 3,693 ; W. M. Murphy (AP), 1,096 — Parnellite majority, 2,597.
1895 : W. Field (P), unopposed.
Mr. William Field is a butcher, and President of the Irish Cattle Traders' and Stockowners' Association. He was educated at the Catholic University, and later in life became Chairman of the Dublin County Council. He is now President of the Dublin Bimetallic League, and has convictions on railway matters. To these varied successes and accomplishments Mr. Field adds the appearance of a poet laureate or Sarasate.

MR. W. FIELD.
Main Street, Blackrock, co. Dublin.

image is that of a car race, was published in December 1904, when there were virtually no cars in Ireland. On Bloomsday there is also a motor car, with the sun on its windscreen, seen by Mr Kernan in 'Wandering Rocks' (*U* 10.759). The references to television in *Finnegans Wake* may well be used by future historians to trace some early responses to the age of television.

With the construction of the new Dublin tramway system, Joyce noticed that the centre of the city had shifted. Formerly, it could be argued that the centre was Dublin Castle, the seat of British rule in Ireland, or Christ Church Cathedral, or Trinity College, or the Bank of Ireland, the site of Grattan's eighteenth-century Parliament, or some other site. But Edwardian Dublin swept all that aside and Nelson's Pillar on Sackville Street became the heart of the

3 (*cont.*) (Metal Bridge on map, E4), with Bachelor's Walk on the right and beyond that Ormond Quay. *Photograph Dan Harper.*

4 Nicknamed 'Hamlet' by John Joyce (*DD* 20–1), William Field, despite his appearance, was in fact a butcher and leading representative of the Irish Cattle Traders. In his capacity as president of that organization he receives a letter from Mr Deasy with a solution to the foot-and-mouth disease. (In 1912 Joyce had written to Field on the same topic on behalf of Henry Blackwood Price.) Later on Bloomsday we learn that Field and Councillor Nannetti are going to London to ask a question in the House of Commons about the disease. This sketch of Field appeared in the special issue of the *Pall Mall Gazette* on the 1900 general election.

5   Sackville Street (F4; now O'Connell Street) with the imposing Nelson's Pillar opposite the General Post Office. 'Hackney cars, cabs, delivery waggons, mailvans, private broughams, aerated mineral water floats with rattling crates of bottles, rattled, rolled, horsedrawn, rapidly' (*U* 7.1047–9). *Courtesy of the National Library of Ireland.*

Hibernian metropolis. Here was the hub of the tramway system, the new 'heart', pumping out blood through the city, the organic image doing duty for a mechanical system. At the beginning of 'Aeolus', Joyce's use of capital letters – especially noticeable in the Shakespeare and Company edition – affords a fitting salute to his 'capital'.

IN THE HEART OF THE HIBERNIAN METROPOLIS

★ Before Nelson's pillar trams slowed, shunted, changed trolley, started for Blackrock, Kingstown and Dalkey, Clonskea, Rathgar and Terenure, Palmerston Park and upper Rathmines, Sandymount Green, Rathmines, Ringsend and Sandymount Tower, Harold's Cross. The hoarse Dublin United Tramway Company's timekeeper bawled them off:
– Rathgar and Terenure!
– Come on, Sandymount Green!
   Right and left parallel clanging ringing a doubledecker and a singledeck moved from their railheads, swerved to the down line, glided parallel.
– Start, Palmerston Park!

(*U* 7.1–13)

'Aeolus' is set in a newspaper office in Abbey Street (E4). The image of the title, taken from Homer's myth of Aeolus, hints at the way newspapers in the modern world veer and tack with every wind that blows. But the myth, while there, is kept in the background, for Joyce seems more interested in the newspaper office itself where telephones whirr and printing presses interrupt conversation and interior monologue alike:

   Sllt. The nethermost deck of the first machine jogged forward its flyboard with sllt the first batch of quirefolded papers. Sllt. Almost human the way it sllt to call attention. Doing its level best to speak. That door too sllt creaking, asking to be shut. Everything speaks in its own way. Sllt.

(*U* 7.174–7)

'Aeolus', complete with typographical errors in the Shakespeare and Company edition, is laid out like a newspaper with a series of subheadings which are by turns pointed, amusing, ridiculous, and rude.

```
HOW A GREAT DAILY ORGAN IS TURNED OUT

WE SEE THE CANVASSER AT WORK

HOUSE OF KEY(E)S

ORTHOGRAPHICAL

???

KYRIE ELEISON !

LENEHAN'S LIMERICK

OMNIUN GATHERUM

CLEVER, VERY

YOU CAN DO IT !

LET US HOPE

DEAR DIRTY DUBLIN

K. M. A.

K. M. R. I. A.

RASING THE WIND

THOSE SLIGHTLY RAMBUNCTIOUS FEMALES

DIMINISHED DIGITS PROVE TOO TITILLATING
FOR FRISKY FRUMPS. ANNE WIMBLES, FLO
WANGLES — YET CAN YOU BLAME THEM?
```

6 A list of subheadings (in sequence but incomplete), taken from the 1928 Shakespeare and Company 10th printing of *Ulysses*.

Joyce's sophisticated eye could see there was something odd about the relationship between a subheading and the ensuing passage. Most people skip the subheading to prevent interference with the storyline. In 'Aeolus', by contrast, the subheadings constantly halt the flow of the narrative. Such a self-conscious, intrusive mode, so out of keeping with the style of the first half of

7 'How A Great Daily Organ Is Turned Out': Richard Hamilton's 'aeolian' representation of *Ulysses*. Mixed media plates. Among the scenes depicted are: the advert for the House of Keyes; portraits made from photos of Joyce, Wilde, Mulligan, and Nora; Tuohy's portrait of John Joyce; drawings of Molly; sketches of Bloom in 'Cyclops' and 'Lestrygonians'; the funeral at Glasnevin; Private Carr; the mangy dog Garryowen. *Courtesy of Richard Hamilton and Waddington Graphics, London.*

112

Ulysses, anticipates the second half of the book, which is dominated by self-conscious techniques such as parody, correspondences, lists, and by stylistic exuberance. In the process of composition, and only after the bulk of 'Aeolus' was written, did Joyce return to the episode and insert the sub-headings; here was further *graphic* proof of their intrusiveness.

When remarking on changes in communications or technology, Joyce rarely forgets the human contribution or consequence. In 'Wandering Rocks', the secretary, Miss Dunne, hides a copy of Wilkie Collins's *The Woman in White*, which she has borrowed from the Capel Street library (E3). Rolling a sheet of gaudy notepaper into her type-writer, she settles again to her work:

> Too much mystery business in it. Is he in love with that one, Marion? Change it and get another by Mary Cecil Haye.
> The disk shot down the groove, wobbled a while, ceased and ogled them: six.
> Miss Dunne clicked on the keyboard:
> – 16 June 1904.
>
> (*U* 10.371–6)

The disk, in point of fact, refers to a method of identifying acts in a continuous variety show, the whole sentence being an intrusion from a later section in the episode. Change the vowel in 'six' to 'e' and you have a thumbnail sketch of Miss Dunne, the bored secretary, mindlessly answering telephones and sitting at a typewriter which 'ogled them'. Miss Dunne clicks on the keyboard and inserts into the covers of a novel a date now known internationally as Bloomsday. Joyce discerned that the human world was both dependent on technology and also – at least in Ireland – independent of technology and the machine.

Elsewhere in *Ulysses*, the new technology receives comic treatment. Bloom gives serious thought to telephones being installed in every coffin just in case the person is not really dead. 'Whew! By jingo, that would be awful! . . . Just as well to get shut of them as soon as you are sure there's no' (*U* 6.866–71). For 'Blazes' Boylan, the phone provides a new line in suggestive chat; 'May I say a word to your telephone', he asks the fruit and flower assistant in Thornton's (*U* 10.336). By the time Joyce came to write *Finnegans Wake*, the telephone had become 'telephony' (*FW* 52.18), and the telephone directory a 'tellafun book' (*FW* 86.14).

Joyce's Dublin is saturated with signs and visual material. Eighteenth-century Dublin was by comparison an empty city. Consider James Malton's comments on town plan-ning made in the 1790s, at the end of the remarkable period when modern Dublin was effectively built:

> To promote the health and convenience of the city, wide and clean streets are certainly of principal importance; yet, if by an unforeseen event, a picturesque object should obtrude itself, so as to impede the view from one end of the street to the other, and uninterrupted prospect the only advantage to be gained by its removal, it certainly should not take place; as in the first instance a real beauty would be lost, and it is not certain an equivalent would be gained.[4]

The passage reminds us of the care which went into the making of Georgian Dublin. A century later, the city seems caught in the mire of poverty and commercialism, the great age of improvement past when art and nature rather grandly complemented each other. Joyce does not lament the passing, though he often reminds us through his characters that the city they inhabit was once

9 After receiving Martha Clifford's letter at the Westland Row post office (F4) Bloom's thoughts are set jingling with the language of flowers, a well-worked theme with Edwardian postcard manufacturers on both sides of the channel. 'Angry tulips with you darling manflower punish your cactus if you don't please poor forgetmenot how I long violets to dear roses when we soon anemone meet all naughty nightstalk wife Martha perfume' (*U* 5.264–6).

graceful, beautiful, and spacious. The streets of Joyce's Dublin give the impression of being closed in, noisy with information and people. The shop-fronts and window displays seduce the eye away from vistas and impressive thoroughfares and the city becomes just a place full of shops. And look at them all! In Westland Row (F4) there is the Belfast and Oriental Tea Company, in Lincoln Place (F4) Sweny's the chemists ('Chemists rarely move' [*U* 5.463–4], thinks Bloom), in Grafton Street (F4) Brown Thomas. There is the Rover cycle shop, Moses Dlugacz the pork butchers, James W. Mackey, seed merchants, Fullam's the ship chandlers, Flower and MacDonald, coal merchants, Meade's timber yard, Henry Price makers of chinaware (and commodes), George Mesias, tailors, D.B.C. or 'damn bad cakes' (*U* 10.1058), as 'Buck' Mulligan calls the Dublin Bakery Company in Dame Street (E4), O'Neil's funeral establishment, Connellan's bookshop, Dillon's auction rooms. Joyce does more than any Edwardian guidebook to Dublin, for he insists on giving us the actual name, the type of shop, and, more often than not, its location.

8 'Was the guest conscious of and did he acknowledge these marks of hospitality? His attention was directed to them by his host jocosely, and he accepted them seriously as they drank in jocoserious silence Epps's massproduct, the creature cocoa' (*U* 17.366–70). From *Ward Lock Guide to Worthing and South-West Sussex* (1906).

10 'hes very young to be a professor I hope hes not a professor like Goodwin was he was a potent professor of John Jameson' (*U* 18.1332–3). From *Ward Lock Guide to Worthing and South-West Sussex* (1906).

As the various characters make their way about the city – and Joyce's characters are more often than not in transit – they are assaulted by a range of visual material, much of it originating in adverts on hoardings or in newspapers. There are the drink adverts: Tunney's tawny sherry; Cantrell and Cochrane's Ginger Ale; Benedictine ('They had a gay old time while it lasted. Healthy too, chanting, regular hours, then brew liqueurs' [*U* 5.406–7]); Bushmills and John Jameson, Bass and Guinness; Dr Tibble's Vi-Cocoa and Epps's soluble cocoa.

There are also the medicinal adverts: William Gilbey and Company's white invalid port, Hamilton Long's syringe, and the 'Wonderworker', which Joyce could not resist quoting in full:

It heals and soothes while you sleep, in case of trouble in breaking wind, assists

nature in the most formidable way, insuring instant relief in discharge of gases, keeping parts clean and free natural action, an initial outlay of 7/6 making a new man of you and life worth living. Ladies find Wonderworker especially useful, a pleasant surprise when they note delightful result like a cool drink of fresh spring water on a sultry summer's day. Recommend it to your lady and gentlemen friends, lasts a lifetime. Insert long round end. Wonderworker.

(*U* 17.1826–33)

Even though he relishes excess, Joyce insists on accuracy. Everything has to be correctly named: Lisle suspender tops, Crown Derby saucer, Muratti's Turkish cigarettes,

DUBLIN—ST. STEPHEN'S GREEN.
Mr. James McCann—N... 3,429

*Mr. J. H. M. Campbell—C 2,873
Nationalist majority... —— 556
Electorate : 8,714.

1886 poll ; E. D. Gray (N), 5,008 ; Sir E. Sullivan (LU), 2,565—Nationalist majority, 2,443.
1888, May 4 (on the death of Mr. Gray): T. A. Dickson (N), 4,819 ; R. Sexton (C), 2,932—Nationalist majority, 1,887.
1892 poll ; Wm. Kenny (LU), 2,893 ; J. M. Meade (P), 2,876 ; Wm. Pearson (AP), 615—Liberal Unionist majority, 15.
1895 poll : W. Kenny (LU), 3,190 ; Count Plunkett (P), 2,634—Liberal Unionist majority, 556.
1895, Sept. 2 (on Mr. Kenny accepting office): Kenny (LU), 3,661 ; Pierce Mahoney (P), 2,893—Unionist majority, 768.
1898, Jan. 21 (on Mr. Kenny being made a Judge): J. H. M. Campbell (C), 3,525 ; Count Plunkett (P), 3,387—Conservative majority, 138.
Mr. James McCann, who has somewhat unexpectedly won back the St. Stephen's Green division to Nationalism, is one of the great commercial men of the Irish capital. Educated under the Jesuits, who stood him in good stead when he started in Dublin as a stockbroker, Mr. McCann has always refused in his business to have anything to do with "booms," such as the disastrous cycle boom of a few years ago, either as stockbroker or speculator. As chairman of the Grand Canal Company, Mr. McCann controls perhaps the greatest of Irish waterways, and he has managed so well

MR. JAMES McCANN.

that it is now a paying concern. The new member for St. Stephen's Green is a very devoted Catholic. His son is a Jesuit priest, one of his daughters is a nun.

11   On their way to Glasnevin Cemetery (D1), the funeral cortège passes the house where Thomas Childs was murdered in 1899. 'A gruesome case,' comments Simon Dedalus. 'Seymour Bushe got him off. Murdered his brother. Or so they said' (*U* 6.470–1). To Joyce, Dublin was a 'prismatic' community, always there and subject to ceaseless refraction. In the next episode, 'Aeolus', Myles Crawford and J. J. O'Molloy refer to the same case and Bushe's expertise in the court of law. '– One of the most polished periods I think I ever listened to in my life fell from the lips of Seymour Bushe' (*U* 7.747–8). More comically, in 'Ithaca', Bloom imagines he might have had a successful career at the bar with Seymour Bushe, KC, as his 'exemplar' (*U* 17.792). This photo of Bushe appeared in Michael McCarthy, *Five Years in Ireland 1895–1900* (1901).

12   As the cortège crosses the Royal Canal (E2), Bloom thinks of the course of the canal through the Irish Midlands and the possibility of taking a walking tour by the canal to see Milly. 'Developing waterways. James McCann's hobby to row me o'er the ferry. Cheaper transit. By easy stages. Houseboats. Camping out. Also hearses. To heaven by water' (*U* 6.447–9). From the *Pall Mall Gazette* we learn that James McCann, a successful businessman, was also MP for 'my green', namely St Stephen's Green. We are also told (perhaps there is an intended irony) that the Jesuits 'stood him in good stead' when he started in Dublin as a stockbroker, precisely the phrase the less successful Jesuit-educated Stephen Dedalus uses at the end of *A Portrait*. *Pall Mall Gazette* 1900.

13 Clara Butt was associated with 'Love's Old Sweet Song', 'Land of Hope and Glory', and 'Softly Awakes My Heart'. In 1901 Stanislaus went to a concert at the Rotunda given by her. He was alone, seated next to a 'handsome, dark-haired woman, between thirty and forty years old'. They struck up a conversation and at the end shook hands. 'Out of this unpromising material which he found in my diary, my brother made the story "A Painful Case".' (*MBK* 159).

14 and 15 The popular Victorian comedian Dan Leno (1860–1904) surrounded himself on stage with imaginary figures like Mrs Kelly, and used a patter reminiscent of Anna Livia: 'Ah y'know Mrs Kelly, you must know Mrs Kelly . . . she's a cousin of Mrs Niplet's and her husband keeps the what-not shop in the – ah, y'must know Mrs Kelly. Everybody knows Mrs Kelly'. 'Well, you know Anna Livia? Yes, of course we all know Anna Livia. Tell me all. Tell me now. You'll die when you hear.' (*FW* 196.4–6). According to Watters and Murtagh, London loved him but Dublin, where he wandered as a boy in a 'white hat shaped like a basin and a pair of elastic boots which he shared with his mother', was less enthusiastic.

MADAME CLARA BUTT.

"Abide with Me."

A bide with me fast falls the ev en tide The dark ness deep ens

116

Matterson's fat ham rashers, bottles of Jeyes's Fluid, Dockrell's wallpaper, Henry Clay cigars, Commerfords party oranges and lemonade. And Bloom's mind resonates all the time, as with the name of Scottish Widows: 'Takes it for granted we're going to pop off first' (*U* 13.1228).

The music hall

Joyce devotes considerable attention to another feature of late-Victorian/Edwardian life – the music hall. In the first episode of *Ulysses*, we learn of Stephen's mother laughing when old Royce sang: '*I am the boy / That can enjoy / Invisibility*' (*U* 1.260–2). In 'Circe', Bloom's mother Ellen appears '*in pantomime dame's stringed mobcap, widow Twankey's crinoline and bustle*' (*U* 15.283–4). Music-hall numbers can be heard throughout *Ulysses* and *Finnegans Wake*, and some, such as 'Love's Old Sweet Song' in *Ulysses* or Tom Costello's 'At Trinity Church I Met My Doom' in *Finnegans Wake*, function as leitmotifs. Frank Budgen remembers Joyce in Zurich in 1918–20 singing tunes from those 'vintage years of popular song associated with the names of Dan Leno, Harry Randall, Tom Costello, Gus Elen, Arthur Roberts, and the other music-hall giants of that time.'[5] One of Joyce's party pieces, which both Curran and Budgen remember him singing, was Charles Coburn's 'The Man Who Broke the Bank at Monte Carlo'.[6] There is no snobbery in Joyce; he was as interested in popular entertainment as he was in Italian opera. Indeed, for him, as Stanislaus reminds us, it is not poetry that affords an Arnoldian criticism of life, but music hall (see *DD* 38).

In *Finnegans Wake*, Joyce draws on his memory of music hall, pantomime, and melodrama to provide a comic introduction to 'The Mime of Mick, Nick and the Maggies':

Every evening at lighting up o'clock sharp and until further notice in Feenichts Playhouse. (Bar and conveniences always open, Diddlem Club douncestears.) Entrancings: gads, a scrab; the quality, one large shilling. Newly billed for each wickeday perfumance. Somndoze massinees. By arraignment, childream's hours, expercatered. Jampots, rinsed porters, taken in token. With nightly redistribution of parts and players by the puppetry producer and daily dubbing of ghosters, with the benediction of the Holy Genesius Archimimus and under the distinguished patronage of their Elderships the Oldens from the four coroners of Findrias, Murias, Gorias and Falias, Messoirs the Coarbs, Clive Sollis, Galorius Kettle, Pobiedo Lancey and Pierre Dusort, while the Caesar-in-Chief looks. On. Sennet. As played to the Adelphi by the Brothers Bratislavoff (Hyrcan and Haristobulus), after humpteen dumpteen revivals. Before all the King's Hoarsers with all the Queen's Mum. And wordloosed over seven seas crowdblast in celtelleneteutoslavzendlatinsoundscript. In four tubbloids. While fern may cald us until firn make cold. *The Mime of Mick, Nick and the Maggies*, adopted from the Ballymooney Bloodriddon Murther by Bluechin Blackdillain (authorways 'Big Storey'), featuring:
(*FW* 219.1–21)

Joyce's mind buzzes with detailed memories associated with the music hall of his childhood. He recalls the billboards, that music hall was the poor man's entertainment, the names of the theatres such as the Queen's and its predecessor, the Adelphi, the names of pantomimes such as *Humpty Dumpty*, how children would pay with jam pots for admission, and he does not forget St

16 Harry Randall (1860–1932) performed in all the leading music halls, making his first panto appearance in 1871. In her letter to Bloom, Martha Clifford calls him a 'naughty boy': 'So now you know what I will do to you, you naughty boy, if you do not wrote' (*U* 5.252–3). And he remembers Molly chiding him in similar terms: 'Are you not happy in your home you poor little naughty boy?' (*U* 8.612).

"AH! NAUGHTY BOY!"

17 'Bella Bello' from an original embossed colour engraving by Saul Field. (From Saul Field and Morton P. Levitt, *Bloomsday*, Greenwich, Conn: New York Graphic Society, 1972). *Courtesy of Jean Townsend-Field.*

118

Genesius, the patron saint of actors. Hump – the HCE figure – is played by Mr Makeall Gone, Michael Gunn, that is, the 'enterprising' manager of the Gaiety, who made all and went. It is a 'wickeday' performance because popular entertainment in Dublin always risked clerical attack. It is a 'Diddlem Club' because money was made out of people unfairly.

Joyce found irresistible the music hall's mixed genres and rapid changes of scene, its rogues, gangsters, and children's dreams, its evocation of exotic scenes from the East. With only a small adjustment, he could quickly incorporate all this into the many-layered programme of *Finnegans Wake*. In the above passage, for example, the immediate context of the mime and music hall suddenly opens out on to the whole field of politics, history, and culture with Joyce's allusions to an Elizabethan company of players, 'firn make cold' (Finn MacCool), the Tuatha de Danaan, and Patrick Pearse's Sword of Light ('Clive Sollis' is *Claidheamh Solais*, the title of Pearse's newspaper).

The Edwardian period saw the final flourishing of the British music hall, and it is right that it should be given prominence in Joyce's novel of 1904. 'Circe', the Night-town sequence or phantasmagoria that takes place in Bella Cohen's brothel, is the episode that best captures the music-hall flavour. Most of the characters previously mentioned in *Ulysses* make a further appearance, only this time they are cast as actors in a play. There is no escape from Joyce's compulsive desire to recycle. Stephen's dead mother, and Paddy Dignam, whose funeral took place that morning, are both 'revived'; Bloom's Hungarian father 'Virag Lipoti of Szombathely', who committed suicide in the Queen's Hotel in Ennis, County Clare, returns to taunt Bloom for associating with a 'drunken goy' (*U* 15.253); and there are walk-on parts also for Edward VII, Elijah and a figure called 'The End of the World'. Father Dolan, whom we last encountered in *A Portrait*, also appears, making the same threatening noises: 'Any boy want flogging? Broke his glasses? Lazy idle little schemer. See it in your eye' (*U* 15.3671–2). Even Dolly Gray, the figure in Costello's patriotic song from the Boer War years, has a part, waving goodbye from a balcony: 'Safe home to Dolly. Dream of the girl you left behind and she will dream of you' (*U* 15.4419–20).

'Circe' is awkward, larger than life, conscious of the audience, loud, capable of every kind of ribaldry, full of belly laughs, and in this regard not unlike music hall or a scene from an expressionist play. It belongs to the world of drag, pantomime dames and principal boys, ventriloquists, and courtroom drama. People dress up, change names, change sex, adopt impersonations. The keeper of the brothel, a '*massive whoremistress*' (*U* 15.2742) Bella Cohen, becomes Bello Cohen, a transformation that recalls the stage performance of the popular male impersonator Vesta Tilley. To his cost Bloom learns that Bella/Bello is 'Master! Mistress! Mantamer!' (*U* 15.3062). Tim Harrington, the late Lord Mayor of Dublin, enters in scarlet robe with mace, gold mayoral chain, and large white scarf.

Needless to say, it is Bloom, entering carrying in one hand a lukewarm pig's crubeen and in the other a cold sheep's trotter, who steals the show. With rapid changes of clothes, he attempts to appease in turn his different accusers: in 'smart blue Oxford suit' and 'brown Alpine hat'; dinner jacket with 'blue masonic badge in his buttonhole'; 'purple Napoleon hat with an amber halfmoon'; 'oatmeal sporting suit, a sprig of woodbine in the lapel'; in 'red fez, cadi's dress coat with broad green sash';

18 Vesta Tilley, the 'London Idol', spent most of her stage career as a male impersonator. A popular performer with Irish audiences, she appeared seven times at Dan Lowrey's Star of Erin music hall in Dublin, the last time in 1895. An Edwardian postcard.

19 When Joyce went to Paris in 1902 to study medicine, he carried with him a testimonial from Tim Harrington, one-time Mayor of Dublin and friend of John Joyce. Harrington appears in 'Circe' dressed in his mayoral robes. This is how he appeared in the *Pall Mall Gazette* in October 1900.

DUBLIN CITY—HARBOUR DIV.

*Mr. T. Harrington—N......Unopposed

Electorate : 11,018.

1886: T. Harrington (N), unopposed.
1892: T. Harrington (P), 4,482 ; J. McDonnell (AP), 1,376—Parnellite majority, 3,106.
1895: T. Harrington (P), unopposed.

The greatest piece of good luck which befell Mr. Parnell when he had fallen on evil days was probably the capture of Mr. Tim Harrington, and with him most of the machinery of the National League. For Mr. Harrington was the Carnot-Schnadhorst of Ireland. He had his hand on the machinery of public opinion, and he had perfected his engine till it responded to his lightest touch. That so many branches should have declared against Mr. Parnell was almost a miracle ; for Tim was a caucus boss à l'Américaine,

MR. T. HARRINGTON.

and as much down on unregulated enthusiasm as on the use of alcohol, which he never tastes. In this character he has in past years done really good service in the suppression of crime and extreme measures. His master-stroke was the carving up of the Paris funds with the Anti-Parnellites. In the late Parliament, having split off from Mr. Redmond, he founded the only harmonious Irish party on record. It consisted of one member, Mr. Tim Harrington ; but, in the interests of Irish unity, this party eventually consented to amalgamate with the others on terms of equality. His physique has given him a special prominence on the Irish benches, and the House has often been startled by the boisterousness of his cheers and the loudness of his voice. He is 49, was educated at Trinity College, Dublin, and, as a barrister, appeared before the Parnell Commission.

6 Cavendish Row, Dublin ; Artane Lodge, Artane.

'housejacket of ripplecloth' and 'heelless slippers'; in 'workman's corduroy overalls'; in 'dalmatic and purple mantle'; in 'a seamless garment marked I.H.S.'; in 'Svengali's fur overcoat'; in 'flunkey's prune plush coat and kneebreeches, buff stockings and powdered wig'. He performs juggler's tricks, draws a spectrum of silk handkerchiefs from his mouth, 'turns each foot simultaneously in different directions', 'seats himself in the pillory with arms crossed, his feet protruding'. Joyce is in his element writing about clothes. As a child he wore an Eton suit for the family Christmas dinner; as a young man back from Paris he sported a

wide-brimmed hat; as a grown man, he came complete with walking-stick, headgear, and fashionably dressed wife.

'Circe' is at once psychologically intense and ruthlessly detached, mixing pathos and

to a world of desire rather than actuality. But he is also rooted in a particular time and place. His thoughts, half-thoughts, personality, conversation, occupation, reading, all proclaim pre-First World War Dublin. He seems too real to be confined to the realms of fiction. Indeed, Peter Costello has assembled his biography as if Bloom were an actual historical person,[7] and when writing about the character, Joyce critics are often tempted to say not that he lives but that he lived at No. 7 Eccles Street (E2) – in a house that Joyce saw was vacant in *Thom's Directory of Dublin* for 1904. So real is Bloom that many Joyceans felt a genuine sense of violation when the Eccles Street house was demolished in 1982 to make way for a hospital extension.

Certain aspects of Joyce's placing of Bloom remain more shadowy than others. We need reminding, for example, that this was an era driven by the export of capital and marked in consequence by the beginnings of anti-colonial struggles in Egypt, South Africa, and Ireland. In South Africa, for example, Maud Gonne's husband, Captain John MacBride, fought with the Boers against the British. Dublin-born Robert Noonan, who was later to write, under the name Robert Tressell, a classic Edwardian novel about the British working class, *The Ragged Trousered Philanthropists*, was also involved in the anti-colonial struggle in the Transvaal at this time. In 1907–9, Dubliners William Maloney and Fred Ryan went to Cairo to edit the *Egyptiam Standard*, ever conscious, as their letters to their socialist friend Francis Sheehy-Skeffington reveal, that they too were involved in a struggle against British imperialism. Some of this material, especially the rise of Sinn Fein, surfaces in Joyce's book – there is even the fanciful suggestion that Arthur Griffith, author of *The Resur-*

22 A portrait of 7 Eccles Street (E2) by Flora H. Mitchell. *Courtesy of the University of Southern Illinois Library.*

rection of Hungary (1904), lifted some of his ideas from the Hungarian Jew Leopold Bloom.

References to the Boer War punctuate *Ulysses*. The day Joseph Chamberlain, for example, receives an honorary degree at Trinity College, Bloom, caught in the commotion, is chased by a mounted policeman down Abbey Street (E4):

– Up the Boers!
– Three cheers for De Wet!
– We'll hang Joe Chamberlain on a sourapple tree.

(*U* 8.434–6)

In 'Circe' Bloom defends himself against the charge of using seditious slogans by saying that he 'fought with the colours for king and country in the absentminded war under

general Gough in the park and was disabled at Spion Kop and Bloemfontein', that he was 'mentioned in dispatches', and that he 'did all a white man could' (*U* 15.794–7). 'I'm as staunch a Britisher as you are, sir.' Bloom's double identification – with the Irish general Gough who distinguished himself in the Peninsular War and whose statue was erected seventy years later in the Phoenix Park (B3), and with the British who fought the Boers – reveals his sense of unease about national identity and the need to compensate for his Hungarian Jewish origins. Skin-the-Goat, on the other hand, entertains no such doubts about his identity and 'stated *crescendo* with no uncertain voice' that:

> The Boers were the beginning of the end. Brummagem England was toppling already and her downfall would be Ireland, her Achilles heel. . . .
>
> (*U* 16.1002–3)

Bloom is accused of being a 'whiteeyed kaffir' (*U* 12.1552) in a passage in which Roger Casement, the man responsible for exposing the atrocities of King Leopold in the Belgian Congo, is mentioned. The Citizen's prejudice against foreigners and blacks is momentarily checked – for Casement is an Irishman (later executed by the British in 1916 for gun-running). Joyce seems reluctant to make a connection between Leopold the King of the Belgians and Leopold Bloom: Bloom is called Leopold the First, but Joyce distances him from the man who helped create Conrad's 'heart of darkness'. However, there is enough in the text to make us pause before concluding that the Boer War is used simply as background by Joyce. There are many indictments against the British in *Ulysses* but one of the most telling occurs in the 'Scylla and Charybdis' episode when Stephen mentally

connects Hamlet, the concentration camps established by the British to terrorize the Boers, and the jingoism of one of England's leading poets: 'Khaki Hamlets don't hesitate to shoot. The bloodboltered shambles in act five is a forecast of the concentration camp sung by Mr Swinburne' (*U* 9.133–5).[8]

As to the character of Bloom himself, he is Joyce's master stroke. Bloom is both an idiosyncratic individual and Everyman, a lower-middle-class hero and *l'homme moyen sensuel*, the father looking for a son, the Jew in a Catholic country, the kind-hearted protector of women and children, the rescuer of fallen women, a husband-victim, the man of feeling, at one with the world's suffering. In the words of *Ulysses* he is the 'plebeian Don Juan', 'a cod', an 'allround man', the citizen with 'a touch of the artist', a 'distinguished phenomenologist', a 'public nuisance to the citizens of Dublin', 'a cuckold', the 'greekjew' and the 'Jewgreek', the 'outsider', an 'acclimatised Britisher', the 'departing guest', the 'limp father of thousands', 'the new womanly man'. He is, in short, someone who is simultaneously dispossessed, in exile, and at home. As a salesman, a 'space-hound' whose job it is to sell advertising space in newspapers to the business community, he understands instinctively that his first duty towards others is not to assert his opinion but to accommodate theirs. He is the outsider who takes the pulse of his city not by introspection but by observing what people read and how they conduct themselves. He is not quite all things to all men, for he has his principles. But he possesses sufficient qualities and, indeed, defects to make him someone the modern reader can instantly identify – and identify with.

> I stand for the reform of municipal morals and the plain ten commandments. New

worlds for old. Union of all, jew, moslem and gentile. Three acres and a cow for all children of nature. Saloon motor hearses. Compulsory manual labour for all. All parks open to the public day and night. Electric dishscrubbers. Tuberculosis, lunacy, war and mendicancy must now cease. General amnesty, weekly carnival with masked licence, bonuses for all, esperanto the universal language with universal brotherhood. No more patriotism of barspongers and dropsical impostors. Free money, free rent, free love and a free lay church in a free lay state.

(*U* 15.1685–93)

The Edwardian aspect of Bloom's character is especially noticeable in the context of advertising and 'physical culture'. Joyce meticulously recreates the street furniture for 16 June 1904, even down to the advertising hoardings. In doing so he reminds us of what is today a commonplace, namely the pervasiveness of advertising in our lives. In his professional capacity, Bloom has first-hand knowledge of the new world of mass advertising. 'No use canvassing him for an ad', he thinks to himself about Larry O'Rourke (*U* 4.112); 'must nail that ad of Keyes's', he reminds himself in 'Nausicaa' (*U* 13.1243), having spent part of the morning proposing the idea to Myles Crawford the editor and Councillor Nannetti the printer: '– The idea, Mr Bloom said, is the house of keys. You know, councillor, the Manx parliament. Innuendo of home rule. Tourists, you know, from the isle of Man. Catches the eye, you see. Can you do that?' (*U* 7.149–51). Molly, on the other hand, is thoroughly bored with 'Billy Prescotts ad and Keyess ad and Tom the Devils ad', knowing that 'if anything goes wrong in their business we have to suffer' (*U* 18.1342–4).

24 Eamonn Morrissey dressed as Bloom inside the Martello Tower at Sandycove. In the opening paragraph of 'Calypso', Joyce finally discovers in the character of Bloom his counter to the remoteness of Stephen Dedalus: 'Mr Leopold Bloom ate with relish the inner organs of beasts and fowls. He liked thick giblet soup, nutty gizzards, a stuffed roast heart, liverslices fried with crustcrumbs, fried hencods' roes. Most of all he liked grilled mutton kidneys which gave to his palate a fine tang of faintly scented urine' (*U* 4.1–5). *Photograph Dan Harper.*

Bloom reshapes the world according to adverts. For him the most suitable place to catch a woman's eye is on a mirror (*U* 13.919–20). If he cannot remember the restaurant advertising cheap lunches, he can look it up in the National Library (*U* 8.369), but some adverts, such as the one featuring a luminous crucifix (*U* 8.18–19), escape the powers of his prodigious memory. The best paper for a small advert 'by long chalks' is the *Irish Times* – and it has 'got the provinces now' (*U* 8.334). That very morning Bloom has received a (further) reply to his request in the personal columns for 'smart lady typist to aid gentleman in literary work' (*U* 8.326–7). In spite of the presumably suggestive

125

25 In 'Aeolus' Bloom nervously seeks permission for the House of Keyes ad from Councillor Nannetti, the foreman printer at the *Freeman's Journal* (which also published the *Evening Telegraph*). Nannetti is both an MP at Westminster and a city councillor (hence 'councillor'). 'I could ask him perhaps about how to pronounce that *voglio*. But then if he didn't know only make it awkward for him' (*U* 7.152–3). This is how the Councillor appeared in the hostile *Pall Mall Gazette* in 1900.

DUBLIN—COLLEGE GREEN.

Mr. J. P. Nanetti—Ind N... 2,467

*Mr. J. L. Carew—N 2,173
Nationalist majority ...... —— 294

Electorate : 10,223.

1886 : T. D. Sullivan (N), unopposed.
1892 : Dr. J. E. Kenny (P), 2,568 : Sir H. Cochrane (LU), 1,441 : T. D. Sullivan (AP), 1,116 —Parnellite majority, 1,127.
1895 : Kenny (P), unopposed.
Mr. Joseph Patrick Nanetti, who challenged Mr. Carew's right of succession because that free and independent member had dared to attend a levée of the Duke of York's in London, was the foreman printer of the Dublin *Evening Telegraph*, is a member of the Dublin Corporation, the Dublin Port and Docks Board, and the Dublin Trades Council. He was one of the candidates nominated by Mr. William O'Brien's United Irish League, and on the eve of his selection he stated that in 1887 he was a sworn Fenian and trusted in the inner ranks of that organisation. He was the Dublin correspondent of the *Board of Trade Gazette*. As his name indicates, he is of Italian extraction.
19 Hardwicke Street, Dublin.

MR. J. P. NANETTI.

contents of his own letter, Martha Clifford 'Answered anyhow' (*U* 5.65). Stephen Dedalus's degree from the National University is 'a huge ad in its way' (*U* 16.1827). The Church's use of repetition is similar to the way adverts function: 'Good idea the repetition. Same thing with ads. Buy from us. And buy from us' (*U* 13.1123–4). And Bloom's mind immediately clicks into the humour of graffiti as with 'POST NO BILLS', which 'some chap with a dose burning him' has changed to 'POST IIO PILLS' (*U* 8.101).

Throughout the day Bloom's expert eye fixes on adverts around the city. The horseshoe poster over the gate of College Park with the cyclist doubled up like a cod in a pot is a 'damn bad ad': 'Now if they had made it round like a wheel. Then the spokes: sports, sports, sports; and the hub big: college. Something to catch the eye' (*U* 5.552–4). In the same episode, having collected the letter for 'Henry Flower' from Westland Row post office (F4), Bloom pauses at the corner of Brunswick Street and Cumberland Street (G4), 'his eyes wandering over the multicoloured hoardings. Cantrell and Cochrane's Ginger Ale (Aromatic). Clery's Summer Sale. No, he's going on straight. Hello. *Leah* tonight' (*U* 5.192–4). At this point Bloom is anxious to read Martha Clifford's reply and to escape from the clutches of McCoy, whom he imagines for a moment might be pimping him: 'No, he's going on straight.' Just prior to this, Bloom glances at the Plumtree's potted meat advert in the newspaper he has rolled up into a baton: 'What a stupid ad!' he thinks later (*U* 8.743).

Folded into Bloom's internal emotional landscape is the impersonal 'serial' language of advertising.[9] Although publicly displayed, adverts are for the most part addressed to the individual. Adverts need to suppress the thought that they are also being read by another million individuals, for this would undermine their efficacy and remind the individual that s/he is but one of a series and not the fully human subject s/he imagines. Present in most adverts therefore is the Other. In Joyce's depiction of Bloom, a link is established between the Other in the advert and the Other inside Bloom himself, which can be defined as that which needs suppressing, that which cannot be thought, or perhaps which emerges as a Freudian slip. Bloom's angry dismissal of the Plumtree's potted meat advert reveals as much about his own state of mind as about the advert's inane jingle, for, with Boylan on his way to seduce Molly, Bloom half-consciously

recognizes that without his potted meat home is not 'an abode of bliss'.

Joyce dwells on the serial nature of advertising – he seems less interested in the role advertising plays in appealing to the collective subject or in producing a group identity. In the funeral cortège on its way to Glasnevin, Bloom notices on the hoardings under the railway bridge past the Queen's Theatre (F4) 'Eugene Stratton' (*U* 6.184). In 'Wandering Rocks', Father Conmee sees on a different hoarding 'Mr Eugene Stratton' grimacing at him with 'thick niggerlips' (*U* 10.141–2). On yet another hoarding at the Royal Canal bridge (actually McKenna Bridge [G5] over the Grand Canal – a rare Joycean slip), His Excellency the Earl of Dudley passes 'Mr Eugene Stratton, his blub lips agrin, [bidding] all comers welcome to Pembroke township' (*U* 10.1273–4). With his thick lips and his enigmatic grin, Stratton stares out from the hoardings round the city. The same advert, seen by different people in different parts of the city, triggers in turn a range of different responses. Father Conmee alights on Stratton's 'niggerlips' and thinks of the 'souls of black and brown and yellow men' (*U* 10.142–4); elsewhere in the city the

advert is wrongly interpreted as belonging to the welcoming celebrations for the Earl of Dudley's cavlacade. A grinning face demands a response, especially when the face is black and the society predominantly racist. Stratton's advert is directed at a potential theatre audience, but it is read by many others. It exists, therefore, within a much more widely dispersed field of cultural signs. Joyce throws into relief the 'surplus value' of advertising. Bloom is involved in a constant battle to make sense of all the

26 '*What is home without Plumtree's Potted Meat? Incomplete. With it an abode of bliss.*' (*U* 5.144–7)
Private Collection.

27 An advertisement in the *Freeman's Journal* and the *Evening Telegraph* for 16 June 1904 announces: 'Eugene Stratton, the World Renowned Comedian' at the Theatre Royal. Born in Buffalo, New York, in 1861, Eugene Stratton came to London in the 1880s and quickly established himself with his song and dance routine as a sought-after black entertainer. With songs such as 'The Whistling Coon' and 'The Dandy Coloured Coon', he made much of his racial origins. On stage he wore a black frock coat, silk top hat and bow tie, using a single spotlight on his face for dramatic effect. He was popular with other professionals, and in 1896 and again in 1900 he was named King Rat. The Chieftains play a hornpipe named after him. An Edwardian postcard.

28 A striking array of advertisements in a poorer district of Joyce's Dublin. Such bits and pieces form the basis of Joyce's seamless world of signs. Whether the advert is announcing the date of a cycling tour, cajoling people to buy the *Sunday World* ('The Only Sunday Paper'), exhorting the faithful to be mindful of their religious duties (saying the Rosary, eschewing mixed marriages), or seducing people to buy alcohol ('Ask for it and try it'), they are all reminders that advertising obeys its own rules, being simultaneously value-free and value-laden. The one thing adverts rarely address is poverty and class conflict. *Courtesy of the National Library of Ireland.*

reading matter and cultural images and signs around him; his head whirls as he tries to absorb the scattered bits of information; he develops a nervous tic and finds himself repeating the jingles. Joyce was alive to this new kind of phenomenon, the war in the market-place between the advertiser and the public. He does not labour the point, but Joyce clearly recognized an emerging 'recuperative' struggle: the use and control of language was contentious; the personal image in an anonymous environment was subject to distortion.

Sandow's exercises

Among the books on Bloom's shelf, we are informed in 'Ithaca', is one by Eugen Sandow entitled *Physical Strength and How to Obtain It* (U 17.1397). Complete with photographs of Sandow's manly body, an Anatomical Chart, a system of exercises, and readers' letters vouching for the method, the book is designed for those who 'wish to be strong' and who 'yearn for health'. 'Its ultimate object', Sandow proclaims, 'is to raise the average standard of the race as a whole.' He assures his reader that, prior to turning to his system, many of his pupils 'had been rejected as unsound by Life Insurance Companies', and, for good measure, he informs us that he himself is insured by the Norwich Union.[10] Bloom, with his feelings of inferiority, his generalized anxiety, and his search for the key to a successful life, is an ideal candidate for the Sandow treatment. At one point the author uncannily expresses what could be Bloom's philosophy in life: 'There is no better guide to good living than moderation.'[11]

Sandow's exercises were very popular in the Edwardian era – even the dream-led and sedentary Yeats spent time doing them. Sandow schools were established in

29   Eugen Sandow, author of the Sandow system of physical exercise. Billed as 'The Strongest Man in the World', his name was used to advertise everything from corsets to cocoa. Ironically, in 1925, while attempting to retrieve his car from a ditch, he suffered a stroke and died at the age of fifty-eight.

several parts of Britain, and Sandow himself travelled widely giving exhibitions – in May 1898 he performed at the Empire Palace in Dublin. The Edwardian age, with its stress on physical exercise and the outdoor life, laid the foundations for today's interest in physical culture. The bicycle, or as Joyce called it the 'bisexycle' (*FW* 115.16), enabled people to travel out of the city at weekends and into the countryside, the women dressed in 'peak caps and the new woman bloomers' (U 18.839). To cater for this new audience, the *Irish Cyclist* and other magazines for Touring Clubs were launched.

Bloom belongs to this new body-and-fitness culture, hoping that its magic aura

129

30 Bloom's relationship with the body is by turns hopeful, jejune, secretive, abusive, and obsessive. He is conscious of the need for exercise, to 'get the hands down', but is equally interested in the female anatomy, and during the day he makes a special trip to the Museum and National Library (F5) to inspect the female statues in the entrance hall – he thinks of them as 'aids to digestion' (*U* 8.922). Bloom's name suggests bloomers, the new fashion in women's clothes. Molly goes further: 'I suppose theyre called after him I never thought that would be my name Bloom when I used to write it in print to see how it looked on a visiting card' (*U* 18.840–2). *Courtesy of the National Library of Ireland.*

will transform him into an active participant. Earlier in the day on his way from the pork butchers after purchasing a kidney for his breakfast, the thought of exercise occurs to him: 'Got up wrong side of the bed. Must begin again those Sandow's exercises. On the hands down' (*U* 4.233–4). The phrase repeats itself in 'Circe', when Bloom, running away from danger, develops a stitch. 'Close shave that but cured the stitch. Must take up Sandow's exercises again. On the hands down' (*U* 15.199–200). Sandow's exercises are mentioned again in 'Ithaca':

Were there no means still remaining to him to achieve the rejuvenation which these reminiscences divulged to a younger companion rendered the more desirable?

The indoor exercises, formerly intermittently practised, subsequently abandoned, prescribed in Eugen Sandow's *Physical Strength and How to Obtain It* which, designed particularly for commercial men engaged in sedentary occupations, were to be made with mental concentration in front of a mirror so as to bring into play the various families of muscles and produce successively a pleasant rigidity, a more pleasant relaxation and the most pleasant repristination of juvenile agility.

(*U* 17.509–18)

Sandow's seriousness we can accept, but Bloom's cultivation of physical culture, partly because he is so obviously deluded

130

by appearances, is rightly amusing. 'Telemachus' evokes the ancient Greek ideal regarding the male body, but when Bloom appears in 'Calypso', the companion episode, the contrast is plain to see. Bloom is the little man dissatisfied with his size who constantly idealizes the agility of his youth, when 'he had excelled in his stable and protracted execution of the half lever movement on the parallel bars in consequence of his abnormally developed abdominal muscles' (U 17.521–4). The 'inflated' language of 'Ithaca' reflects Bloom's inflated sense of his physique. Sandow himself had experienced the magical transformation and the leap in social status that Bloom desires. In his youth Sandow challenged and defeated on opponent known as 'Cyclops'. Until that point in his career, he was not regarded. 'But when I took off my coat [to fight "Cyclops"] and the people could see the muscular development, the tone of indifference changed immediately to surprise and curiosity.'[12] By contrast, in the 'Cyclops' episode in *Ulysses*, Bloom is unceremoniously ejected from Barney Kiernan's pub by the citizen, and has a biscuit tin thrown after him.

CHAPTER SIX
Ulysses *and the Unmaking of Modern Ireland*

1   At the beginning of *Ulysses* Stephen Dedalus has just returned from Paris, sporting a wide-brimmed Latin Quarter hat, the would-be artist looking for recognition. His clothes he borrows from Mulligan, but in his mind the bohemian Stephen feels perhaps not unlike the young man in this drawing which appeared in the *Pall Mall Gazette* in May 1901. 'God, we'll simply have to dress the character' (*U* 1.515–6). By contrast, as Padraic Colum reminds us in *Our Friend James Joyce*, when he returned to Dublin in 1909, Joyce was no longer 'the "character", the "card", the "artist" of Dublin conversation'.

THE DISPOSSESSED SON IN STRUGGLE

QUOTATION MOVES UNEASILY BETWEEN the centre and not so much the periphery as the surface of modernism. When a modernist writer quotes from a past text, the chord struck is often uncertain. At times there is a profound resonance, as for example when Eliot at the beginning of *The Waste Land* (1922) invokes Chaucer's General Prologue and the Anglican service for the Burial of the Dead; or when Malcolm Lowry begins his Faustian novel *Under the Volcano* (1947) in a style that recalls both Prescott's *History of the Conquest of Mexico*, written almost a century before, and Conrad's Latin-American novel *Nostromo* (1904). Quotation here serves to deepen our appreciation of the text, to establish a field of reference against which the writer seeks to have his or her text measured. At other times the achievement or purpose of quotation is less clear, and we are detained by the surface feature of a text, by its use of puns or parody or burlesque, for example. Joyce brings to this debate both a reassessment of hierarchical relationships in a text between centre and surface and also an awareness that quotation is associated with power and with struggle.

Joyce's continuous and generous use of Homer, his close alignment of *Ulysses* with

The Odyssey, serves to reinforce the way quotation is integral to his theme. Joyce is also a 'doublin' writer (*FW* 3.8) and reading him invariably implies therefore a form of double reading, a constant shifting between the text he is writing and the one(s) to which he is alluding. In 'Telemachus' this double reading can be tracked in Stephen's resistance to, among others, the Church, the *aisling* tradition of Irish verse, his mother's strictures, Matthew Arnold's Hellenism, the nineties Yeats. 'Telemachus' thus centres on the struggle between the young Irishman's desire for authentic existence and the more likely prospect of merely reproducing a known pattern. Inscribed in the opening episode to *Ulysses* are a variety of sources and contexts – religious, linguistic, cross-cultural, formal, biographical, political, the cultural representations of the female – but all these are held in check by the Homeric theme of 'the dispossessed son in struggle'.[1] Expressed slightly differently, Stephen's predicament is initially mapped out by Joyce in the context of Irish Catholicism, Arnoldian Hellenism, and the colonial encounter between Britain and Ireland.

★ Stately, plump Buck Mulligan came from the stairhead, bearing a bowl of lather on which a mirror and a razor lay crossed. A yellow dressinggown,

132

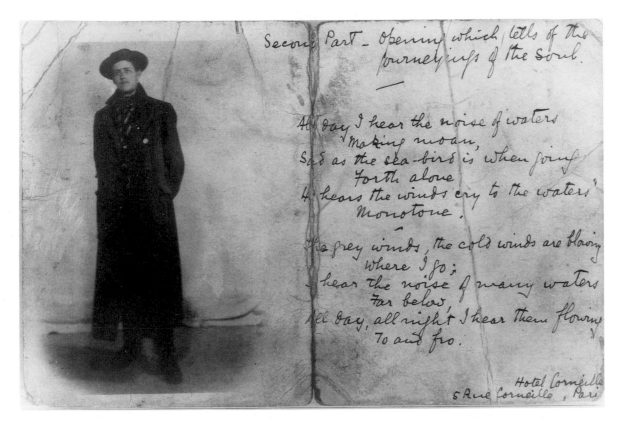

Second Part – Opening which tells of the journeyings of the soul.

All day I hear the noise of waters
    Making moan,
Sad as the sea-bird is when going
    Forth alone
He hears the winds cry to the waters'
    Monotone.

The grey winds, the cold winds are blowing
    Where I go;
I hear the noise of many waters
    Far below,
All day, all night I hear them flowing
    To and fro.

5 Rue Corneille, Pari
Hotel Corneille

2   Photo-postcard sent by Joyce to his friend J. F. Byrne from Paris in 1902, telling of 'the journeyings of the soul'. This first trip was cut short by a telegram from his father: MOTHER DYING COME HOME FATHER. It was Good Friday 1903. 'You were going to do wonders, what?' (*U* 3.192). 'Fabulous artificer. The hawklike man. You flew. Whereto? Newhaven–Dieppe, steerage passenger. Paris and back' (*U* 9.952–3). *Courtesy of the Beinecke Rare Book and Manuscript Library, Yale University.*

ungirdled, was sustained gently behind him on the mild morning air. He held the bowl aloft and intoned:
– *Introibo ad altare Dei.*

(*U* 1.1–5)

The religious struggle is evident in the very opening sentence, which transforms the readers of *Ulysses* into a 'congregation' of readers. The first words heard are spoken in Latin and 'intoned'; they are words recited by the priest at the beginning of the Mass: 'I will go up to the altar of God'. We are present at a parody of the Mass, an Irish black Mass conducted at the top of a Martello Tower amid the military trappings of the Napoleonic era. 'Buck' Mulligan – a descendant of the eighteenth-century

'bucks' who lived in a spirit of adventure and dressed in the devil's livery to show their contempt for superstition – assumes the role of celebrant with his dressing gown the priest's alb, the bowl of lather the chalice, and the mirror and the razor occult implements in a sacred rite. In the background are the Church's heretics, several of whom are mentioned in this episode – Photius, Arius, Valentine, Sabellius. *Ulysses* begins with a performance, a parody, and with an absence of spontaneity. There is a knowing acceptance, therefore, that the text's origins lie elsewhere, for a performance implies a known script, a parody an original, and intoning the more natural form of speaking, namely conversation.

The linguistic struggle is signalled in the

133

ἄνδρά μοι ἔννεπε μοῦσά πεμἰτροπον ὡς μάλά πόλλ

very first word. Is 'stately' an adjective or an adverb? Is Mulligan stately or is it his walk? It matters because in reading aloud there is a slight pause or otherwise between 'stately' and 'plump'. In terms of its meaning, the word 'stately' is decisive, but deployed here it produces hesitation. Is it a pun on the word 'state', on the British State, on the Secretary of State for War, who owned the Martello Tower? Is it meant to illustrate the doubt that straddles speech and writing?

Now take the opening sentence as a whole, and set it out, as Hugh Kenner suggests,[2] as a line of epic verse:

Státelў, plúmp Búck Múllĭgăn cáme frŏm thĕ stáirhéad, béarĭng

ă bówl óf láthĕr ŏn whĭch ă mírrŏr ănd ă rázŏr láy cróssed.

The awkwardness of this opening sentence seems designed to suggest the confrontation between two linguistic systems, English and Greek. Partly because of the grammatical structure, partly the strange word order, the sentence is profoundly un-English – indeed 'crossed'. Possibly Joyce has in his sights nineteenth-century critics who sought to parse English, which is an accentual language, as if it were a syllabic one like Latin and Greek. At stake is Joyce's attempt to free the language and criticism from its classical models, and to provide from the outset a *graphic* example of the necessity for a double reading of his 'usylessly unreadable Blue Book of Eccles' (*FW* 179.26–7).

134

In cross-cultural terms, *Ulysses*, as its title indicates, speaks directly to Homer and the Greeks. Joyce insisted that the binding of the Shakespeare and Company edition of *Ulysses* should be blue (with the title in white), the colours of the Greek flag. In the vestibule of his apartment in Paris there was a Greek flag on the wall, a relic of his days in Trieste: 'The Greeks have always brought me good luck,' he once told Padraic Colum.[3] The Greek motif is repeated throughout this first episode. The name Malachi Mulligan, like that of his model in real life, Oliver St John Gogarty, is double-dactylic (a dactyl being stressed, unstressed, unstressed). Indeed, 'Telemachus' affords a characteristically Joycean reply to Homer's *Odyssey*. *The Odyssey* begins with an invocation to the Muse and with a reference to Odysseus himself:

> Goddess of song, teach me the story of a hero.

Joyce's *Ulysses* opens more 'prosaically' with no mention of the 'hero' and with a parody for an invocation.

In terms of literary form, Homer's *Odyssey* is an epic; Joyce's *Ulysses* is a modern novel. Is it possible to write an epic set in the modern world? Joyce is nothing if not ambitious, and in *Ulysses* he attempts to achieve for Ireland what Homer's *Odyssey* had done for Greece, Virgil's *Aeneid* for Rome, Dante's *Divine Comedy* for Italy, and Milton's *Paradise Lost* for England. According to the English critic E. M. Tillyard, an epic should display four characteristics: high seriousness, amplitude, control, and choric quality. Strictly defined, Joyce's novel is not an epic, but with its high seriousness, dazzling variety, absolute control on the part of the author, and 'the feelings of a large group of people living in or near his own time',[4] it has all the expansiveness and

COPY

60 Shelbourne Road,
Dublin.

Dear Gogarty

I sent you back the budget. I am still alive. Here is a more reasonable request. I am singing at a garden-fete on Friday and if you have a decent suit to spare or a cricket shirt send it or them. I am trying to get an engagement in the Kingstown Pavilion. Do you know anyone there? My idea for July & August is this - to get Dohnetchi to make me a lute and to coast the South of England from Falmouth to Margate, singing old English songs. When are you leaving Oxford? I wish I could see it. I don't understand your allusions. "Chamber music" is the title for the suite. I suppose Jenny is leaving in a day or so. I shall call to say farewell and adieu. Her letter did not annoy me. The others did. I enclose one lest you should plume yourself. Elwood is nearly cured. I have a rendezvous with Annie Laryton - but you forget her? I have no news to report. Their Intensities and Their Bullockships continue to flourish. His particular Intensity walks now unencumbered. Mackmliffe is going for Greenwood Pine's job in C P I - desires to be remembered to you. You will not have me faithfully. Adieu, then, Inconsequent.

Stephen Dedalus.

3 June 1904

4 Joyce's communication with Gogarty a fortnight before Joyce met Nora. It is full of banter, plans for the summer ('those lovely seaside girls'), together with a fair share of the Dubliner's proneness to character assassination ('His Particular Intensity' is J. F. Byrne, at one time Joyce's closest friend). *Courtesy of the Beinecke Rare Book and Manuscript Library, Yale University.*

seriousness of the form. Writing in Italian to Carlo Linati in September 1920, enclosing a schema for the novel, Joyce is nothing if not ambitious:

> It is an epic of two races (Israelite–Irish) and at the same time the cycle of the human body as well as a little story of a day (life). The character of Ulysses always fascinated me – even when a boy. Imagine, fifteen years ago I started writing it as a short story for *Dubliners*! For seven years I have been working at this book – blast it! It is also a sort of encyclopaedia. My intention is to transpose the myth *sub specie temporis nostri*.
>
> (*Letters* I. 146–7)

Less serious though no less accurate is Mulligan's comment to Stephen after breakfast, 'You have eaten all we left, I suppose'

135

5 The Martello Tower at Sandycove, now the James Joyce Museum. Joyce once prophetically remarked to Gogarty in the tower, 'We could stand a siege here', for what is *Ulysses* but an open declaration of war on literary conventions? *Photograph Dan Harper.*

(*U* 1.524) – this too is an apt description of Joyce's relationship with the fragments left him by western history and culture.

In biographical terms, *Ulysses* begins with Gogarty and Stephen/Joyce. The mood is bitter but not self-indulgent. Gogarty recalls the time when he and Joyce were occupying the Tower:

> One morning back in Sandycove I was shaving on the roof of the Tower, because of the better light – it is a good idea to shave before going into salt water – when up comes Joyce.
>
> 'Fine morning, Dante. Feeling transcendental this morning?' I asked.
>
> 'Would you be so merry and bright if you had to go out at this hour to teach a lot of scrawny-necked brats?'[5]

Mulligan's coarse banter serves to bring out the sensitivity of Stephen's private thoughts and the inner drama he is both witnessing and experiencing. Mindful of his 'dogsbody' and wrapped in the past, Stephen, unlike Mulligan, feels nothing of the pagan excitement about the morning, the awaking mountains, the sea, or his body. He is wearing a pair of second-hand trousers; his shiny black coat sleeve is fraying at the edge; his handkerchief is snotgreen – and Mulligan takes care to let him know how he appears to the world: '– Look at yourself, he said, you dreadful bard!' (*U* 1.134).

The dispossessed son is also enmeshed in the colonial encounter between Ireland and Britain. Here, Matthew Arnold is the key figure. In *On the Study of Celtic Literature* (1867), Arnold contended that the English

genius was characterized by energy with honesty, the Germanic genius by steadiness with honesty, while the Celt, who is 'always ready to react against the despotism of fact', he summed up in the one word – 'sentimental'. Furthermore, he associated the Celt with the Greek, claiming that, while the Celt lacks the 'sense of measure', both possess the 'same emotional temperament'.[6] Arnold failed to appreciate the insulting nature of such comments, and it is one of the ironies of Anglo-Irish relations that he should have contributed in the late nine-

teenth century – as is especially evident in the line from Standish James O'Grady to Yeats – to the emergence of a national identity which found its most vocal expression in the Irish Literary Revival.

The discussion in 'Telemachus' takes its cue in part from Arnold's view of the Celt – Joyce even includes a reference to a deaf gardener 'masked with Matthew Arnold's face' who pushes his mower across the sombre lawn, 'watching narrowly the dancing motes of grasshalms' (*U* 1.173–5). Arnold's tidy mind, preoccupied with con-

6   Men bathing nude in the Forty Foot Hole just below the Tower. '– Look at the sea. What does it care about offences? Chuck Loyola, Kinch, and come on down. The Sassenach wants his morning rashers' (*U* 1.231–2). *Photograph Dan Harper.*

137

verting the Irish into the little people dancing on the lawn, misses the greater 'mote' in his own eye, while his attempt to emphasize cultural difference merely reveals and underlines a dominant ideology working in the opposite direction.[7] Stephen is usurped of his country and simultaneously forced to listen to Mulligan, a fellow countryman, urging him to Hellenize Ireland, create a new paganism, and establish a new *omphalos* (*U* 1.544), a new centre of the world in Ireland. The suggestion that Stephen could bring Arnoldian culture to Ireland is quietly ridiculed by Joyce. Stephen can have recourse neither to the pagan body nor to the Hellenic mind as filtered through Arnold, for such returns are possible only to people with the freedom to ignore the Act of Union and its colonial legacy.

The Sassenach, Haines, the third occupant of the Tower, is the other English voice heard in this opening episode. The previous night, disturbed by a nightmare about a panther, Haines reaches for the gun in the gun case. Shots ring out. Stephen, terrified, and ever alert to signs of betrayal, determines to leave the Tower. Haines, over from Oxford to do some field work 'on' the Irish, is the enlightened and sympathetic colonial who inadvertently transforms the Irish into 'folk': Mulligan suggests that he ought to collect Stephen's sayings and put them in a book (*U* 1.365). There is a telling moment as Stephen sets off for class: '– We'll see you again, Haines said, turning as Stephen walked up the path and smiling at wild Irish' (*U* 1.731–2). Haines smiles not at 'a wild Irishman', but at 'wild Irish'. Here is the historical condescension that in Spenser's time banished the native Irish to the woods and in the post-Romantic era calls them up again to savour their exoticism. Stephen knows the course of this whole history, and tellingly refuses it by screening his thoughts from the stranger's observation: 'Horn of a bull, hoof of a horse, smile of a Saxon' (*U* 1.733). Haines is an embodiment of the image the Irish have of the English ruling class: ponderous, inconsequential, superior, outwardly seeking control but inwardly at the mercy of monsters.[8] When Stephen complains about being the servant of two masters, one English, the other Italian, Haines 'detached from his underlip some fibres of tobacco before he spoke':

– I can quite understand that, he said calmly. An Irishman must think like that, I daresay. We feel in England that we have treated you rather unfairly. It seems history is to blame.

(*U* 1.647–9)

This is the reasonable English voice dealing with what is for Stephen the 'nightmare' of history (*U* 2.377). For those actually experiencing the force of history from within, such detachment is impossible; in Ireland, as Yeats also knew only too well, the Arnoldian voice of sweetness and light was not available:

Out of Ireland have we come.
Great hatred, little room,
Maimed us at the start.
I carry from my mother's womb
A fanatic heart.[9]

Yeats spent much of his life holding down emotion; Stephen, on the other hand, is enervated by the colonial encounter and the Catholic Church. 'Telemachus' affords a brilliant, if pessimistic summary of what happened to Ireland in the nineteenth century under British rule. The language was lost, the political will sapped, the key handed over, history forgotten, the people turned into 'folk', the culture deformed and twisted into a grotesque parody of itself, and overseeing it all – the twin forces of Rome and the Crown. When the old woman enters the Tower to deliver their morning milk, she is drawn into conversation:

— Do you understand what he says? Stephen asked her.
— Is it French you are talking, sir? the old woman said to Haines.

Haines spoke to her again a longer speech, confidently.
— Irish, Buck Mulligan said. Is there Gaelic on you?
— I thought it was Irish, she said, by the sound of it. Are you from the west, sir?
— I am an Englishman, Haines answered.
— He's English, · Buck Mulligan said, and he thinks we ought to speak Irish in Ireland.
— Sure we ought to, the old woman said, and I'm ashamed I don't speak the language myself. I'm told it's a grand language by them that knows.
(*U* 1.424–34)

The banality of her response – 'I'm told it's a grand language by them that knows' – carries a measure of bathos, but it also conveys Stephen's impatience with those who fail to recognize that he too shares their heritage of dispossession. Not everything is taken away, for 'Telemachus' is told from Stephen's perspective and therefore contains a counter-movement. Thus, although the episode begins with a possible pun on the State, it finishes with the single, resolute, accusatory, word-sentence 'Usurper'.

Oscar Wilde's presence in 'Telemachus' provides an instructive warning. Haines is introduced by Mulligan in Wildean fashion: the Englishman is 'bursting with money and indigestion' (*U* 1.52–3). Just as Haines treats Ireland as material for his research, Wilde, the Oxford-educated Irishman, undertook a similar project on the English. At one

THE SPHINX BY OSCAR WILDE

MEL AN CHO LIA

WITH DECORATIONS BY CHARLES RICKETTS
LONDON MDCCCXCIV
ELKIN MATHEWS AND JOHN LANE · AT THE SIGN OF THE BODLEY HEAD

7 Charles Ricketts's design for Wilde's *The Sphinx* (1894). 'Telemachus' is the most 'Greek' episode in *Ulysses*, not least in its enigmatic quality. Stephen's journey begins amid the twisted cultural roots of his country, the old identities and interminable failures. He is excited neither by the '*Thalatta! Thalatta!*' (*U* 1.80), the sea, the sea, the cry uttered by the Greek soldiers on their return from the wars against the Persians, nor by Mulligan's wish that he establish an *omphalos* (*U* 1.544), a Greek centre, in Ireland.

point, Stephen himself is linked with Wilde when Mulligan suggests with reference to Stephen's wit that 'We have grown out of Wilde and paradoxes' (*U* 1.554). Stephen, less sure, lifts from *The Picture of Dorian Gray* (1891) an image that occurs in a discussion about art and life, and applies it specifically to the fate of art in Ireland: to Stephen, the symbol of Irish art is 'the cracked lookingglass of a servant' (*U* 1.146). Stephen refuses to play the role either of source for the folklorist or of court jester for the Crown. Wilde was Joyce's cautionary model, whose destruction by the English courts was a reminder to disfranchised sons of Ireland that wit was not enough to save them.

The son is also involved in a struggle with his mother and with cultural representations of the female. Stephen is weary, depressed by his own voice, and reluctant to join in the repartee with Mulligan. Wherever he looks – at the world around him or in the mirror – the Irish Hamlet encounters not so much a reflection of himself as images of oppression. He broods on his part in the death of his mother and on his refusal to fulfil his religious obligations. Her figure haunts him, 'her wasted body within its loose graveclothes giving off an odour of wax and rosewood' (*U* 1.270–1). In April 1903, when his own mother was dying of cancer, Joyce knelt by her bedside and recited the lines 'Who Goes with Fergus' from Yeats's play *The Countess Cathleen* (1892).[10] In 'Telemachus', Mulligan cruelly taunts Stephen with the same lines as he descends the staircase, booming out:

> – *And no more turn aside and brood*
> *Upon love's bitter mystery*
> *For Fergus rules the brazen cars.*
> (*U* 1.239–41)

Stephen is deprived not only of his mother but also of the tender affection he once had for her. Joyce deliberately exaggerates Stephen's antipathy towards his mother. In reality, as their exchange of letters in 1902–3 when he was in Paris confirms, he was very fond of her. In December 1902 his mother writes to him: 'Do not wear your soul out with tears but be as usually brave and look hopefully to the future. Let me have a letter *by return*, and for Gods sake take care of your health' (*Letters* II. 22). In March 1903 Joyce showed himself equally solicitous:

Ask Benson about your own glasses, I am sure they are ruining your sight. Get him to prescribe *proper* glasses for you. Don't fail to do this. Do you go out as I told you? I think you are in good health. I never saw you look better than the night I went home and you came into the hall.

(*Letters* II. 38)

In *A Portrait* and *Ulysses*, the tender side to Joyce's character is hidden beneath layers of bitterness and rebellion: 'Ghoul! Chewer of corpses!' (*U* 1.278). In reality, as his sister Eileen later recalled, Mrs Joyce's death was devastating for Joyce and the family:

Oh, years later in Trieste, he was still deploring her death. You see, Mother was wonderfully understanding with Jim. She always wanted him to go on with his studies and his writing. . . . She always did everything in her power to help him follow his bent.[11]

Stephen is comfortless, sustained by no mythology or religion, and pursued by his mother's accusing image. '– No, mother! Let me be and let me live' (*U* 1.279). He broods but does not mourn, and he searches for some representation in life or art or literature that will reflect his mood. The lines from Yeats help but only because of their enigmatic quality; Yeats's words are sufficiently removed from actual life not to be confused with it. Commentators often remind us that Stephen is searching for a father, but the only certainty we have – given that *Ulysses* is set in 1904, a year after his mother's death – is that he is living on after the death of his mother.

Without the physical presence of his mother, the other female figures in *Ulysses* acquire a special significance. Stephen is particularly sensitive to women and to cultural representations of women. His mother is not just the woman who bore him but also

Mother Ireland. In this light, references to his mother have a profound resonance. It is Ireland that comes to haunt him; it is Ireland that is the 'chewer of corpses'; it is Ireland that won't let him live. 'In a dream, silently, she had come to him' (U 1.270). His mother is here associated with the Ireland of the *aisling* visionary poems of the eighteenth century. In such poems the poet has a vision of a destitute woman, who tells him her tragic story, how her land is oppressed by the stranger, but how one day the yoke will be cast off. She then reveals her beauty and – in the words which mark the visionary ending of Yeats's *Cathleen ni Houlihan* (1902) – 'the look of a queen'. Stephen's mother comes to him after death, but in this case she offers him no release from suffering. Something similar happens when the 'Poor Old Woman' enters the Tower. She represents the Shan Van Vocht of Irish folklore. But the female figure who in the eighteenth century was associated with a political struggle for Irish freedom is here reduced to a more lowly task – delivering milk. Again, Stephen is drawn towards the symbolic representations of the female. She is not only the Poor Old Woman and Cathleen ni Houlihan but also Athene in disguise, come to encourage Telemachus to tackle the suitors and find his father. Once more the harshness of reality intervenes, for the irony is that the woman fails to recognize either her own language or her true sons. 'A wandering crone, lowly form of an immortal serving her conqueror and her gay betrayer, their common cuckquean, a messenger from the secret morning' (U 1.404–6).

Without his mother, Stephen is bereft of an Athene, someone among the gods to take his side, and to this extent *Ulysses* constitutes Joyce's attempt to replace through writing the loss of his mother. Isolated in a country that is both conquered and full of betrayers, Stephen is not only sensitive to the traditional female images of Ireland but is oppressed by that sensitivity, for he recognizes that such images can be activated only with irony. It could be argued that *Ulysses* records a journey to discover the authentic self in a world without God, but it is more exacting than this.[12] Directly opposite the Martello Tower, across Dublin Bay, lies Howth Head. *Ulysses* opens with the phallic symbol and closes with Molly's memories of lovemaking on Howth and the seedcake in her mouth. It begins with Stephen's 'no', his intellectual rejection of Ireland, and ends with Molly's 'yes', her physical acceptance of life. It starts with Mrs Dedalus, the dead mother, and closes with the living woman, Molly, lying in bed remembering her past lovers. In Homeric terms, it begins with Penelope, the dead woman haunting the young Telemachus, and it ends with Penelope in the next room wishing she may not be too old for the young house guest who has just returned with her husband. In biographical and psychological terms, the novel begins with Joyce's mother, with the son, and ends with Joyce's wife, that is with the lover. But the patterns themselves – whether at the level of geography, biography, history, culture, intertextuality or textual cohesion – constantly reveal or collide with the non-linear and more intractable issue of gender.

Ulysses ends not with thoughts of the dispossessed son, who is haunted by his dead mother, but with female pleasure and the assuaging of male guilt. The son returns with his 'father' to 7 Eccles Street, a house occupied both by the long-suffering housewife and mother Penelope and – in Joyce's *Ulysses* – by the temptress Calypso. Perhaps Joyce structures his book in this way to suggest that before a modern Ireland can

8   Henry Sharpe's view of
'The Mummers': Synge, AE,
Lady Gregory, and Yeats.
(From Mairéad Byrne and
Henry Sharpe, *Joyce – A Clew*,
Dublin: Bluett and Co., 1981.)
Courtesy of Henry Sharpe.

emerge, there has to be an unmaking, a casting off, an expunging of the guilt of the old world. If so, central to that process is the replacement of certain traditional images of Ireland with an acceptance of life as ordinary, unheroic, physical, and pleasurable. The Poor Old Woman, Cathleen ni Houlihan, chiding her sons to take up arms, has to yield to the less hectoring Mother Earth figure, the genuine feminine principle. The ending thus marks Joyce's attempt to reconcile the male and the female, and at the same time reveals a 'movement downwards upon life, not upwards out of life' – a movement that Yeats had himself embarked upon some years earlier, in 1906.[13]

THE CULTURAL FERMENT

The Abbey Theatre

After the fall of Parnell in 1890 a space opened for a different kind of politics in Ireland. Agrarian agitation and parliamentary action gave way to cultural politics and to a struggle over the role of culture in the shaping of modern Ireland. One of the flash-points in that struggle came in the area of drama, and it centred largely on the depiction of rural Ireland. It would be wrong, however, to assume the dispute was about art versus propaganda: that is how the *Playboy* riots of 1907 are frequently interpreted, largely because Yeats's lofty opinion has prevailed. But there was another equally impassioned view from inside the culture clamouring for expression in the new Ireland. In reality, it is more accurate to speak of a mismatch between the city audiences, anxious to see a wholesome image of rural Ireland presented on the stage, and the Abbey directors, who were motivated by different ideals.

The prime movers behind the formation of the Abbey in 1904 were Yeats and Lady Gregory, but, as with any national movement, many other individuals also played important roles. The project was subsidized by Annie Horniman, daughter of the chairman of a Manchester tea company. The idea of a non-commercial theatre in Ireland was promoted initially by Edward Martyn and George Moore. In the first five years of the Abbey, the contribution of the Fay brothers, Willie and Frank, with their practical work in travelling fit-up companies and Dublin theatre groups, was invaluable, as was the

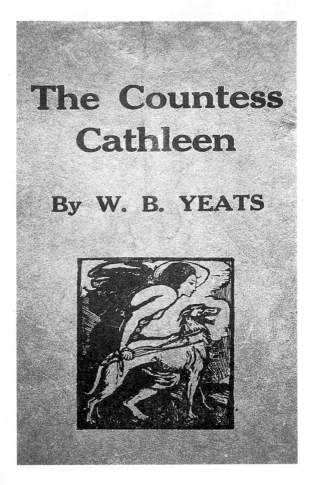

The Countess Cathleen

By W. B. YEATS

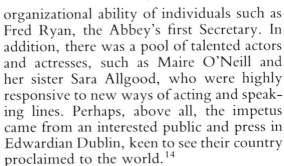

organizational ability of individuals such as Fred Ryan, the Abbey's first Secretary. In addition, there was a pool of talented actors and actresses, such as Maire O'Neill and her sister Sara Allgood, who were highly responsive to new ways of acting and speaking lines. Perhaps, above all, the impetus came from an interested public and press in Edwardian Dublin, keen to see their country proclaimed to the world.[14]

Arguably the leading playwright of the Edwardian era is J. M. Synge, and his work alone would justify the Abbey Theatre experiment. In plays such as *Riders to the Sea*

(1904), *The Well of the Saints* (1905), and *The Playboy of the Western World* (1907), Synge explored his lyrical obsession with rural Ireland. His plays embody what Lady Gregory sought in her ideals for the new theatre, 'a base of realism, with an apex of beauty',[15] but in Synge's case there is a tension between the realism and the beauty, a reflection within his work of a wider cultural conflict. The richness of the dialogue seems to have a life of its own, drawing its strength from its proximity to rural life, but seemingly blind to the plight of the rural poor. Tensions are also apparent in Synge's choice of characters and themes: he begins in search of community, but almost at once he finds his mind peopled with the outcasts of that rural world – beggars and tramps, blind

9 Elinor Monsell's famous emblem of the legendary Queen Maeve with the Irish wolfhound appeared on Abbey Theatre programmes for over fifty years. *Courtesy of the Abbey Theatre.*

10 J. B. Yeats's sketch of Synge in 1907. *Courtesy of Special Collections, Colby College, Waterville, Maine.*

11 Castle Kevin, the house at Annamoe in County Wicklow, which the Synge family rented for their summer holidays. *Photograph Dan Harper.*

12 (*facing page*) Glenmalure in the Wicklow Mountains, the setting for Synge's play *In the Shadow of the Glen. Photograph Dan Harper.*

men and wrongdoers – figures like himself at odds with society.

Synge's achievement is especially remarkable when set against his narrow Protestant family background. As a boy while staying at the family's summer retreat of Castle Kevin, at Annamoe, he roamed among the Wicklow Mountains, finding his solitude reflected in the shadow of Glenmalure. But nothing could have prepared him for the intensity of his encounter with the west. His family's attitude towards Irish Ireland was contemptuous, best expressed in 1853 by one of his uncles, the first Protestant rector in the Aran Islands, when he wrote, 'Here am I Lord of all I survey – surrounded with dirt and ignorance'. Forty-five years later, the playwright's first visit to the Aran Islands generated a different response. He was enchanted by the simplicity of the islanders and felt compelled to spend part of each of the following five summers among

them. He stayed in their homes, played the violin for their dances, and listened intently to their language and their stories. Landing in Galway after one trip, he wondered if he was not leaving on Inishmaan 'every symbol of the cosmos'.[16] Within five years of his first trip to the Aran Islands, Synge had composed *Riders to the Sea*; within ten years he had written himself into the Irish imagination.

No one, not even the prime movers of the Abbey project, could have predicted in 1898 the major contribution that Ireland would make to the European stage in the twentieth century. In 1898, Lady Gregory, enthralled by Yeats's folklore collection, *The Celtic Twilight* (1893), invited him to her country estate at Coole in the west of Ireland; Synge was in Paris, contemplating a musical career; George Moore had not yet discovered his enthusiasm for Ireland; only Yeats perhaps knew what he wanted. Step ahead six years,

to the opening of the Abbey Theatre on Tuesday, 27 December 1904. The programme consisted of four plays: Yeats's *On Baile's Strand*, the first play in what was to become his Cuchulain cycle of plays; a one-act comedy by Lady Gregory entitled *Spreading the News*; a revival of Yeats's highly political play *Cathleen ni Houlihan*, in which the title role in the 1902 production had been played by Maud Gonne; and Synge's *In the Shadow of the Glen*. A national theatre had been established and a new Ireland was in the making on the stage.

The first decade of the new century was especially promising for the younger generation of writers. Irish publishers discovered a renewed interest in Irish material; newspapers, weeklies, and other journals were keen to publish imaginative and critical work; and a reading public was there to be sought out and entertained. Second-hand printing presses were coming on to the market at an affordable price and enterprising individuals were quick to seize the opportunity of becoming editors overnight. From his base in Kilkenny, Standish James O'Grady published his fortnightly journal *All-Ireland Review* (1900–7); in 1904, 'John Eglinton' and Fred Ryan founded and edited a free-thinking monthly magazine entitled *Dana*; the Yeats family established the Dun Emer Press in 1903, later to become the Cuala Press; the Tower Press booklets, published by Maunsel & Co. of Dawson Street, Dublin, began publication in 1906 with a series of essays by AE (George Russell), Moore, Eglinton, Ryan, and poems by Seamas O'Sullivan, Thomas Keohler, and Ella Young. Many such ventures folded before they could become established. This was not surprising, given that there was no audience research beforehand and little or no advertising revenue; there was only enthusiasm, ideology, and a desire to

persuade. There was something unpredictable about all this activity, and readers could never be sure in advance what they might encounter in a weekly paper or journal. Griffith's political weekly the *United Irishman* (1899–1906), for example, often contained heated exchanges about the image of Ireland on display in the new plays. Perhaps the most striking mismatch occurred in AE's farming weekly, the *Irish Homestead*, which in 1904 carried three of Joyce's stories that later appeared in *Dubliners*, 'The Sisters', 'Eveline', and 'After the Race' (see pp. 148–9).

Joyce and Yeats

It would be wrong to imagine that there was a single phenomenon called the Irish Dramatic Movement or even the Irish Literary Revival. These are umbrella terms which in fact concealed enormous differences, not least concerning the role literature should play in the making of modern Ireland. In 1906, for example, several new playwrights, including Padraic Colum, dissatisfied with the high-handedness of Yeats, Synge and Lady Gregory, the Abbey's 'Anglo-Irish' directors, formed their own Theatre of Ireland Company. But neither did Yeats have his way. By 1910 he himself was beginning to realize, especially after the *Playboy* riots, that he would not be able to create a new audience in Ireland, and so turned to a more private, less popular form of theatre, to be performed in masks. In 1916 Yeats's first Noh play, *At The Hawk's Well*, was performed not in Dublin but in Lady Cunard's drawing-room in London before a private audience which included T. S. Eliot and Ezra Pound. A fortnight later, the Easter Rising of 1916 'changed utterly' the face of Ireland, leaving Yeats

That evening my aunt visited the house of mourning and took me with her. It was an oppressive summer evening of faded gold. Nannie received us in the hall, and, as it was no use saying anything to her, my aunt shook hands with her for all. We followed the old woman upstairs and into the dead-room. The room, through the lace end of the blind, was suffused with dusky golden light, amid which the candles looked like pale, thin flames. He had been coffined. Nannie gave the lead, and we three knelt down at the foot of the bed. There was no sound in the room for some minutes except the sound of Nannie's mutterings—for she prays noisily. The fancy came to me that the old priest was smiling as he lay there in his coffin.

But, no. When we rose and went up to the head of the bed I saw that he was not smiling. There he lay solemn and copious in his brown habit, his large hands loosely retaining his rosary. His face was very grey and massive, with distended nostrils and circled with scanty white fur. There was a heavy odour in the room—the flowers.

We sat downstairs in the little room behind the shop, my aunt and I and the two sisters. Nannie sat in a corner and said nothing, but her lips moved from speaker to speaker with a painfully intelligent motion. I said nothing either, being too young, but my aunt spoke a good deal, for she is a bit of a gossip—harmless.

"Ah, well! he's gone!"

"To enjoy his eternal reward, Miss Flynn, I'm sure. He was a good and holy man."

"He was a good man, but, you see . . . he was a disappointed man. . . . You see, his life was, you might say, crossed."

"Ah, yes! I know what you mean."

"Not that he was anyway mad, as you know yourself, but he was always a little queer. Even when we were all growing up together he was queer. One time he didn't speak hardly for a month. You know, he was that kind always."

"Perhaps he read too much, Miss Flynn?"

"O, he read a good deal, but not latterly. But it was his scrupulousness, I think, affected his mind. The duties of the priesthood were too much for him."

"Did he . . . peacefully?"

"O, quite peacefully, ma'am. You couldn't tell when the breath went out of him. He had a beautiful death, God be praised."

"And everything . . . ?"

"Father O'Rourke was in with him yesterday and gave him the Last Sacrament."

"He knew then?"

"Yes; he was quite resigned."

Nannie gave a sleepy nod and looked ashamed.

"Poor Nannie," said her sister, "she's worn out. All the work we had, getting in a woman, and laying him out; and then the coffin and arranging about the funeral. God knows we did all we could, as poor as we are. We wouldn't see him want anything at the last."

"Indeed you were both very kind to him while he lived."

"Ah, poor James; he was no great trouble to us. You wouldn't hear him in the house no more than now. Still I know he's gone and all that. . . . I won't be bringing him in his soup any more, nor Nannie reading him the paper, nor you, ma'am, bringing him his snuff. How he liked that snuff! Poor James!"

"O, yes, you'll miss him in a day or two more than you do now."

Silence invaded the room until memory reawakened it, Eliza speaking slowly—

"It was that chalice he broke. . . . Of course, it was all right. I mean it contained nothing. But still . . . They say it was the boy's fault. But poor James was so nervous, God be merciful to him."

"Yes, Miss Flynn, I heard that . . . about the chalice. . . He . . . his mind was a bit affected by that."

"He began to mope by himself, talking to no one, and wandering about. Often he couldn't be found. One night he was wanted, and they looked high up and low down and couldn't find him. Then the clerk suggested the chapel. So they opened the chapel (it was late at night), and brought in a light to look for him. . . And there, sure enough, he was, sitting in his confession-box in the dark, wide awake, and laughing like softly to himself. Then they knew something was wrong."

"God rest his soul!"

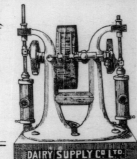

hopelessly wrong-footed and aggrieved that he had not been consulted by the insurgents. The older form of politics, which had gone underground in 1890 with the fall of Parnell, had returned, banishing overnight the breathing space for culture. The old 'nightmare', as James Stephens wrote in May 1916, was about to ride Ireland all over again.[17]

Joyce belongs, with Yeats, Synge, Lady Gregory, George Moore, and AE – and with the 'wildeshaweshowe' which moved 'swiftly sterneward' (*FW* 256.13–14) – to a group of Irish writers who ensured Ireland a place on the modern literary map. A more

150

difficult question to determine is how far Joyce was a product of Ireland's cultural renewal. Without him the Revival would have been dependent on Shaw and Moore for its negative critique. In this company, Joyce's work is a powerful reminder of Bakhtin's concept of 'heteroglossia', the jostling, different voices which refuse incorporation into a dominant culture.[18] But from the outset of his career as a writer, as is evident from his attack on Yeats for his 'treacherous instinct of adaptability' in the early pamphlet 'The Day of the Rabblement', Joyce maintained his distance and resisted all attempts to enlist him in the services of the Revival.[19] To further his occult or poetic ambitions, the dream-led Yeats joined coteries such as the Order of the Golden Dawn or the Rhymers' Club which met at the Cheshire Cheese in Fleet Street, but Joyce always recoiled from the idea of a common cause. The attitude he adopted – like Yeats, he was fond of the self-dramatizing gesture – was similar to the *non serviam* expressed by Stephen in *A Portrait*. Before he could entertain a common identity, Joyce needed to establish a negative identity, a mark or show of difference from his rivals, which meant in this case demonstrating his superiority over them. He enjoyed writing against the grain. He rebelled against the Father, took whatever he needed from his literary heritage, and invented his own heterodox tradition, where Swift was stern and Sterne was swift. But without Moore's *The Untilled Field* (1903), for example, or Yeats's *The Wind Among the Reeds* (1899), or Synge's *Playboy* (1907), the early Joyce would have had to struggle more than he did to discover his own voice either in fiction or verse.

The idealist AE also alights on the dialectical nature of the relationship between Yeats and Joyce:

16 J. B. Yeats's pencil drawing of George Moore. Joyce was indebted to Moore perhaps more than he appreciated – or more than he was prepared to admit. *Dubliners* reworks material in *The Untilled Field* (1903), 'Eveline' owes something to *Evelyn Innes* (1898), and *A Portrait*, especially in its symbolism of flight, has similarities to *The Lake* (1905). *Courtesy of Special Collections, Colby College, Waterville, Maine.*

17 The First International James Joyce Symposium was held in Dublin in 1967. Among the guests were Giorgio Joyce and his wife Astra, Padraic Colum, and Donagh MacDonagh, author of *Happy as Larry* and son of Thomas MacDonagh, the Sinn Fein leader executed in 1916. Colum, whose early poems were collected in *Wild Earth* (1907), was well known to Joyce from his Dublin days and became a close friend of his in Paris in the inter-war years. *Courtesy of Fritz Senn and Zurich James Joyce Foundation.*

It is perhaps the imp in me which makes me speculate whether James Joyce was not made inevitable by W. B. Yeats, is not in a sense the poet's creation, his child, born to him, not out of his loins, but supplied to him by Nature, being called forth by a kind of necessity to balance in our national life an intense imagination of beauty, by an equally intense preoccupation with its dark and bitter opposites. It amuses me to consider this parentage. Father and son have this in common, that they are stylists even to elaboration. There was also a little poetry in the youth of James Joyce, and if Nature, or the national being, had not to preserve the balance of things, if there was not a force pulling the pendulum of literature from the height of dream it had

swung to in Yeats, Joyce might never have written *Ulysses*. He might have gone on writing *Chamber Music* and further innocencies of that kind.[20]

Of all his contemporaries or near-contemporaries, 'Doubbllinnbbayyates' (*FW* 303.7–8) exerted the strongest impression on Joyce. In his teens Joyce took to writing verse and committed to memory many of Yeats's lines – in the 1930s he could still recite them to friends. Joyce learnt the craft of writing in part through the time-honoured classical method of imitation. He admired Yeats and wanted to write like him. The character of Stephen Dedalus in *Ulysses* owes as much to the nineties Yeats as to Homer. Stephen is the Druid king in retreat from the world, brooding upon 'love's bitter mystery'; he is the dreamy nineties aesthete attempting to resolve his problems through literature rather than through life; he is the Symbolist poet hoping to find in language a corresponding image for the soul.

Woodshadows floated silently by through the morning peace from the stair-head seaward where he gazed. Inshore and farther out the mirror of water whitened, spurned by lightshod hurrying feet.

White breast of the dim sea. The twining stresses, two by two. A hand plucking the harpstrings, merging their twining chords. Wavewhite wedded words shimmering on the dim tide.

(*U* 1.242–7)

Such a passage is not unlike an Imagist poem, a series of separate, accumulating images. It is also redolent of the symbolism and incantation often associated with Yeats's early verse. The repetition of sound and image is designed to suggest a mood, to lure the reader, as Yeats puts it in his 1900 essay 'The Symbolism of Poetry', to 'the threshold of sleep'. 'Literature differs from explanatory and scientific writing in being wrought about a mood, or a community of moods, as the body is wrought about an invisible soul', he writes in 'The Moods', while in 'The Autumn of the Body', another essay relevant to understanding Stephen, he declares, 'Our thoughts and emotions are often but spray flung up from hidden tides that follow a moon no eye can see'.[21]

Stephen's eye gazes over Dublin Bay but his mind is preoccupied with language and imagery: the water is like a 'mirror', the spray 'lightshod hurrying feet', a 'white breast', a sexual image which is continued in 'twining stresses' and a 'hand plucking the harpstrings'. The final sentence beginning with 'wavewhite wedded words' links the (Greek) sea with whiteness, marriage, and language, and the poetic reverie is brought to an end on the sad (Victorian) note of 'dim tide'. The debt to Yeats can be felt throughout, not only in the rhythmic structure but also in Joyce's recourse to similar images. 'You waves, though you dance by my feet like children at play' is the opening line in Yeats's 'The Meditation of the Old Fisherman'; in 'The Fiddler of Dooney', 'folk dance like a wave of the sea'.[22] In *The Wanderings of Oisin*, Oisin recounts to St Patrick how at one stage in his travels he shouted out to the stars: the stars are held by the iron rod of God, but 'we in a lonely land abide/Unchainable as the dim tide'.[23] The same phrase, 'dim tide', resurfaces inside Stephen, only now the mood is more sombre and less defiant. 'Wandering Aengus of the birds' (*U* 9.1093) is the epithet Mulligan requisitions to chide Stephen in 'Scylla and Charybdis', and again Yeats is there, for Aengus, the god of youth, beauty, and poetry, is a figure often employed by the early Yeats both in his long quest romances such as *The Wanderings of Oisin* and *The Shadowy Waters* as well as in a shorter lyric such as 'The Song of Wandering Aengus'.

Yeats also functions as Stephen's role-model, the figure of the poet as bard, at once remote and respected, marginal and yet central to the culture. Stephen returns from Paris sporting a wide-brimmed Latin quarter hat. His pose is self-conscious, reminiscent of the nineties Yeats who took to wearing a cape, flowing cravats and black clothes. But, with his second-hand clothes, Stephen cannot quite pull it off. He is mocked by Mulligan, patronized by Haines, unrecognized by the Poor Old Woman, and has difficulty discovering his own voice as a poet. Like his counterpart in *A Portrait*, he is 'wooed by grace of language and gesture' (*U* 7.776), but a novel which aspires to be the Irish epic requires a more interventionist character, certainly not someone who languishes in 'wavewhite wedded words'. Yeats, as he tells us in *Autobiographies*, had to abandon the 'slight, sentimental sensuality' present in some of his early work, the temptation to linger 'between spirit and sense',[24] but Stephen seems incapable of advance. Stephen is the artist as a 'young man', the Yeatsian figure Joyce jettisoned at

phanies; they discussed literature; Joyce scoffed at Yeats for reading Balzac; Yeats spoke of the importance of folklore and of the popular tradition underlying poetry; Joyce replied (as Yeats recorded it) that 'his own mind . . . was much nearer to God than folklore'. Joyce was intent on wounding Yeats, to make a mark. At one stage Yeats thought he had conquered Joyce, but the twenty-year-old retorted that 'generalizations aren't made by poets; they are made by men of letters. They are no use.' To rub salt in the wound Joyce added, 'I have met you too late. You are too old' (*JJ* 100–4). The phrase must have tickled Joyce, for its jingle recurs throughout *Finnegans Wake* as 'We have meat two hourly' (*FW* 60.29–30) or in the Fable of the Mookse and the Gripes as 'we first met each other newwhere so airly' (*FW* 155.12). It is difficult to know what to believe of this meeting, for, as Con Curran writes: 'It is inconceivable to me that as a young man [Joyce] would have waited upon his senior, sought his opinion unasked on his verses, and then turned him and his criticism down in such arrogant terms.'[25]

However he achieved it, Joyce succeeded; clearly he made a deep impression on Yeats. Yeats kept a copy of the epiphanies and verses, penned some complimentary remarks about them, and in his account of the meeting confirmed AE's impression that 'the younger generation is knocking at my door' (*JJ* 103). In November 1902, Yeats invited Joyce to dinner at the Nassau Hotel (F4) with Lady Gregory and his father, J. B. Yeats; in early December, he offered to introduce him to some of his literary friends in London, and to help him find some reviewing work. Later, in 1915, Yeats was instrumental in securing a grant for Joyce from the Royal Literary Fund; the same year, he persuaded Ezra Pound to use his influence with the editors of the *Egoist* to

18   This photograph of the youthful Yeats by Elliott and Fry was chosen by Katherine Tynan as a frontispiece for the fourth and final volume of her *Cabinet of Irish Literature*, published in 1903. It is sometimes forgotten that when Joyce and Yeats first met, Ireland's leading writer was still a relatively young man, with the 'pretty plumage' he refers to in his poem 'Among School Children'.

some point after 1909 in favour of Bloom and Molly. We might want to go further: in order to come upon a different kind of writing that allowed scope both for his lyrical impulses and for his 'ordinary' mind, Joyce had to write his way through Yeats.

Yeats and Joyce first met in October 1902. Joyce was anxious to obtain Yeats's opinion of his epiphanies and his verse, and through AE had arranged a meeting. Joyce arrived at the Antient Concert Rooms, where Yeats was rehearsing *Cathleen ni Houlihan*, and managed to persuade the Abbey Theatre director to withdraw to the more intimate setting of a café near by. Once there, Joyce is reputed to have subjected Yeats to an ordeal for which the poet was quite unprepared. The younger man recited some of his epi-

have *A Portrait* serialized. Yeats was always keen to promote Joyce's work, and in 1932 invited him – without success – to become a founder member of the Irish Academy.

Joyce welcomed patronage but he never allowed himself to be patronized, and though he referred to Yeats as a friend he maintained a wary distance. In 1906 he called Yeats and some others 'the blacklegs of literature'; in 1907 he thought Yeats 'quite out of touch with the Irish people' (*Letters* II. 187, 211); and in the 'Scylla and Charybdis' episode of *Ulysses* he mocks the mystical Yeats: 'Seven is dear to the mystic mind. The shining seven WB calls them' (*U* 9.27–8). By the time he came to *Finnegans Wake*, however, Joyce's old rancour towards Yeats had disappeared: he is no longer the aspiring writer out to prove a point but the low jester confident of his prowess and income. Yeats is the 'specious aristmystic unsaid' (*FW* 293.28); his poem 'Lapis Lazuli' becomes 'the lazily eye of his lapis' (*FW* 293.11); Yeats's gyre is also duly mocked in 'Gyre O, gyre O, gyrotundo! Hop lala!', and Joyce adds that this 'makes us a daintical pair of accomplasses!' (*FW* 295.23–7). 'You, allus for the kunst and me for omething with a handel to it. *Beve*!' (*FW* 295.27–9) (You always for art and me for business – or perhaps something less printable.)[26] But when Joyce heard of Yeats's death in 1939, he commented in private that he thought his former rival the greater writer (*JJ* 660n.).

'Scylla and Charybdis'

In the 'Scylla and Charybdis' episode of *Ulysses*, Joyce makes telling use of dramatic irony to provide a lively picture of the world of his youth he had rejected. The episode was written in Zurich in October 1918 when Joyce was considerably distanced both in time and space from the Dublin of 1904. He jeers at the pseudo-intellectual, provincial atmosphere of 1904 Dublin, flashes his 'antlers' at the literary establishment, whom he felt had excluded him, and everywhere insists on his own survival.

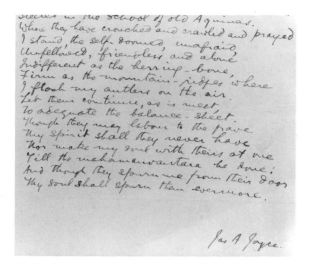

Ms 1. *Courtesy of the Beinecke Rare Book and Manuscript Library, Yale University.*

'Scylla and Charybdis' continues where 'The Holy Office' and 'Telemachus' left off. Stephen exposes the shallowness of his contemporaries, their predictable responses, and their inability to recognize the new Homer in their midst. For them, the new literary surprise will come from younger poets such as Padraic Colum or Walter Starkey (Seamas O'Sullivan), or from a more established writer like George Moore. But, as the reader infers, it is Joyce who has written the national epic. It is Joyce, the hawklike man bent on wreaking a lasting vengeance, who has consigned to history the 'brood of mockers' (*U* 9.492) who once controlled his future as a writer. 'Scylla and Charybdis' is an act of revenge, but it has

none of the animosity that is to be found in, say, Djuna Barnes's *Nightwood* (1936). By 1918 Joyce must have known as he was listing the names of his rivals that for many of them he was their passport to perpetuity.

'Urbane, to comfort them, the quaker librarian purred' (*U* 9.1). Nothing shakes the literary establishment. The very syntax of the opening sentence reproduces and carries to excess the episode's titular principle, and gently mocks both the character of the Librarian T. W. Lyster and, more widely, the intellectual's belief in an ordered universe. The opening word 'urbane' is especially appropriate, given the setting of the National Library on Kildare Street, for the idea of western culture is rooted in the Latin concept of *urbanitas*, in books and libraries, and in the consolation stemming from intellectual inquiry. But as is apparent in the mixture of warmth and contempt in the opening sentence, Joyce both values and

21 The Reading Room in the National Library (F5) in Dublin. Joyce used to sit at the front near the main desk. On the Library staff was Richard Best, a fictional portrait of whom appears in 'Scylla and Charybdis'. Long after Joyce's

scoffs at such an idea. The quaker librarian purrs; Joyce by contrast refuses to comfort his rivals.

Synge is one of those singled out early on for attack. Mulligan tells Stephen that Synge is looking for him 'to murder you. He heard

you pissed on his halldoor in Glasthule. He's out in pampooties to murder you.' 'Me!' Stephen exclaims. 'That was your contribution to literature' (*U* 9.569–72). The Synge style is also ridiculed when Mulligan recalls Stephen holding up proceedings at the Ship

THE TOWER PRESS BOOKLETS
NUMBER FIVE ✿ ✿ ✿
BARDS AND SAINTS. BY
JOHN EGLINTON.

THE TOWER PRESS BOOKLETS
NUMBER SIX ✿ ✿ ✿
CRITICISM AND COURAGE
AND OTHER ESSAYS. BY
FREDERICK RYAN.

26 'Scylla and Charybdis' continues the theme of dispossession initiated in the tower scene in 'Telemachus'. Interestingly, the image of the tower was used on the cover of the Tower Press Booklets series published in 1906–8. Perhaps Joyce intended his 'tower' as a gesture of defiance against not only the English but also those in Ireland who were arbiters of taste. The more we know the more we realise Joyce has much in common with those he spurns in *Ulysses*. Fred Ryan stood, like Joyce, for 'criticism and courage', and John Eglinton was also involved in deconstructing the accepted tradition of Irish literature.

9.1158–9); a joke is cracked about Moore being Martyn's wild oats (*U* 9.307–8); Blessed Margaret Mary Alacoque, the seventeenth-century saint who promoted the Devotion to the Sacred Heart, a devotional practice especially popular in Ireland, becomes Blessed Margaret Mary Anycock (*U* 9.646); Mr Best becomes Mr Secondbest Best (*U* 9.715); 'Buck' Mulligan becomes Puck Mulligan (*U* 9.1125) and Ballocky Mulligan (*U* 9.1176). No one escapes from the (often adolescent) onslaught, not even the master of puns, Shakespeare himself, for 'if others have their will Ann hath a way' (*U* 9.256–7).

'Scylla and Charybdis', as Patrick McGee persuasively argues, steers a course between the rock and the whirlpool towards the space that lies between two established or known positions.[27] In western culture, and the one upheld by the assembled company, the convention is that 'the truth is midway' (*U* 9.1018). This is the middle ground of certainty, but, for Stephen, the midway position is invariably associated with the in-between world of doubt. He is troubled in particular by aesthetic and philosophical issues. He finds no solution to the questions he poses: the relationship between Shakespeare's life and his art; the part that Anne Hathaway played as both wife and muse; the link between *Hamlet*, the play,

159

and Hamnet, the dead son; Shakespeare's presence in his plays, whether as Hamlet's ghost, or as the banished figures in *The Two Gentlemen of Verona* or *The Tempest*; the relationship between Stratford, his birthplace, and London, the site of his plays and fame.

Stephen, too, is suspended between two positions, between his desire to impress and his instinct to disdain, between his public deliberations on aesthetics to the assembled company and private ruminations about the permanence of the self through time: 'Every life is many days, day after day. We walk through ourselves, meeting robbers, ghosts, giants, old men, young men, wives, widows, brothers-in-love, but always meeting ourselves' (*U* 9.1044–6). By contrast, Bloom shrugs off such a dilemma. In 'Calypso', he is daydreaming about the east, dandering along all day. 'Might meet a robber or two. Well, meet him' (*U* 4.91–2). The permanence of the self through time would for Bloom be resolved accordingly: 'well, meet him'. Later in the same episode, Molly comes across the word 'metempsychosis' in her reading and asks Bloom to explain:

– Met him what? he asked.
– Here, she said. What does that mean?
   He leaned downward and read near her polished thumbnail.
– Metempsychosis?
– Yes. Who's he when he's at home?
– Metempsychosis, he said, frowning. It's Greek: from the Greek. That means the transmigration of souls.
– O, rocks! she said. Tell us in plain words.

(*U* 4.336–43)

For Molly the issue of change is simply a word; for Bloom an opportunity here to display knowledge. But Stephen, not unlike the Pre-Socratics in this regard, wrestles with doubt, and in the process underlines for us the 'navigational' position of the author in his text, who has so 'arranged' it that a similar phrase appears in the thoughts of both Stephen, Molly and Bloom.[28]

ONE-EYED NATIONALISM

'Cyclops' is the most disturbing, the most unattractive, and, at the same time, perhaps the funniest episode in *Ulysses*. Hanging menacingly over its course is the figure of Homer's one-eyed giant, who fills his great belly with human flesh, who cares nothing for Zeus, and who nearly destroys Odysseus and his men. In Homer, the meaning of the Cyclops episode is closely integrated into the narrative. The episode tends to be read neither symbolically nor as a metaphor of, say, the fear the Greeks had of the unknown, but as a gripping account of Odysseus' escape from the jaws of death. In his attempt to depict corresponding modern equivalents to the Cyclops, Joyce invests in several of the Homeric devices – the cave-like setting, the incipient violence, the coarseness of the language and thinking – but he has a certain advantage over Homer. He can switch the discourse from the literal to the metaphoric, from modern Dublin to ancient Greece, simply by one word or image. Thus, whenever the word 'I' or 'eye' appears in Joyce's 'Cyclops', it resonates against the Homeric text, and summons up Homer's famous pun on the word 'Noman'. Such alternation interrupts the flow of the narrative and systematically calls attention to what I take to be a central discourse of the episode, the critique of narrow-minded nationalism.

Joyce was in general too impatient to argue logically or philosophically, preferring to persuade through telling detail, indirect statement, imaginative leaps, and wilful exaggeration. The primary technique deployed in 'Cyclops' is what Joyce calls 'gigantism', which is here the humorous spoofing – through lists – of the so-called special qualities of Ireland and Irish life. Only someone inside the culture, engaged yet detached and certain of his ground, could have written such a reproach. Joyce parades the worst excesses of Irish chauvinism and excuses nothing. In other episodes the blame is laid elsewhere – on the colonial encounter, the past, the literary establishment. But here there is no escaping the suffocating claustrophobia of Irish life.

'Cyclops' begins as it means to continue. After the internal doubt and disintegration of language and personality in the previous episode, 'Sirens', the thoroughgoing coarseness of 'Cyclops' is especially marked:

★I was just passing the time of day with old Troy of the D.M.P. at the corner of Arbour hill there and be damned but a bloody sweep came along and he near drove his gear into my eye. I turned around to let him have the weight of my tongue when who should I see dodging along Stony Batter only Joe Hynes.

(*U* 12.1–5)

There is no room here for doubt, hesitation, or reflection. 'I' has destroyed any sense of personal identity, filling that space with the impersonality of prejudice, the 'weight of my tongue'. To this extent 'I' resembles the 'Noman' of the Homeric story, the name the crafty, punning Odysseus uses to fox the Cyclops. But unlike Odysseus, 'I' is a prisoner of his own language, ever conscious that the world is all 'my eye':

'How are you blowing?' (*U* 12.6): a polite form of greeting.
'the most notorious bloody robber you'd meet in a day's walk' (*U* 12.25): a character reference.
'waiting for what the sky would drop in the way of drink' (*U* 12.120–1): the citizen quietly waiting for someone to buy him a round.
'I was blue mouldy for the want of that pint' (*U* 12.242–3): an expression of satisfaction.
'– What's that bloody freemason doing, says the citizen, prowling up and down outside?' (*U* 12.300–1): the eye of the unprejudiced observer.
'Begob he was what you might call flabbergasted' (*U* 12.337): a response to the news of Dignam's death.
'– Could you make a hole in another pint?' (*U* 12.756): a bar-room invitation.
'Gob, he had his mouth half way down the tumbler already' (*U* 12.821): the citizen quaffing his pint.
'– Put it there, citizen, says Joe' (*U* 12.886): an example of male camaraderie.
'– Half and half I mean, says the citizen. A fellow that's neither fish nor flesh' (*U* 12.1055–6): unmanly men, like Mr Breen (and Bloom).
'– Their syphilisation, you mean, says the citizen. To hell with them! The curse of a goodfornothing God light sideways on the bloody thicklugged sons of whores' gets!' (*U* 12.1197–9): an ancient Irish curse on the English.
'They were never worth a roasted fart to Ireland' (*U* 12.1386): an impartial view of the French.
'– Repeat that dose' (*U* 12.1413): an exhortation to a barman.
'he spat a Red bank oyster out of him right in the corner' (*U* 12.1433): a colourful form of expression.

27 Geo. Webb's bookstore down by the quays (E4). With their almost exclusive devotion to books about Ireland, Dublin bookshops are a colourful reminder of the claustrophobia of Irish life. Perhaps it was less oppressive in Joyce's day, when George Webb sat outside his shop 'with his one closed and his one open eye'. 'Some of your Italian books, Mr Joyce?' *Photograph Dan Harper.*

'(gob, must have done about a gallon)' (*U* 12.1567–8): thoughts while urinating.

'flabbyarse of a wife' (*U* 12.1568): a reference to Molly.

'– We don't want him, says Crofter the Orangeman or presbyterian' (*U* 12.1634): a comment on the limits of Irish hospitality, the 'him' being Bloom, and 'Crofter' Crofton.

'– I wonder did he ever put it out of sight' (*U* 12.1655): a reference to Bloom's sex life.

'Cyclops' affords an unflattering picture of pub talk, its venom, and the part it plays in Irish life. The type is well known both inside and outside Ireland, the person who turns a pub conversation into a court of law with himself as judge, jury, and hangman. Joyce modelled his Cyclops in part on Michael Cusack, the Clareman who in 1884 founded the Gaelic Athletic Association to promote Irish sports. Cusack belonged to that generation who sought a thoroughgoing separation from Britain. In 1893 the Gaelic League was formed to de-Anglicize Irish life and culture and to promote the fortunes of the Irish language. In 1905 Arthur Griffith launched Sinn Fein, a separatist political party which had for its slogan a Gaelic name: 'We Ourselves' or 'Ourselves Alone'. To many Irish people today, such events are recalled with pride as registering key moments in the making of modern

Ireland. But Joyce, ever alert to the 'old pap of racial hatred', was more suspicious: '– *Sinn Fein!* says the citizen. *Sinn fein amhain!* The friends we love are by our side and the foes we hate before us' (*U* 12.523–4).

In 'Cyclops', in characteristic fashion, Joyce censures all this enthusiasm for things Irish. The citizen is seated in a bar in Little Britain Street (E4 – continuation of Great Britain Street) and not with the famous Irish wolfhound but with his mangy dog, Garryowen.

> The figure seated on a large boulder at the foot of a round tower was that of a broadshouldered deepchested stronglimbed frankeyed redhaired freelyfreckled shaggybearded widemouthed largenosed longheaded deepvoiced barekneed brawnyhanded hairylegged ruddyfaced sinewyarmed hero. . . . He wore a long unsleeved garment of recently flayed oxhide reaching to the knees in a loose kilt and this was bound about his middle by a girdle of plaited straw and rushes. . . . From his girdle hung a row of seastones which jangled at every movement of his portentous frame and on these were graven with rude yet striking art the tribal images of many Irish heroes and heroines of antiquity, Cuchulin, Conn of hundred battles, Niall of nine hostages, Brian of Kincora . . . Michael Dwyer . . . the Village Blacksmith . . . Theobald Wolfe Tone, the Mother of the Maccabees, the Last of the Mohicans, the Rose of Castile, the Man for Galway, The Man that Broke the Bank at Monte Carlo, The Man in the Gap, The Woman Who Didn't . . . the first Prince of Wales . . . Sidney Parade, Ben Howth . . . Adam and Eve . . . Jack the Giantkiller . . . Lady Godiva. . . .
>
> (*U* 12.151–97)

Joyce's onslaught on Irish chauvinism is

deliberately exaggerated. He consciously picks up on the style and language of a particular kind of writing or speaking and subjects it to remorseless parody. He mocks the veneration for ancient Irish heroes, for those 'tribal images' (*U* 12.175) such as Cuchulain, who became through the advocacy of O'Grady and Yeats the dominant mythological figure of the Revival. He chides the kind of 'unfurling', memorializing, banner sensibility which sees Irish history as a list of heroes composing a single story of Ireland's great epic past. But, for all its murderousness, the dominant note of 'Cyclops' is pleasure, pleasure from writing,

29   Barney Kiernan's pub on the appropriately named Little Britain Street (E4, unmarked). On account of its proximity to the Four Courts it was known as 'The Court of Appeal'. In Joyce's world it is both remarkable – and then unremarkable – how everything fits. It is also fitting that in an episode about all things Irish the Citizen and his friends are absorbed in the outcome of the *cross-channel* Ascot Gold Cup. *Courtesy of the University of Southern Illinois Library.*

164

further release from the restrictions that characterize the first half of *Ulysses*, release from the nightmare of Irish history. What daring to insert into this long line of Irish heroes figures such as the Last of the Mohicans or the Woman who Didn't, or Dick Turpin or Ben Howth. Joyce is outlandish, a scandal, the writer who at one level insists on the text's cohesiveness and at another refuses to integrate his material. Almost anything could be added to this list; it is infinitely extensible, in this respect exactly mirroring Joyce's process of composition. The Irish chauvinist would seek to keep Ireland confined/coffined within defined limits and condemned to repeat sanctioned formulae at traditional shrines. Through his emphasis on the bits and pieces which make up our modern world and which resist incorporation into the single view, Joyce exposes the hollow, ritualistic quality of such prejudices.

One reason for the company's dislike of Bloom in 'Cyclops' is that he interrogates their assumptions, asks awkward straightforward questions, seeks answers. He is interested in a scientific way, for example, in the 'phenomenon' of hanged men having erections:

– That can be explained by science, says Bloom. It's only a natural phenomenon, don't you see, because on account of the . . .
And then he starts with his jawbreakers about phenomenon and science and this phenomenon and the other phenomenon.
(*U* 12.464–7)

Bloom does not help his case 'with his knockmedown cigar putting on swank with his lardy face' (*U* 12.501–2), but, then, in the cave of prejudice where 'ruling passion' (*U* 12.463) prevails, everything he is or does will count against him. Bloom's role is to probe the 'naturalness' of things. He is the outsider in Irish life, the scientist, the Jew, the son of a Hungarian immigrant, the cuckold, the spacehound, the person whose job is to fill empty spaces in newspapers. For Bloom, the world is only a 'natural phenomenon', precisely what the citizen embodies but would want to deny. Prejudiced people assume they are at the centre of existence, that history culminates in them, that they are the subject of history. Their opinions are 'natural' and it is unnatural to treat their views as a 'phenomenon'. Bloom is unnatural precisely because he cannot accept things as natural.

The company take particular exception to his remarks about Jesus being a Jew. To counter their racism Bloom is forced to raise the stakes and state simply his own most basic attitude to life:

– But it's no use, says he. Force, hatred, history, all that. That's not life for men and women, insult and hatred. And everybody knows that it's the very opposite of that that is really life.
– What? says Alf.
– Love, says Bloom. I mean the opposite of hatred.
(*U* 12.1481–5)

Bloom is given to faltering. '– You don't grasp my point, says Bloom. What I mean is . . .' (*U* 12.522). But he is not allowed to finish. With a slip of the tongue, he refers to 'the wife's admirers' instead of the wife's 'advisers' (*U* 12.767–9). His uncertainty is ridiculed by those who deploy language as a weapon, those for whom fluency is a sign of power and *hesitancy* a mark of weakness. But Bloom's agitated ineffectual voice, a voice to be heard again in the character of HCE in *Finnegans Wake*, also has a part to play in the unmaking of modern Ireland.

CHAPTER SEVEN
Finnegans Wake *and Exile in Europe*

1 Joyce's final resting-place, the Fluntern Cemetery in Zurich. The sculpture is by Milton Hebald. Close by is the Zoo. 'He was awfully fond of the lions,' Nora once remarked. 'I like to think of him lying there and listening to them roar' (*JJ*, 743). *Photograph the author.*

JOYCE'S CONTINENTAL CITIES

AFTER LEAVING IRELAND IN 1904, Joyce's horizons dramatically altered. Dublin remained the focus of his imaginative attention, but other cities – Pola, Trieste, Rome, Zurich, Paris – now 'sent for him' (*U* 2.1). From 1904 to 1915 Joyce lived in Trieste, a stay interrupted in 1904–5 by six months in Pola and in 1906–7 by seven months in Rome. From 1915 to 1919 he lived in Zurich, from October 1919 to July 1920 in Trieste again, and from 1920 to 1939 in Paris. The twelve months from December 1939 until December 1940 he spent at Saint-Gérand-le-Puy near Vichy. Then, fearing for his family's safety under German occupation, he fled once more to neutral Zurich, where he died on 13 January 1941. On only three occasions did Joyce revisit Ireland: twice in 1909 in connection with the publication of *Dubliners* and with the Volta cinema project, and once in 1912 in another attempt to secure a publisher for *Dubliners*.

In Trieste Joyce wrote *Chamber Music*, *Dubliners*, *A Portrait*, *Giacomo Joyce*, and *Exiles*; in Zurich he completed most of the writing of *Ulysses*; in Paris he revised and completed *Ulysses*, wrote *Pomes Penyeach*, and from 1923 until 1938 composed 'Work in Progress', which was eventually pub-

lished in 1939 as *Finnegans Wake*. In his native city, by comparison, Joyce did apprentice work: 'Ibsen's New Drama' in 1900, 'The Day of the Rabblement' in 1901, some epiphanies and poems, a philosophical-cum-literary essay entitled 'A Portrait of the Artist' in 1904, and part of the unfinished *Stephen Hero*. Like many Dubliners – and the irony would not have been lost on him – Joyce needed to be free of his native country before he could produce works of lasting value.

Only in *Giacomo Joyce* did Joyce use a continental setting for his fiction: in his major work his imagination dwelt almost exclusively on Irish material. As Ettore Schmitz once said of Joyce's years in Trieste, 'A piece of Ireland was ripening under our sun'.[1] But as if to emphasize its European dimension, Joyce ended *Ulysses* with the words 'Trieste–Zurich–Paris 1914–1921'. There is a further irony – especially given Joyce's topographical imagination – for the presence of these European cities is glimpsed only occasionally in *Ulysses*.

On first arriving in Trieste in 1904 to take up a post at the Berlitz School, Joyce fell into conversation with three drunken English sailors in the Piazza Grande. Because of the noise they were making, the three sailors were arrested for drunken

167

2   The Piazza Della Borsa in Trieste taken in 1902. According to Joyce's Florentine friend Alessandro Francini Bruni, 'Who could avoid noticing this eccentric during the years that he strolled the streets of Trieste? Agile and lean, his rigid legs like the poles of a compass, he went about with an abstracted look. In summer he wore a Panama hat of indescribable colour and old shoes, in winter, a shabby overcoat with raised fur collar.' *Courtesy of the Civici Muse: Di Storia Ed Arte, Trieste.*

behaviour. Joyce attempted to intervene on their behalf, and accompanied them to the police headquarters to act as their translator, but once there he too was thrown into gaol, and only after the grudging intervention of the British consul was he released. In spite of this initial hostile reception, Joyce grew to like Trieste, a city which boasted an opera house, a warm climate, and a lively political atmosphere. Today Trieste is an Italian city, but in 1904 it was the leading port of the 'old Auster and Hungrig' (*FW* 464.27–8), the Austro-Hungarian empire that ruled from Vienna. It was not unlike Dublin, therefore, a city held by a foreign power. In their struggle to regain their city from the German-speaking imperialists, the Italian Irredentists found ready sympathy from the Irish exile. When his two children were born, he gave them Italian names, Giorgio and Lucia, and Italian became the language spoken at home.

Trieste is mentioned in passing in 'Eumaeus', when D. B. Murphy, the modern Ulyssean 'globetrotter', tells Stephen and Bloom: '– And I seen a man killed in Trieste by an Italian chap. Knife in his back. Knife like that' (*U* 16.576–7). In *Finnegans Wake* Trieste is given more prominence. Joyce's drinking bouts there are recalled in the phrase 'trieste, ah trieste ate I my liver!' (*FW* 301.16) – earlier there is a reference to Shem having a 'bladder tristended' (*FW* 169.20). Joyce enjoys playing on the name of the city and its proximity to the Latin word *triste* (sad). 'My animal his sorrafool!' (*FW* 301.15). My soul, my *anima*, is sorrowful, which is an echo of the line in Psalm 42: *Quare tristis es, anima mea*? (Why are you sad, my soul?). Giordano Bruno's motto – *In tristitia hilaris hilaritate tristis* (joy in sadness, sadness in joy) – acts as a refrain in *Finnegans Wake* and carries within it the city's name. In the Tale of the Prankquean and Jarl

van Hoother, the prankquean 'kidsnapped' two little 'jiminies', whose names are 'Tristopher' and 'Hilary', Christopher/ *tristitia* and Hilary/*hilaris* (*FW* 21.5–23.15). Trieste, the meeting-place of opposites, serves to contrast with the more dour motto for Dublin, to which there is allusion at the end of the Tale of the Prankquean: *Obedentia civium urbis felicitas* (the obedience of citizens, the happiness of the city).

Joyce's stay in Rome in 1906–7 was brief but formative. He arrived in Rome on 31 July 1906 to begin work in the Italian correspondence office of the private bank of Nast-Kolb and Schumacher, and was immediately greeted by a tablet near the bank commemorating Shelley's writing of *The Cenci* and *Prometheus Unbound*. Rome failed to stimulate a similar appetite for writing, but it did clarify certain things, reawakened his generosity towards Ireland, and arguably laid the foundations for *Ulysses*. In Rome Joyce had the idea of another story for

3 A view of St Peter's from the Pincian Hill as it appeared in *Picturesque Europe* (1876–9). When Joyce arrived in Rome in July 1906 he toured St Peter's, the Pincio, the Forum, and the Coliseum. 'The Pincio is a fine garden overlooking one gate of the city.' (*Letters* II, 145). (From *Picturesque Europe* 1876–9).

Dubliners about an Alfred H. Hunter, a clerk with dark complexion who was rumoured to have an unfaithful wife and who on 22 June 1904 rescued Joyce after a fracas involving another man's girlfriend. In Rome, however, '*Ulysses* never got any forrader than the title' (*Letters* II. 209). Joyce wished 'someone was here to talk to me about Dublin. I forget half the things I wanted to do' (*Letters* II. 189).

Zurich's muggy climate suited neither Nora nor Joyce, but its political and cultural atmosphere was a different matter. In 1916 Hans Arp, Hugo Ball, Tristan Tzara and other Dadaists, who were engaged in 'a warping process' (*FW* 497.3) much like his own later experiments with language in 'Work in Progress', used to meet in the Cabaret Voltaire. Before his departure from Zurich in 1917 Lenin was a frequent visitor to the Cafe Odeon, a restaurant also patronized by Joyce. If it were possible, Zurich brought out even more of the subversive in Joyce. When he arrived from Trieste in 1915 he commented, 'Zürich ist so sauber' ('clean' but also 'sober' to English ears); at his last Christmas in 1940, he turned to Carola Giedion-Welcker and said (uncannily as it turned out), 'You have no idea how wonderful dirt is'.[2] Among the friendships

that Joyce formed in Zurich, possibly the most important was the one with Frank Budgen. While Zurich as such is not mentioned in *Ulysses*, Joyce does incorporate several incidents that happened to him there. One was his fleeting affair with Martha Fleischmann (about which more below). The other was a row in 1918 with Henry Carr, a member of the British Consulate. Carr took exception to being handed the miserable sum of ten francs for his part in a stage performance of *The Importance of Being Earnest*, and accused Joyce, the business manager of the English Players, of being a swindler. Incensed by such ingratitude, Joyce took out a lawsuit, and wreaked a more lasting revenge in his portrait of 'Private Carr', the crude-mouthed Cockney who attacks Stephen in

4 *L'Asino*, an anti-clerical newspaper, struck many chords in Joyce. The front cover for the edition of 17 February 1907 shows flames engulfing Giordano Bruno of Nola, a sixteenth-century heretic. The caption reads, 'Around the burning stake the priests are still shouting, "Long live freedom of thought".' The back cover – the one reproduced here – depicts the nightmare of Pope Piux X, his bed surrounded by heretics of the Church including Savanorola and Bruno. In his 1901 pamphlet 'The Day of the Rabblement' Joyce enjoyed quoting 'the Nolan', conscious that Bruno would have been known to few of his readers in Dublin. The similarity of Bruno of Nola's name to that of the Dublin booksellers Browne and Nolan must also have impressed him. Bruno's cosmology – a more sophisticated version of Nicholas of Cusa's coincidence of opposites – insists on an ultimate unity with terrestrial divisions into opposites. Bruno's plays, especially *Candelaio* (The Candlemaker), first published in 1582, would also have appealed to Joyce's sense of humour, particularly its word-play, neologisms, and puns on candles. *Courtesy of Carla de Petris and Bulzoni Editore.*

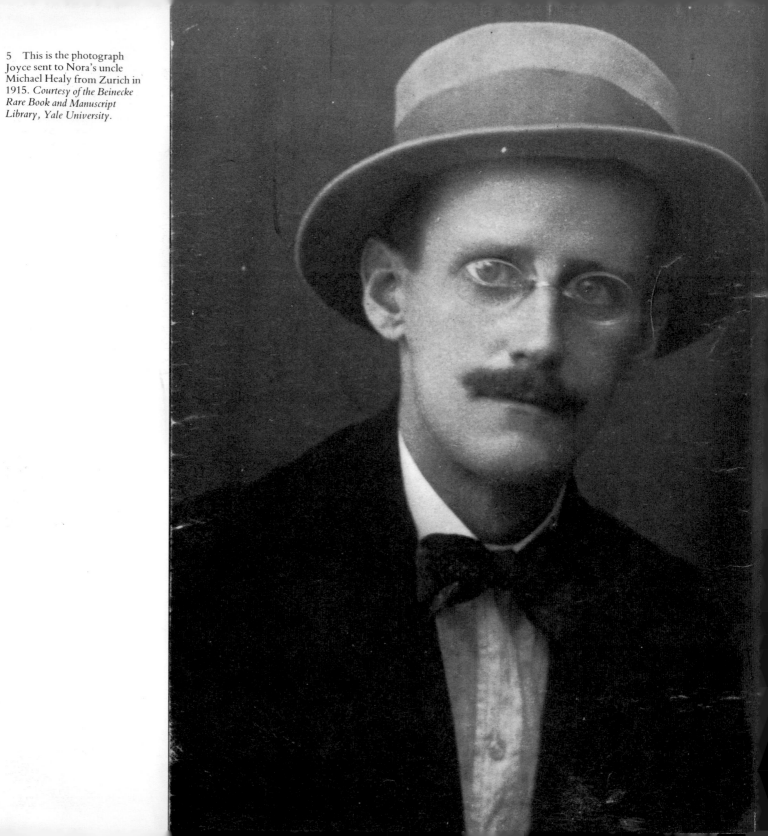

5   This is the photograph Joyce sent to Nora's uncle Michael Healy from Zurich in 1915. *Courtesy of the Beinecke Rare Book and Manuscript Library, Yale University.*

6 The Restaurant and Hotel Pfauen was a favourite meeting place for Joyce and his friends in Zurich. Joyce drank the local white wine, Fendant de Sion, comparing red wine unflatteringly to beefsteak, and white wine to electricity. © *Baugeschichtes Archiv des Stadt Zürich.*

the brothel in 'Circe'. 'I'll wring the neck of any fucker says a word against my fucking king' (*U* 15.4597–8).

In *Finnegans Wake*, Joyce 'swobbing broguen eerish myth brockendootsch' (*FW* 70.8) repays his outstanding debts to Zurich, a city that was twice a sanctuary for him from the two World Wars and – fittingly for a word that resembles *zurück* (the German word 'back') – his final resting-place. The two rivers, the Sihl and the Limmat, which bisect the city, are mentioned – appropriately enough – in ALP's 'river' chapter, where they can be heard in the question 'Yssel that the limmat?' (*FW* 198.13) (Is that the Sihl or the Limmat? Isn't that the limit?). They also provide yet another Meeting of the Waters. 'What a city!' he would exclaim with evident pleasure to Carola Giedion-Welcker, all the time thinking of Dublin. 'A lake, a mountain and two rivers are its treasures.' In the same chapter there is a reference to 'the sillypost' (*FW* 200.22), the GPO in Zurich (*Sihlpost*). In Shem's house of 'O'Shame' we find listed 'cans of Swiss condensed bilk' (*FW* 183.30), which is perhaps what Joyce thought of condensed milk (that is, bilked or cheated of the real thing). On several occasions Joyce plays on the word *Sechselauten*, the Zurich spring fertility festival when bells are rung at six o'clock in the evening: 'there's the Belle for Sexaloitez' (*FW* 213.18–19), says ALP; elsewhere we find 'saxonlootie' (*FW* 58.24), 'saxy luters' (*FW* 492.14–15), and 'silks alustre' (*FW* 528.19). The same festival is

171

invoked in the Irish-sounding phrase, 'Oho, oho, Mester Begge, you're about to be bagged in the bog again' (*FW* 58.16–17), for during *Sechselauten* the winter-demon Böögg was symbolically burnt on the spring bonfire. In the Mookse and the Gripes episode Joyce also alludes to Zurich's heraldic animal, the lion, and to the 'building space in lyonine city' (*FW* 155.6–7). His favourite wine was the 'noble white fat' (*FW* 171.24), a Swiss white wine, Fendant de Sion. After drinking too much, Shem/Joyce 'collapsed carefully under a bedtick from Schwitzer's, his face enveloped into a dead warrior's telemac' (*FW* 176.34–6). During the First World War Joyce retreated to neutral Switzerland, and wrote about the dead warrior Telemachus; a 'bedtick' contains a bed-louse, a 'shuck tick' (a sort of mattress in *Huckleberry Finn*), bought from Switzer's department store in Grafton Street, Dublin, and a clock made in Switzerland.

On over twenty-four occasions in *Ulysses* Paris is mentioned by name, nearly always in connection with Stephen. In 1903 Stephen/Joyce returned from Paris having acquired Paris fads (*U* 1.342) – such as having lemon instead of milk in his tea – and wearing a Latin quarter hat (*U* 1.519). At night, when he was in Paris, he read Aristotle in the Library of Ste Geneviève, 'sheltered from the sin of Paris' (*U* 2.70). During his first stay in Paris in 1902–3, Joyce became friends with Joseph Casey, an old Fenian who worked as a typesetter for the *New York Herald* in Paris and who was the model for 'Kevin Egan'. Casey's son, Patrice, was in the French army:

> Patrice, home on furlough, lapped warm milk with me in the bar MacMahon. Son of the wild goose, Kevin Egan of Paris. My father's a bird, he lapped the sweet *lait chaud* with pink young tongue, plump bunny's face. Lap, *lapin*.
>
> (*U* 3.163–6)

As befits an episode with 'Proteus' for its title, the label 'change' is constantly on display. Casey is compared to the Wild Geese (Catholic earls who fled to the continent in the seventeenth and eighteenth centuries after suffering defeat and persecution in Ireland). He is metamorphosed into a wild goose (the switch from metaphorical to literal meaning and from plural to singular adds a humorous touch). His son is a French soldier – hence 'home on furlough'. As Patrice – French for Patrick – laps his milk, he in turn is transformed into a *lapin*, a rabbit with 'plump bunny's face'. Another 'change' becomes apparent when this episode is juxtaposed with the first, for while 'Telemachus' deals with the usurper in Ireland, 'Proteus' is concerned with exile and possible assimilation in Europe.

Paris was an exile's city not only for the Irish in the eighteenth and nineteenth centuries, but also for the lost generation in the 1920s who came to Paris as to a modern shrine. At some point in the 1920s most of the leading and aspiring writers turned up in Paris: Hemingway, Fitzgerald, Faulkner, Djuna Barnes, Carlos Williams, Dos Passos, Borges, Beckett. The war was over, prices were cheap, and Fitzgerald's 'jazz age' was about to commence. If Paris was the exile's city, then it was also a real home for other Americans, including Gertrude Stein and Sylvia Beach. Joyce is not part of the lost generation, and when he arrived in Paris in 1920 the 'paleoparisien' (*FW* 151.9) was in nearly every important sense at home. *Ulysses* was almost complete and the references to exile confined to the Paris of 1902–3. By 1930 most of the Americans had moved on, the cheap days of Paris having come to an end; Joyce remained, cushioned against rising prices and the world slump by the generosity of his English patroness, Harriet Shaw Weaver. Joyce was also tied to Paris for another reason: Sylvia Beach's agreement in 1921 to publish *Ulysses*.[3]

THE CITY UNDER KALEIDOSCOPE

Living in continental cities for nearly all his adult life, Joyce was exposed to the different languages that make up the community of Europe. In Zurich, and to some extent in Paris, whenever he stepped out of his apartment into the street or into a restaurant he could never be sure which language he would hear. This must have reinforced his consciousness of the limits of a language community, but it must also have underlined the possibilities of writing for a truly European audience. His city is not only topographically precise, as we saw in Chapter 4, it is also a city of words. Where Wordsworth, hushed, heard London's mighty heart beating, a life force the city shared with nature, Joyce hears not so much hearts as voices. Joyce's city is surrounded by the walls of language. From 'tight in his inkbattle house' (*FW* 176.30–1), Joyce felt safe against the threat from outside. The year he spent at Saint-Gérand-le-Puy near Vichy in the French countryside was not one

173

8   View of Zurich or 'Turricum' (*FW* 228.22) by night looking towards the Munster Bridge with the Fraumunster's steeple centre left and the faces of four clocks telling exactly the same time. 'Ding dong! Where's your pal in silks alustre?' (*FW* 528.18–19). *Photograph the author.*

9 Posing again in Paris 1923. Joyce, Pound, John Quinn, and Ford Madox Ford. *John Quinn Memorial Collection, Rare Books and Manuscripts Division, The New York Public Library, Astor, Lenox and Tilden Foundations.*

he enjoyed: after all, what was the world but a 'cell for citters to cit in' (*FW* 12.2). The view of nature in *Finnegans Wake* is essentially a view of the country in the city: rivers with bridges carrying people and traffic, large public parks, walks by the sea along promenades, clouds, fog, rain, and rainbows.

In *Ulysses* Paris is observed through a lens or filter, through a glow of nostalgia, through a particular memory of Joyce's first stay there in 1902–3. But in *Finnegans Wake* the emphasis falls more on simultaneous evocation. At times we can hear – through the fog of a hangover – Paris in the 1920s, the 'shout in the street' (*U* 2.387) just beyond his apartment window, the noises of cars:

rollsrights, carhacks, stonengens, kisstvanes, tramtrees, fargobawlers, autokinotons, hippohobbilies, streetfleets, tournintaxes, megaphoggs, circuses and wardsmoats and basilikerks and

175

aeropagods and the hoyse and the jolly-
brool and the peeler in the coat and the
mecklenburk bitch bite at his ear and the
merlinburrow burrocks and his fore old
porecourts

(*FW* 5.29–36)

Small wonder that his 'howd feeled heavy,
his hoddit did shake' (*FW* 6.8–9)!

This kind of brainstorm, a piling up of
words and concepts, mirrors a characteristic
Wakean approach to history and the world.
Nothing is lost and everything is retriev-
able by the dual movement of the tele-
scopic method. Ancient civilization is
're-presented' by the Rollright Stones near
Chipping Norton or Carhaix in Brittany or
Stonehenge. Bygmester Finnegan, laid out
for his wake, is taunted by 'kisstvanes'

176

(*kistvane* is Welsh for a box-shaped tomb)
and is kissed 'in vain' by the mourners (for
he will rise again). He hears 'fargobawlers'
(*fág an bealach* is Irish for clear the way,
the title of Charles Gavan Duffy's stir-
ring *Nation* ballad composed in 1842),
'megaphoggs' ('mega' fogs and mega-
phones), the 'mecklenburk bitch bite at his
ear' (Mecklenburg Street is the red-light area
of Dublin and the setting for 'Circe'). His
body feels heavy, and, like Merlin, he risks
being buried alive along with his 'fore old
porecourts' (his body is here identified with
the Four Courts in Dublin, a building nearly
completely destroyed during the Civil War).
Outside, people have been busy in history,
constructing, assembling, hacking away,
rolling stones, cutting down trees, making
moats, basilicas, aeroplanes (gods of the
sky), turning taxis, hobbling along on
'hippos' (Greek for horse) or driving in
'autokinotons' (self-moving objects in
Greek) or in Rolls-Royces (rollsrights).

As a hod-carrier, Finnegan has also played
a 'constructive' role in history, but now,
lying out, he feels guilt-ridden, possibly
as a result of some sexual misdemeanour.
Ancient history, the history of transport and
the various modes of modern transport, the
building of cities, the story of Finn MacCool
(for Finnegan is Finn again), wakes and
burial customs, the similarities between
stone circles in antiquity and modern-day
circuses, the sounds in the street, the psychology of Finnegan, the experience of a
hangover – where does it all end? It is
an obvious question to ask and one that
prompts another question equally difficult
to answer – how can all this material be
gathered together and properly ordered?
History is always there, Joyce seems to be
saying, waiting to be rescued from the dark
pool, the Dublin (*dubh linn* is dark pool in
Irish), of language.

One morning Tim was rather full,
  His head felt heavy which made him
    shake,
He fell from the ladder and broke his
    skull,
  So they carried him home his corpse to
    wake,
They rolled him up in a nice clean sheet,
  And laid him out upon the bed,
With a gallon of whiskey at his feet,
  And a barrel of porter at his head.

His friends assembled at the wake,
  And Mrs. Finnegan called for lunch,
First they brought in tay and cake,
  Then pipes, tobacco, and whiskey
    punch,
Miss Biddy O'Brien began to cry,
  'Such a neat clean corpse, did you ever
    see,
Arrah, Tim avourneen, why did you die?'
  'Ah, hould your gab,' said Paddy
    McGee.

Then Biddy O'Connor took up the job,
  'Biddy,' says she, 'you're wrong, I'm
    sure,
But Biddy gave her a belt in the gob,
  And left her sprawling on the floor;
Oh, then the war did soon enrage;
  'Twas woman to woman and man to
    man,
Shillelagh law did all engage,
  And a row and a ruction soon began.

Then Micky Maloney raised his head,
  When a noggin of whiskey flew at him,
It missed and falling on the bed,
  The liquor scattered over Tim;
Bedad he revives, see how he rises,
  And Timothy rising from the bed,
Says, 'Whirl your liquor round like
    blazes,
  Thanam o'n dhoul, do ye think I'm
    dead?'

91.—FINNEGAN'S WAKE

Tim Fin-ne-gan liv'd in Wal-kin Street a gen-tle-man Ir-ish mighty odd. He had a tongue both rich and sweet, an' to rise in the world he car-ried a hod, Now Tim had a sort of a tip-plin' way With the love of the li-quor he was born, An' to help him on with his work each day, He'd a drop of the craythur ev-'ry morn.

CHORUS
Whack fol the dah, dance to your partner Welt the flure yer trot-ters shake, Was-n't it the truth I told you, Lot's of fun at Fin-ne-gan's Wake.

11 Ms of opening stanza with music of 'Finnegan's Wake'. (From Colm O Lochlainn, *Irish Street Ballads*, Dublin: The Three Candles, 1939.)

Finnegans Wake ceaselessly recomposes the city in history. Its continuity is best captured through the image of the river, and *Finnegans Wake* celebrates not only the Liffey flowing through Dublin but also the Seine. In the opening chapter, for example, Joyce takes care to list the Seine's beautiful bridges: 'clouds roll by' (*FW* 7.36) (Pont de St Cloud); 'Redismembers invalids' (*FW* 8.6) (Pont des Invalides); 'royal divorsion' (*FW* 9.35) (Pont Royal); 'hiena hinnessy' (*FW* 10.4) (Pont d'Iena); 'foder allmicheal' (*FW* 11.23) (Pont St Michel);

'marriedann' (*FW* 12.6) (Pont Marie); 'several tones' (*FW* 12.30) (Pont de Sèvres). The river flowing through Paris is the 'Sein annews' (*FW* 277.18), the same anew. In terms of Being (*Sein* is the verb 'to be' in German), the rivers of the world, and especially the Seine and the Liffey, are the same: they are bridges to the past. The connections between the Seine and the Liffey provided Joyce with an analogue from the natural world to complement his work in language, for, while he lived far from his native city, with his 'patternmind' and a 'paradigmatic ear' (*FW* 70.35–6), observing patterns in sounds and sounds through history, he made up for the loss of his native city through language.

Finnegans Wake is a kaleidoscope, a potpourri of associations, where past civilizations and contemporary history, different cities and cultures, private stories and public myths, are all potentially present in the fragments that compose the mosaic. It is appropriate that when Bygmester Finnegan – Ibsen's Master-Builder and the hod-carrier Tim Finnegan – 'rises' in the morning, he should do so against a Paris landmark:

> his roundhead staple of other days to rise in undress maisonry upstanded (joygrantit!), a waalworth of a skyerscape of most eyeful hoyth entowerly, erigenating from next to nothing and celescalating the himals and all, hierarchitectitiptitoploftical, with a burning bush abob off its baubletop and larrons o'toolers clittering up and tombles a'buckets clottering down.
>
> (*FW* 4.34–5.4)

This particular passage collects together all the following and more: St Laurence O'Toole, the patron saint of Dublin, and the murder of his contemporary St Thomas à Beckett 'clottering down'; the Himalayas, the highest mountain range in the world; Moses and the burning bush; the Irish philosopher John Scotus Erigena; Moore's song 'The Light of Other Days'; the heavens and their modern equivalents, namely escalators; the work of the mason on a *maison*, dressing a house, as it were; and perhaps also Parnell's use of a fire escape to avoid discovery by Mrs O'Shea's husband at her Hove residence. The phrase 'eyeful hoyth entowerly' is simultaneously Howth Head, one of the round towers of Ireland, 'an awful house/height entirely', and also the Eiffel Tower; moreover, like the Woolworth Building in New York, it is a 'waalworth of a skyerscape', that is a skyscraper. This last word is especially important, for 'skyerscape' anticipates a key concept in *Finnegans Wake* – 'collideorscape' (*FW* 143.28).

Finnegans Wake is more than a kaleidoscope: it is also a 'collide or escape'. Things come together and there is a collision, possibly – following Nicholas of Cusa (1401?–64) a 'coincidence of opposites'. But there is also something that escapes (from) that collision, something new that is disclosed, a changed perception. One of the rewards of reading *Finnegans Wake* is a renewed attention to the liberating effects of language, for reality can be other than that imposed by a governing ideology. A fresh pattern, a different ordering, can emerge. The erect penis, a 'roundhead', undressed (joygrantit! – joy grant it, joy granite, gigantic) is here compared to the Eiffel Tower, originating from next to nothing, and reaching up as far as it can go 'hierarchitectitiptitoploftical' (higher, architect, hierarchy, tip, top, tiptoe, toploftical, loft, oft, optical). There is a happy coincidence of opposites. Each term is read in terms of the other, but in *Finnegans Wake* no term is privileged at the expense of the other. 'Three

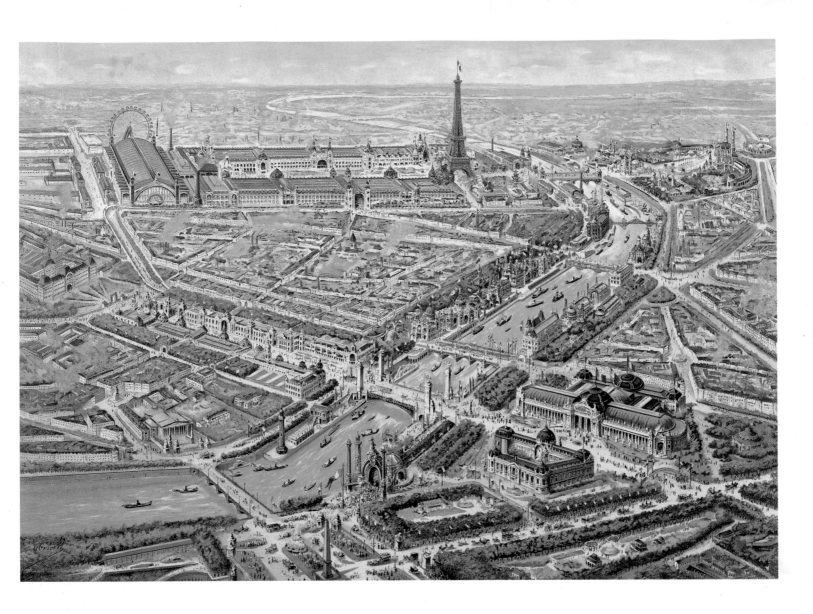

score and ten toptypsical readings' are possible in this 'book of Doublends Jined' (*FW* 20.10–11). Shake the kaleidoscope and the world changes. One moment there is a collision; the next an escape. You can collide, or you can escape; one moment 'clittering up', the next 'clottering down'. Words and ideas collide and new meanings arise. The phrase 'eyeful hoyth entowerly' sets up in turn its own paradigm, independent of its Parisian and other associations at this point; later, we read of 'a wanderful noyth untirely' (*FW* 59.13), and 'vely lovely entiley' (*FW* 299.25).

Paradoxically, such a flood of associations, such 'lashons of languages' (*FW* 29.32), often prevents us from thinking there is a world outside the text. Consequently, while we might begin by concentrating on the immediacy with which Joyce evokes the world, within a short space we are lost in the skein of language. This, however, needs another counter-weight, for the free play of language is tied in Joyce's case to his own exiled condition in the kaleidoscopic meeting-place of 1920s Europe. In Paris Joyce's experiments with the English language found a ready audience in the group round *transition*, the avant-garde magazine which published regular instalments of 'Work in Progress' from 1928 onwards. After Dada in 1916 Zurich, after the 1917 Revolution in Russia, *The Waste Land* in 1922, anything seemed possible. 'Being' not 'meaning' was the new driving force in the modern movement of art. Avoid at all cost the possibility of being paraphrased. In Pound's words, 'Direct treatment of the "thing" whether subjective or objective.'[4] Or in Beckett's words on 'Work in Progress':

> Here form is content, content is form. You complain that this stuff is not written in English. It is not written at all. It is not to be read – or rather it is not only to be read. It is to be looked at and listened to. His writing is not *about* something; it is that something itself.[5]

'This is nat language at any sinse of the world' (*FW* 83.12). Here the confusion of word and world, a confusion that Martha Clifford inadvertently draws attention to in her letter to Bloom in *Ulysses*, overturns the traditional mimetic view of the relationship between language and reality, and serves to remind us how language not only crucially intervenes in our perception of the world but also helps construct that world.

OPENING PAGES OF A WORK IN PROGRESS
by JAMES JOYCE

riverrun brings us back to Howth Castle & Environs. Sir Tristram, violer d'amores, fr' over the short sea, had passencore rearrived from North Armorica on this side the scraggy isthmus of Europe Minor to wielderfight his penisolate war: nor had topsawyer's rocks by the stream Oconee exaggerated themselse to Laurens County's gorgios, while they went doublin their mumper all the time; nor avoice from afire bellowsed mishe mishe to tauftauf thuartpeatrick: not yet, though venissoon after, had a kidscad buttended a bland old isaac; not yet, though all's fair in vanessy, were sosie sesthers wroth with twone nathandjoe. Rot a peck of pa's malt had Jhem or Shen brewed by arclight and rory end to the regginbrow was to be seen ringsome on the waterface.

The fall (badalgharaghtakamminarronnkonnbronntonnerronntuonnthunntrovarrhounawnskawntoohoohoordenenthurnuck!) of a once wallstrait oldparr is retaled early in bed and later on life down through all christian minstrelsy. The great fall of the offwall entailed at such short notice the schute of Finnigan, erse solid man, that the humptyhillhead of humself promptly sends an unquiring one well to the west in quest of his tumptytumtoes: and their upturnpikepointandplace is at the knock out in the park where oranges have been

— 9 —

Equally, the different languages that compose and define *Finnegans Wake* remind us of another kind of relativity. In learning a foreign language the emphasis falls on finding equivalents between the native speaker's language and that being studied; it is a translation, not a philosophical exercise. Joyce put to good use his time spent teaching English as a foreign language in Berlitz schools, for at least at one level *Finnegans Wake* is like a school for foreign languages. The pupil/reader walks through the different classrooms picking up snatches of Norse, French, German, Dutch, Hebrew, Portuguese, Gaelic, Italian, listening to the rote learning and substitution exercises, the use of word lists, and the mechanical chant-

14 Harry Fenn's drawing of Howth in *Picturesque Europe* (1876–9). *Ulysses* ends with Molly remembering a day in 1888 lying among the rhododendrons on Howth head: 'the day I got him to propose to me yes first I gave him the bit of seedcake out of my mouth and it was leapyear like now yes 16 years ago' (*U* 18.1573–5). *Finnegans Wake* begins appropriately with the river of life and the male figure of HCE (here, Howth Castle and Environs): 'riverrun, past Eve and Adam's, from swerve of shore to bend of bay, brings us by a commodius vicus of recirculation back to Howth Castle and Environs' (*FW* 3.1–3).

15 Joyce's letter to Weaver in November 1926 in which he provides a key to the opening paragraph of *Finnegans Wake*. *Courtesy of the Beinecke Rare Book and Manuscript Library*, Yale University.

brings us back to

Howth Castle & Environs. Sir Tristram, violer d'amores, had passencore rearrived on the scraggy isthmus from North Armorica to wielderfight his penisolate war; nor had stream rocks by the Oconee exaggerated themselse to Laurens County, Ga, doublin all the time; nor avoice from afire bellowsed mishe mishe to tauftauf thuartpeatrick; not yet, though venisoon after, had a Kidscad buttended a bland old Isaac; not yet, though all's fair in vanessy, were sosie sesthers wroth with twone jonathan. Rot a peck of pa's malt had Shem or Shen brewed by arclight and rory end to the regginbrow was to be seen ringsome on the waterface.

James Joyce

Paris. 15/xi/926

Dear Madam: Above please find prosepiece ordered in sample form.
Also key to same. Hoping said sample meets with your approval

yrs trly

Jeems Joker

Howth (pron Hoaeth) = Dan Hoved (head)
Sir Amory Tristram 1st earl of Howth changed his name to Saint
    Lawrence, b in Brittany (North Armorica)
Tristan et Iseult, passim
viola in all moods and senses
Dublin, Laurens Co, Georgia, founded by a Dubliner, Peter Sawyer,
    on r. Oconee. Its motto: Doubling all the time.
The flame of Christianity kindled by S. Patrick on Holy Saturday in
    defiance of royal orders
Mishe = I am (Irish) i.e. Christian
Tauf = baptise (German)
Thou art Peter and upon this rock etc (a pun in the original
    aramaic)
Lat: Tu es Petrus et super hanc petram
Parnell ousted Isaac Butt from leadership
The venison purveyor Jacob got the blessing meant for Esau

2 (continuation of 15.xi.926)

Miss Vanhomrigh and Miss Johnson had the same christian name
Sosie = double
Willy brewed a peck of maut
Noah planted the vine and was drunk
John Jameson is the greatest Dublin distiller
Arthur Guinness "   "   "   "   brewer
rory = Irish = red
rory = Latin, roridus = dewy
At the rainbow's end are dew and the colour red
    bloody end to the lie in Anglo-Irish = no lie
regginbrow = German regenbogen + rainbow
ringsome = German ringsum, around
When all vegetation is covered by the flood then are no eyebrows
    on the face of the Waterworld
exaggerare = to mound up
themselse = another dublin 5000 inhabitants
Isthmus of Sutton a neck of land between Howth head and the plain
Howth = an island for old geographers
passencore = pas encore and ricorsi storici of Vico
rearrived = idem
wielderfight = wiederfechten = refight
bellowsed = the response of the pestfire of faith to the windy
    words of the apostle

181

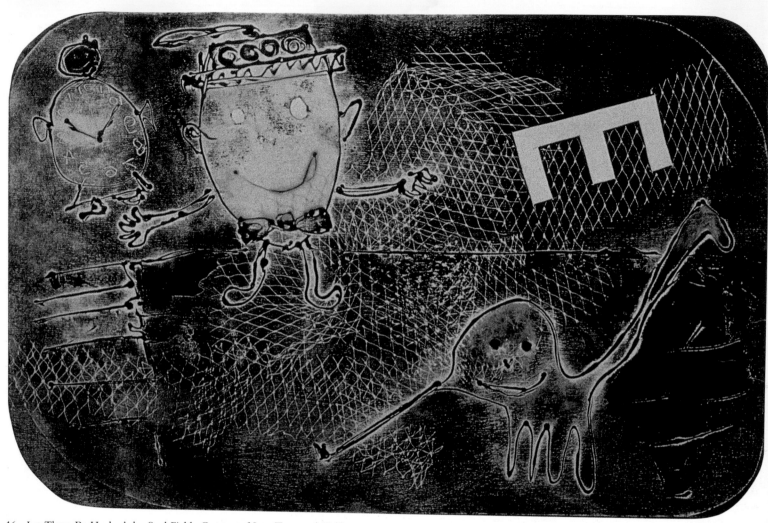

16   Let There Be Horlog', by Saul Field. *Courtesy of Jean Townsend Field.*

ing, conscious only of rhythms and words, their physical shape, and how they might be pronounced. The Berlitz method was almost designed to detach words from meaning. Like Ferdinand de Saussure, Joyce seemed to sense that the detachment of words from meaning, a principle underlying both high modernism and Saussurian linguistics, was a necessary limitation in order for new ideas about language to emerge. To Saussure, language was a system which could be explained without constant reference to meaning; signs, composed of signified and signifier, were arbitrary; words gained meaning in opposition to other words. Saussure was a French-speaking Swiss linguist who diplomatically respected language boundaries. Joyce, on the other hand, regarded all the languages he knew as part of his school for foreign languages.

A graduate in modern languages, the 'mimetic' Joyce took delight in practising a form of 'machine translation'. In *Ulysses* he enjoys punning in different languages: lap, *lapin*; *dignum*, Dignam; the joke about who put the Virgin Mary in this 'position' (that is, bent over and pregnant), the answer being '*C'est le pigeon, Joseph*' (*U* 3.161–2); *irlandais*, *Hollandais* (*non fromage*) (*U* 3.220); *corpus*, corpse (*U* 5.350). In 'Circe', Stephen at one point imagines that gesture might be a 'universal language' (*U* 15.105–6), but Joyce knows this is an illusion. What interests him is the surface texture of a language, the family resemblances between languages, and, in *Finnegans Wake*, the interface of languages.

Joyce is 'middayevil down to his vegetable soul' (*FW* 423.28). In *Finnegans Wake* he displays a special interest in the period from the Viking invasion of Dublin in the tenth century through to the establishment of Anglo-Norman Ireland in the twelfth

century. This period witnessed the invasion/ foundation of his native city, the defeat of the Danes at the Battle of Clontarf in 1014 by Brian Boru, the demise of the last High King of Ireland, Roderick O'Connor, the granting of Dublin by the English Pope Adrian IV to Henry II, and Henry II's disposal of the city to the citizens of Bristol. In the 1170s, Henry triumphed: the remaining Danes were driven by the settlers from Bristol to Oxmantown (town of the Eastmen or Danes) north of the river, and King Roderick relinquished his power – 'suck up' (*FW* 381.30) is how Joyce describes this abdication. The first passage of *Finnegans Wake* to be written was the Roderick O'Connor section on pages 380–2, and throughout the text there are numerous references to other incidents in this period – the Mookse and the Gripes, for example, is at one level about Adrian, 'our once in only Bragspear' (*FW* 152.32–3), the Shakespearean upstart Nicholas Brakespear (who became Pope Adrian). Joyce was also fascinated by Dublin's coat of arms – three castles ablaze – and its accompanying motto, *obedentia civium urbis felicitas*; he uses both with ironic and often devastating effect in *Finnegans Wake*.

In 'Proteus' Stephen's historical imagination reconstructs a 'starving cagework city', scene of 'famine, plague and slaughters', where in 1331 a 'horde of jerkined dwarfs' hacked in 'green blubbery whalemeat'. These are 'my people', Stephen remarks, 'their blood is in me, their lust my waves' (*U* 3.304–7). The same historical imagination is at work in *Finnegans Wake*, at once establishing and telescoping difference. Dublin presented Joyce with a case study in the way language might have evolved. In the first chapter of *Finnegans Wake* he recreates the confrontation between Mutt and Jute, the native Irish and the Scandinavian invader.

17 Dublin's coat of arms: three castles ablaze. The city's motto is *Obedentia Civium Urbis Felicitas* (the obedience of the citizens, the happiness of the city). Throughout *Finnegans Wake* Joyce mercilessly plays on this motto, turning it inside out: 'the hearsomeness of the burger felicitates the whole of the polis' (*FW* 23.14–15), 'the obedience of the citizens elp the ealth of the ole' (*FW* 76.8–9), and 'Thine obesity, O civilian, hits the felicitude of our orb!' (*FW* 140.6–7). From James Malton, *A Picturesque and Descriptive View of Dublin* (1792–9).

The scene is Dublin some time after the Battle of Clontarf and the defeat of the Danes in 1014:

Jute. – Yutah!

Mutt. – Mukk's pleasurad.

Jute. – Are you jeff?

Mutt. – Somehards.

Jute. – But you are not jeffmute?

Mutt. – Noho. Only an utterer.

Jute. – Whoa? Whoat is the mutter with you?

Mutt. – I became a stun a stummer.

Jute. – What a hauhauhauhaudibble thing, to be cause! How, Mutt?

Mutt. – Aput the buttle, surd.

Jute. – Whose poddle? Wherein?

Mutt. – The Inns of Dungtarf where Used awe to be he.

Jute. – You that side your voise are almost inedible to me. Become a bitskin more wiseable, as if I were you.

Mutt. – Has? Has at? Hasatency? Urp, Boohooru! Booru Usurp! I trumple from rath in mine mines when I rimimirim!

Jute. – One eyegonblack. Bisons is bisons. Let me fore all your hasitancy cross your qualm with trink gilt. Here have sylvan coyne, a piece of oak. Ghinees hies good for you.

Mutt. – Louee, louee! How wooden I not know it, the intellible greytcloak of Cedric Silkyshag! Cead mealy faulty rices for one dabblin bar. Old grilsy growlsy! He was poached on in that eggtentical spot. Here where the liveries, Monomark. There where the misers moony, Minnikin passe.

Jute. – Simply because as Taciturn pretells, our wrongstory-shortener

he dumptied the wholeborrow of rubbages on to soil here.

Mutt. – Just how a puddinstone inat the brookcells by a riverpool.

Jute. – Load Allmarshy! Wid wad for a norse like?

Mutt. – Somular with a bull on a clompturf. Rooks roarum rex roome! I could snore to him of the spumy horn, with his woolseley side in, by the neck I am sutton on, did Brian d' of Linn.

Jute. – Boildoyle and rawhoney on me when I can beuraly forsstand a weird from sturk to finnic in such a patwhat as your rutter-damrotter. Onheard of and umscene! Gut aftermeal! See you doomed.

Mutt. – Quite agreem. Bussave a sec. Walk a dun blink roundward this albutisle and you skull see how olde ye plaine of my Elters, hunfree and ours, where wone to wail whimbrel to peewee o'er the saltings, where wilby citie by law of isthmon, where by a droit of signory, icefloe was from his Inn the Byggning to whose Finishthere Punct. Let erehim ruhmuhrmuhr. Mearmerge two races, swete and brack. Mor-thering rue. Hither, craching eastuards, they are in surgence: hence, cool at ebb, they requiesce. Countlessness of livestories have netherfallen by this plage, flick as flowflakes, litters from aloft, like a waast wizzard all of whirl-worlds. Now are all tombed to the mound, isges to isges, erde from erde. Pride, O pride, thy prize!

Jute. – 'Stench!

Mutt. – Fiatfuit! Hereinunder lyethey. Llarge by the smal an' everynight life olso th'estrange, babylone the greatgrandhotelled with tit tit tittlehouse, alp on earwig, drukn on ild, likeas equal to anequal in this sound seemetery which iz leebez luv.

Jute. – 'Zmorde!

Mutt. – Meldundleize! By the fearse wave behoughted. Despond's sung. And thanacestross mound have swollup them all. This ourth of years is not save brickdust and being humus the same roturns. He who runes may rede it on all fours. O'c'stle, n'wc'stle, tr'c'stle, crumbling! Sell me sooth the fare for Humblin! Humblady Fair. But speak it allsosiftly, moulder! Be in your whisht!

Jute. – Whysht?

Mutt. – The gyant Forficules with Amni the fay.

Jute. – Howe?

Mutt. – Here is viceking's graab.

Jute. – Hwaad!

Mutt. – Ore you astoneaged, jute you?

Jute. – Oye am thonthorstrok, thing mud.

(*FW* 16.10–18.16)

Mutt and Jute, me and you; Mutt and Jeff, American comic-strip characters; one hardly audible, the other a deaf-mute: the permutations are designed to stress the coincidence of opposites, their similarities as much as their disagreement. The Danes were defeated in history but their legacy in Dublin and Ireland – especially evident in the names of places and people, such as Howth, Dalkey, Broderick, Sigerson – remained. Irish Mutt has fought at the Battle of Clontarf and has developed a stammer. Jute tells him to draw near: 'Become a bitskin more wiseable, as if I were you'. It is difficult to know if we should sympathize with Jute or Mutt: Mutt's stammer and hesitation reminds us that he is a forerunner of HCE and Parnell; Jute's reference, on the other hand, to his 'eyegonblack' recalls Joyce's own black eyepatch. The conciliatory Jute, the invader, offers Mutt a 'piece of oak' and reminds him in Indo-English – a thousand years before the Guinness commercial – that 'ghinees hies good for you'. Mutt wishes Jute – less warmly – a 'cead mealy faulty', *cead mile failte*, a hundred thousand welcomes, and follows this with an attack on Sitric Silkenbeard, the Danish leader at Clontarf.

Jute becomes increasingly agitated: 'Boildolye and rawhoney' (Baldoyle and Raheny) 'I can beuraly forsstand a weird from sturk to finnic in such a patwhat as your rutterdamrotter.' (I can barely understand a word from start to finish in such a patois/patter, you damn rotter.) Jute would see Mutt doomed, and Mutt quite agrees. Mutt then changes tack and asks Jute to wait a moment ('bussave a sec') and he'll show him the site where 'wilby citie', namely Dublin. He then cites the title to a Moore song 'Let Erin Remember' and suggests how the Irish are the 'Mearmerge' of 'two races, swete and brack'. Thousands of 'live-stories' have fallen by this 'plage' (beach/place), 'litters from aloft'. Now they are all dead, ashes to ashes, and 'erde from erde', shit from shit. This is the prize of pride, the victories of history: ''Stench!' Here they lie, by the Liffey, in lethe sleep, large by small, 'alp on earwig' (Anna Livia Plurabelle on Earwicker), in this 'sound seemetery'. This earth of ours is nothing save 'brickdust' and 'being humus [human/earth] the same roturns'. He who runs may read it, deciphering the meaning by stooping close to the earth. Mutt tells Jute to speak ever so softly: 'whisht!' To which Jute replies 'Whysht?' Exclamation is answered by a question-mark. Each stage of history poses problems for subsequent generations. Conquest gives way to assimilation and the eventual accession of the human stage in Vico's cycle of history. The Viking's grave becomes the 'viceking's graab', which produces from Jute the exclamation 'Hwaad' (Danish for 'what'). Mutt wonders if Jute is 'astoneaged' (astonished/ a stone-aged man), to which Jute replies that he is 'thonthorstrok' (Thon/Thor, thunderstruck).

The encounter between Mutt and Jute, where 'beuraly' contains not just barely but also *beurla* – Irish for the English language – and where 'forsstand' recalls *verstand* (the past tense in German for 'understand') and hence the Germanic origins of English, reconstructs an early stage in the development of the English language. As Patrick Parrinder reminds us in connection with the *Wake*'s so-called nonsense language, Joyce's freeplay of language 'is leading somewhere'[6]. In a phrase such as 'a patwhat as your rutterdamrotter', several strands of meaning overlap in what might appear to be at first sight simply an unintelligible insult: (a) patois/patter; (b) rutter (a swindler or a cavalry soldier of the sixteenth and seventeenth centuries), mutter (which is picked up later in the question 'Does your mutter know your mike' *FW* 139.15, that is 'Does your mother know you're out' or 'Does your mother know you're a Mick' or 'Does your mother know your penis', a micky being this in Anglo-Irish since the late nineteenth century); (c) damn, Rotterdam (and by association 'double Dutch'), rotter (its slang meaning, according to the *OED*, first appears in Moore's *Esther Waters* in the accu-

sation 'a regular rotter' – though it sounds more ancient than that), *Götterdämmerung* (Wagner's *The Twilight of the Gods*). In turn, such a phrase acts as a humorous and ironic comment on the *Wake*'s own providential patois or patter, and serves to underscore not the irrationality but the supreme rationality (and good fortune that languages and ideas should so coincide) of Joyce's 'collidabanter' (*FW* 82.15).

In Joyce's account, language cannot be divorced from issues of power, identity, and, in its earliest phase, gesture. But most important is Joyce's sense of 'mearmerge', that the Irish are the product of different races who fought in history. History, which so often has been a story of 'wills gen wonts' (*FW* 4.1), cannot be forgotten, but equally any attempt to uncover a pure thing called 'Irish' is doomed from the start. The English spoken in Dublin today – and for Joyce language is always the model for everything human – has its *roots* in Gaelic, Norse, French, German and English. Contrary, therefore, to Saussure's radical distinction between the two, the paradigmatic axis of history is ever present in the syntagmatic axis of language in use.

JOYCE AND THE JEWS

Joyce came from a country well acquainted with anti-Semitism. In Limerick, for example, in the 1880s, Jews suffered torment partly as a result of not closing their shops on St Patrick's Day. In the same city in January 1904 a Father Creagh advocated a boycott of what he termed the usurious Jewish merchants. Dublin was a more tolerant city than Limerick. In 1892 a new synagogue was opened on Adelaide Road to cater for the Jewish community who lived

same newspaper Joyce read articles by the Dreyfusard journalist Ferrero. In Rome in 1906–7, Jews were again in the forefront of social change; indeed in 1907 Ernesto Nathan, a Jew, was elected Mayor of the Eternal City. At a personal level, Joyce was close to several Jews. In Trieste, one of his pupils was Ettore Schmitz, a middle-aged manager of a paint factory who wrote under the pseudonym Italo Svevo and who in 1909 encouraged Joyce to continue with *A Portrait*. Although he had lost interest in Judaism as a religion, Schmitz provided Joyce with important information on Jewish lore. Moses Dlugacz was another of Joyce's pupils in Trieste. A rabbi and an ardent Zionist, Dlugacz gave classes in Hebrew and Jewish history and Joyce may have studied Hebrew and discussed the Talmud with him – as a reward, Dlugacz is given the pork butcher's shop in 'Calypso'. In Zurich Joyce formed several Jewish friendships: with Ottocaro Weiss, whose brother was one of Freud's early disciples; Edmund Brauchbar, possibly a prototype for Bloom; Rudolph Goldschmidt, a grain merchant who became a friend and pupil of Joyce; and Paul Ruggiero, one of Joyce's companions at the Club de Etrangers. In Paris in the inter-war years, Joyce was surrounded with Jewish friends, most notably Paul Léon, who became his secretary in 1928 and who was later executed in 1942 by the Nazis. Joyce's son Giorgio married an American Jewess, Helen Kastor Fleischman, a cousin of Peggy Guggenheim. In the publishing world, Jews again were prominent in the Joyce story. Benjamin Huebsch, a New York Jew, was responsible for publishing *A Portrait* in 1916; Shakespeare and Company harboured Jewish refugees when Paris was occupied by the Nazis in 1940; Sylvia Beach herself was interned in 1943 because of her Jewish connections; in 1926–7, Samuel Roth published

near the South Circular Road (F6); in 1904 the Jewish population of Dublin numbered around 2,200, over twice what it was in 1891. But as is evident from the attacks on the Jews by Arthur Griffith in the columns of the *United Irishman* in April and May 1904, anti-Semitism in Ireland was not confined to Limerick. According to Louis Hyman, 'the mere concept of the Irish Jew raised a laugh in the Ireland of Joyce's day'.[7]

By way of contrast, in every continental city Joyce took up residence Jews were prominent in public life. In Trieste, a city with nearly 6,500 Jews, *Il Piccolo della Sera*, the Triestine evening newspaper, was edited in 1905 by Teodoro Mayer, the son of a Hungarian-Jewish postcard pedlar who had settled in what was then the leading port of the Austro-Hungarian empire. In the

pirated extracts of *Ulysses* in the United States. That Jews were closely associated with Joyce's career is given a bizarre twist in 1940 when he was intially refused permission to enter Switzerland because it was thought by the authorities that he was a Jew.

Thus, when Joyce left Ireland in 1904 he abandoned the 'Society of Jesus' and, like some Old Testament prophet going into a foreign country, 'caught the europicolas and went into the society of jewses' (*FW* 423.35–6). It was not erysipelas, a febrile disease accompanied by inflammation of the skin, that he caught but the *piccola velocita*, the goods train, to 'europ(e)', the itch, that is, to live on the continent. Inside the word 'europicolas' can also be discerned *Il Piccolo della Sera*, the paper to which Joyce contributed articles from 1907 onwards. Indeed, according to Ira Nadel, this particular sentence from *Finnegans Wake* 'summarises Joyce's longstanding and continual involvement with Jews'.[8]

To read Joyce from a central European perspective is a necessary adjustment after the emphasis on the writer's Dublin roots. 'It is odd,' comments Padraic Colum, 'that the creator of the most outstanding Jew in modern literature did not at that time know any of the Jewish community in Dublin.'[9] 'At that time' – November/December 1903 – Joyce wanted Colum to put him in touch with Jews who might be willing to put up money for the *Goblin*, a proposed daily newspaper (*JJ* 140–1). Not long afterwards, in a letter he sent to Stanislaus from Rome in November 1906, Joyce writes:

I thought of beginning my story *Ulysses*: but I have too many cares at present. Ferrero devotes a chapter in his history of Rome to the Odes of Horace: so, perhaps, poets should be let live. In his book *Young Europe* which I have just read he says there

are three great classes of emigrants: the (I forget the word: it means conquering, imposing their own language, &c), the English: the adhesive (forming a little group with national traditions and sympathies) the Chinese and the Irish!!!!: the diffusive (entering into the new society and forming part of it) the Germans. He has a fine chapter on Antisemitism. By the way, Brandes is a Jew.

(*Letters* II. 190)

Joyce belongs to a generation struggling to articulate new identities at a time when more powerful forces were at work resurrecting old ones. He expresses surprise, however, that as an Irishman he is grouped by Ferrero with the Chinese in a category called 'adhesive'. As an Irish emigrant he constantly risked being defined externally. Yet he realized that while he enjoyed wearing the badge of Irishness he resisted the labels others assigned to him. To those others – at least in 1906 before he became famous – he was Irish (or a Dubliner) first, James Joyce second; to himself he was James Joyce first, Irish second. In the composite figure of Ulysses, the Jew, he could begin to see a way of handling some of these issues in the wider context of 'Young Europe', where a new generation, alert to what the Jew and emigrant represented, looked to a different kind of politics from nineteenth-century nationalism and anti-Semitism.

Mr Deasy, in a remark that recalls Arthur Griffith, tells Stephen in 'Nestor' that Ireland 'has the honour of being the only country which never persecuted the jews.' 'And do you know why? . . . Because she never let them in' (*U* 2.437–42). The Jews, he informs Stephen, repeating familiar anti-Semitic jibes, 'sinned against the light'; they control the financial institutions and the press, and, because of them, England is

19 (*facing page*) Liphitzki's photograph of Paul Léon and Joyce taken in 1936. *Courtesy of the Beinecke Rare Book and Manuscript Library, Yale University.*

dying. Stephen's thoughts carry him back to Joyce's Paris of 1902–3 and the Jews he saw there:

> On the steps of the Paris stock exchange the goldskinned men quoting prices on their gemmed fingers. Gabble of geese. They swarmed loud, uncouth, about the temple, their heads thickplotting under maladroit silk hats. Not theirs: these clothes, this speech, these gestures. Their full slow eyes belied the words, the gestures eager and unoffending, but knew the rancours massed about them and knew their zeal was vain. Vain patience to heap and hoard. Time surely would scatter all. A hoard heaped by the roadside: plundered and passing on. Their eyes knew their years of wandering and, patient, knew the dishonours of their flesh.
>
> (*U* 2.364–72)

In 'Cyclops' there is a companion scene when the citizen, agitated at Bloom's defence of the Jews, accuses him of being 'that bloody jewman'. Bloom replies:

> – Mendelssohn was a jew and Karl Marx and Mercadante and Spinoza. And the Saviour was a jew and his father was a jew. Your God.
> – He had no father, says Martin. That'll do now. Drive ahead.
> – Whose God? says the citizen.
> – Well, his uncle was a jew, says he. Your God was a jew. Christ was a jew like me.
> Gob, the citizen made a plunge back into the shop.
> – By Jesus, says he, I'll brain that bloody jewman for using the holy name. By Jesus, I'll crucify him so I will. Give us that biscuitbox here.
>
> (*U* 12.1804–12)

Joyce uses Bloom, the Irishman with a

Hungarian Jewish background, to censure the citizen's inflated nationalism. By juxtaposing the Jewish question with the Irish one in *Ulysses*, Joyce, 'anarchistically respectsful of the liberties of the noninvasive individual' (*FW* 72.17–18), makes a telling political point: the Jewish unwillingness/inability/failure to assimilate precisely counteracts the narrower forms of nationalism then emerging in Ireland and elsewhere in Europe.

Against Mulligan's advocacy of a Hellenized Ireland, Joyce celebrates an Hebraic culture, but now the terms of the debate are markedly different to Arnold's. For Joyce – at least by comparison with Arnold – embraces but does not subsume a

Jewish view of the world. Joyce is interested in the tension between the Jews' desire for accommodation and their resistance to assimilation by a dominant culture. He is also fascinated with cultural difference and puts into play his own ambivalent attitudes to the issue of identity. In 'Wandering Rocks', a 'darkbacked figure under Merchants' arch scanned books on the hawker's cart' (*U* 10.315–16). The reader recognizes at once that this is Bloom, furtively hunting down a copy of a mildly titillating book for Molly. Joyce knows this is a stereotype: the image of the Jew huddled over reading matter, a dark figure, his back turned, an object of someone else's gaze, 'under Merchants' arch'. The reader would immediately recognize the stereotype if the image was translated into discursive prose: 'the Jews of Europe were invariably outside the mainstream of history, objects of curiosity, suspicion, and often scorn; without a nation, the Jews found comfort among their own people, forming attachments which were at once local and dispersed'. Joyce is no Malamud, no naturalist writer concerned to elicit or track the nature of Jewish experience on the point of assimilation into a modern secular society. But his position is not always clear. Joyce is conscious of Judaism's political significance: the Jew as the outsider, the type, the stumbling-block in the social formation, the Other of western civilization. At the same time he is interested in Jews in sociological and cultural terms: the Jew as inheritor of different customs, life-styles, appearances, calendars, and religious observances. The closer Joyce strays towards the latter the more stereotyped his thinking becomes – or is it the more he dramatizes his own ambivalent attitudes?

In a lecture delivered by John F. Taylor at University College, Dublin in October 1901, Joyce was forcefully reminded of the similarities between the Jews and the Irish. Lady Gregory was also struck by such a similarity, and in her 1911 play *The Deliverer* the links between Moses and Parnell are given formal expression. But Joyce's contacts with European Jews simultaneously brought out and undermined the neatness of such links. *Ulysses* still contains the stereotypes: Bloom is The Jew in a Catholic Country, The Effeminate Jew, The Jewish Victim. But Joyce drains such stereotypes of much of their power. Bloom is also The Unorthodox Jew in Process of Assimilation, The Uncircumcised Baptised Jew Married to a Christian Penelope, The Jewish Father Without Male Heir, The Married Jew about to be Cuckolded, The Jew in the Cave of the Cyclops. Bloom is neither a mythical hero like Moses nor a conventional stereotype – more like the site for interrogating the idea of Jewishness.

In *Finnegans Wake*, as is evident from the wealth of references to Jewish feasts and customs, Joyce puts to good use his knowledge (and his half-knowledge) of Jewish lore. The months of the Jewish year are referred to in the first chapter: 'Nizam' (Nisan), 'Tamuz' (Tammuz), 'Marchessvan' (Marchesvan), 'Adar' (Adar), along with 'Succoth', the Jewish Feast of Tabernacles (*FW* 13.24–8). Rosh Hashanah, the Jewish New Year, can be heard in the name 'Roche Haddocks' (*FW* 34.9), Judenfest, the Jewish holiday, in 'Yuddanfest' (*FW* 82.36), the Jewish Day of First Fruits in the phrase 'fruting for firstlings' (*FW* 12.19), and the Jewish custom of taking an oath with a hat on in 'minhatton' (*FW* 539.2). Echoes of the Old Testament and Hebrew can be heard frequently throughout the book. This is particularly so at the end of the first chapter when a 'big rody ram lad' (*FW* 28.36) is on the premises – that is, when the mythical Finnegan gives way to the historical

Earwicker. The sherif 'Toragh' (Torah, the law), following the 'pinkprophets cohalething' (*quoheleth* is Ecclesiastes in Hebrew), vouches that 'Humme the Cheapner, Esc.' (*hamma* is Hebrew for sun), who is worthy of the 'naym', came to Dublin on board *The Bey for Dybbling*, 'the deadsea dugong updipdripping from his depths', his 'shebi by his shide' (*sebi* is Hebrew for captivity), and that 'ee' is the very same person who 'will be ultimendly respunchable for the hubbub [*hibbub* is Hebrew for love] caused in Edenborough' (*FW* 29.17–36).

Joyce is a 'jewjesuit' (*U* 9.1159), that is someone who deliberately sabotages the elegant divisions between religious faiths and denominations. Joyce 'went into the society of jewses', but he also carried with him the aspirations of the young Stephen who was 'going to do wonders, what? Missionary to Europe after fiery Columbanus' (*U* 3.192–3). It makes sense to think of Joyce as a secular missionary to Europe. In this light, *Finnegans Wake* is Joyce's 'farced epistol to the hibruws' (*FW* 228.33–4), and not unlike, therefore, a Jewish text. Each letter, each syllable, carries meaning: nothing is there by chance. *Finnegans Wake*, the work of a modern monk constructing a twentieth-century Book of Kells or singing a 'mamalujo' (*FW* 398.4) (a rewriting that is of Matthew Mark Luke and John), requires to be pored over like a Rabbinic text. The 'ideal reader', as Joyce half-recognized, is someone 'suffering from an ideal insomnia' (*FW* 120.13–14). No mark can afford to be missed. It is not 'kistvanes' but 'kisstvanes'; not 'the ten commandments' but 'the then commandments' (*FW* 181.31); not 'Hail Mary full of grace' but 'Hail many fell of greats' (*FW* 502.22); not 'domestic husbandry' but 'dumbestic husbandry' (*FW* 38.11); not 'he mourned the flight of the

192

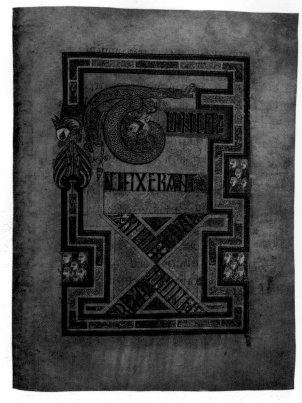

wild geese' but 'he mourned the flight of his wild guineese' (*FW* 71.4); not 'the Oedipus complex' but the 'eatupus complex' (*FW* 128.36); not *Finnegan's Wake* but *Finnegans Wake* (and when the Irish do wake, take care!). It is a work of biblical proportions, but, unlike St Paul's Epistle to the Hebrews, it is designed not to convert the Jews but to show how everything can be assembled and accommodated in Joyce's 'most moraculous jeeremyhead sindbook for all the peoples' (*FW* 229.31–2). *Finnegans Wake* is a Jeremiad, a doleful complaint; like the Bible it is a 'sin book', a book about sin, guilt, and failure; it is also – like Jesus and the Jews – a *sudenbock* (German for scapegoat); and it is, moreover, for 'all the peoples', for Joyce entertained the vain hope that *Finnegans Wake* would be widely read.

At one point in *Finnegans Wake*, Earwicker, his pub closed, is taunted by a Midwesterner to open up: 'come out, you jewbeggar, to be Executed' (*FW* 70.34–5). Here Earwicker is associated with the Jew as victim and linked in this particular case with the hunchback Joseph Biggar, one-time loyal supporter of Parnell who later sided with Healy against Parnell over Captain O'Shea's candidature for Galway. In the list of abuses that follows, Earwicker is called an 'Edomite' (*FW* 72.11), 'Read Your Pantojoke' (*FW* 71.17–18) (read your pantomime joke/your Pentateuch), 'Peculiar Person' (*FW* 71.30–1) (the Jews were 'Peculiar People', that is the chosen people), and 'York's Porker' (*FW* 71.12). A 'porker' is an abusive term for a Jew, but why 'York's Porker'? This is slightly puzzling for someone who lives in York. Perhaps it is associated with York ham, or with the Yorkist Richard III, whose emblem was a boar. Perhaps it contains an allusion to the Jewish massacre in York in 1190, in which case Earwicker is the sole remaining Jew of York, the one who escaped the massacre. A more likely explanation is that Joyce liked the repetition of the vowel sound, just as he liked the phrase 'as different as York from Leeds' (*FW* 576.22) on account of its similarity with the popular expression 'as different as chalk and cheese'. The connection between Earwicker and Jewishness is best observed in such name-calling. In *Ulysses* Joyce attempts a more cohesive framework of identities, especially between Jews and Irish, and Jews and Greeks: Stephen is called a 'jewjesuit' (*U* 9.1159) while in 'Circe' there is a claim that 'Jewgreek is greekjew. Extremes meet' (*U* 15.2097–8). But in *Finnegans Wake* the association is slacker. Earwicker is a Protestant, and in the same list of abuses he is accused of being both Jewish and 'Unworthy of the Homely Protestant Religion' (*FW* 71.21–2), a reference perhaps to the less 'extreme' form of Protestantism, namely Anglicanism.

There is evidence that Joyce associated Jews with Protestants, both religious groups being the most conspicuous outsiders in Catholic Ireland and Europe. In the Picture Gallery chapter, for example, in a series of riddles running to over thirteen pages – Finn MacCool is the catch-all answer – a link is made between Jews and Huguenots. One of the riddles states: 'sucks life's eleaxir from the pettipickles of the Jewess and ruoulls in sulks if any popeling runs down the Huguenots' (*FW* 133.19–21). To make sense of this riddle, we need to know that Halévy's opera *La Juive* was first performed in Paris in 1835, Meyerbeer's *Les Huguenots* the following year, also in Paris; that Eleazar is a character in the former, Raoul the hero in the latter; that both composers were Jewish; that their operas focus on the fate of two persecuted religious groups, the Jews and the French Protestants. We might also call on other bits of information: that Meyerbeer is regarded as the founder of the French Grand Opera and was singled out by Wagner in his anti-Semitic tract *Judaism in Music* (1850); that Huguenots brought cotton to Ireland, as Bloom recalls in 'Lestrygonians'; that when they first met, Bloom tried persuading Molly to sing a song about the Huguenots, but she was tired of his 'explaining and rigmaroling about religion and persecution' (*U* 18.1190–1).

Other references to Jews in *Finnegans Wake* occasionally have sinister undertones. In the incident with the cad in the Phoenix Park, for example, Earwicker is accosted with 'a nice how-do-you-do': 'Guinness thaw tool in jew me dinner ouzel fin?' (*FW* 35.15–16), which sounds more threatening than it actually is – Give us that tool in, jew, me dinner, or else fin. In fact it is Irish for How are you today my fair gentleman? Joyce also makes use of the way the pronunciation of 'Jew' in English often resembles 'do you': 'jew ear that far' (*FW* 180.6). Similarly with the phrase 'jew placator' (*FW* 534.5), behind which can be heard the less threatening word 'duplicator' – although even here there is a suggestion of duplicity and the commonplace prejudice against 'devious' Jews. More playfully, the letter that is found in Chapter 5 contains a reference to 'the froggy jew' (*FW* 116.12), an allusion perhaps to 'The Foggy Dew', a song of the Easter Rising of 1916, or the more licentious song of the English popular tradition 'The Foggy Foggy Dew'. In the Lessons chapter, Anna Livia adds 'gay touches' for 'hugh and guy and goy and jew' (*FW* 273.13–14).

The parallels between the Jews and the Irish, especially in their common experience of exile and oppression, interested Joyce greatly, but he never overcame a lingering suspicion that Jews were a race apart. He notices for example in the 1906 letter cited above that Brandes is a Jew; the character of Bloom comes precariously close at times to a stereotype; when Samuel Roth published pirated extracts from *Ulysses*, Joyce was quick to accuse him of betrayal. But it is in his attitude to Jewish women that Joyce reveals a level of prejudice even less easy to excuse. We are told by commentators that Joyce found Jewish women – his construct was of olive skin, delicate eyelids, and dark hair – particularly sensual. In 1905 he had a brief romance with Anny Schleimer, a student at the Berlitz School, who was part Jewish and the daughter of an Austrian banker. Some time between 1911 and 1914 Joyce fell in love with Amalia Popper, daughter of a Triestine Jewish merchant, a romance that seems to form

the basis of *Giacomo Joyce*. In Zurich, in December 1918, he enjoyed another fleeting voyeuristic affair, this time with Martha Fleischmann, who lived opposite him at No. 6 Culmannstrasse. Having watched her for some time in her flat, he decided to write her a letter in French:

> . . . as I watched you, I noticed the softness and the regularity of your features, and the gentleness of your eyes. And I thought: a Jewess. If I am wrong, you must not be offended. Jesus Christ put on his human body: in the womb of a Jewish woman.
>
> (*Letters* II. 433)

From his reading of Fishberg, Weininger, and Disraeli, Joyce was confirmed in his prejudice about the mystique of the Oriental Jewish woman, but from today's perspective many readers may find Joyce's remarks offensive. Joyce would have been distressed by nineteenth-century scientists measuring Irish skulls and drawing conclusions about Irish intelligence, but here he falls into the same trap, identifying 'race' with physiognomy. As it turned out, Martha was not Jewish.

Joyce enjoyed the intrigue with Martha Fleischmann and invited her to Budgen's studio, possibly to recreate a pose for the 'Nausicaa' scene he was in the process of writing. Budgen reluctantly agreed to Joyce's fantasy and deception and made the studio more bohemian than usual by drawing on the wall in charcoal a large sketch of a female nude. It was Joyce's birthday, 1919, and he brought along with him a Jewish bracketed candlestick, a Menorah, borrowed earlier that day from Goldschmidt. What impressed Budgen as soon as Martha entered the room was that she walked with a limp, precisely what Bloom finds most shocking about Gerty when she leaves the scene of her conquest.[10] This intrigue with Martha finds its literary counterpart in Bloom's letter to Martha Clifford and his anxiety about going too far – 'Answered anyhow'. Joyce may also have been attracted to Nora because of her 'Jewish' looks, if the passing reference in 'Penelope' is auto-biographical: 'we stood staring at one another on account of my being jewess looking after my mother' (*U* 18.1183–5).

What impressed Joyce about 'the gold-skinned men' on the steps of the Paris Stock Exchange was a discrepancy between their public role as citizens and their inner selves. Both Bloom and Earwicker aspire to establishing the right balance between an interior life and the external world; both feel waves of guilt, the need for punishment, and the justness of their cause. The conflict is played out especially inside the family in that complex network of relationships between father and mother, parents and children, husband and wife. *Ulysses* and *Finnegans Wake* are at one level stories about families and they draw on the closeness not only of Joyce's own family in exile but also perhaps on the idea of the Jewish family. Here the similarities in the pattern between *Ulysses* and *Finnegans Wake* are striking: mothers and wives (Molly/ALP); fathers (Bloom/Earwicker); sons (Stephen/Shem); daughters (Milly/Issy). In *Ulysses* the father searches for a substitute son; in *Finnegans Wake* the son mourns the loss of the father. In both texts, however, it is arguably women rather than Jews or Protestants who occupy the most subversive position, for women posed more intractable problems for Joyce's imagination. In this respect, Issy's footnotes in the Lessons chapter, Molly Bloom's soliloquy, ALP's voice, are sharp reminders of a discourse that resists Joyce's 'meandering male fist' (*FW* 123.11).

When Joyce began composing *Finnegans Wake* in March 1923, the Civil War in Ireland was still in progress. In January 1922 de Valera, refusing to accept the treaty ratified by the Dail, proposed instead an alternative course contained in 'Document Number 2'. In April of the same year, Nora, on a visit to her family in Galway, was caught up in the fighting between Free State soldiers and the Irregulars (who were to become the Irish Republican Army). Fearful for the safety of his wife and children, Joyce arranged for an aeroplane to go to Galway and collect them, but they had already caught the train for Dublin. As it happened, the train came under fire and they were forced to take cover by lying on the floor. Just as *Ulysses* belongs to a period of expectancy that found its now perennially hopeful expression in 'Bloomsday', in a parallel way *Finnegans Wake* gives voice to the disorder and disillusionment of Irish politics in the immediate aftermath of the Anglo-Irish War when internecine feuding broke out between the warring brothers Shem and Shaun.

Shaun, as John Garvin argues,[11] is not un-like the figure of de Valera, the 'dogmestic Shaun' (*FW* 411.23), who rose from being a 'mathmaster' (*FW* 4.4) to become 'through deafths of durkness greengrown deeper . . . (the) vote of the Irish, voise from afar' (*FW* 407.12–14). This connection between Shaun and de Valera receives further support from Sean O'Faolain's biography of the Irish leader – a study published in the same year as *Finnegans Wake*. Indeed, one passage might well be about 'frank' Shaun:

Fundamentally his political integrity was unimpeachable . . . . If only . . . de Valera would once or twice say, 'I am not infal-lible. I am no hero. I am no saint. I had to

contradict myself. It was for Ireland' – the heart would open more readily to him, and one could without detriment either to the symbol or the man create the hero in full admiration.[12]

De Valera refused to acknowledge Lloyd George's Anglo-Irish Treaty, negotiated under duress in December 1921 by Arthur Griffith, Michael Collins, and the other Irish leaders. Instead he proposed an amendment which sought a looser association between Ireland and Great Britain. It was a narrow point of principle: effectively, the Irish delegates had been outmanoeuvred by the British, who had used the familiar tactic of

23   The Irish delegation at the Grosvenor Hotel in London during their negotiations with Lloyd George in July 1921. De Valera and Arthur Griffith are seated. Second from left, standing, is Erskine Childers.

divide and rule; equally, as someone once quipped, the only difference between the two documents was that one was signed and the other was not. Throughout *Finnegans Wake* there are references to Documents Number One and Two (see *FW* 358.30, 369.24–5, 386.20–1, 528.32–3, 619.19), and in Chapter 15 'Keven' (a Shaun figure) finds 'dogumen number one . . . an illegible downfumbed by an unelgible' (*FW* 482.20–1). What irritated Joyce about de Valera was his moral uprightness, his dogmatic insistence on a formula of words, his narrow view of Ireland. Above all, de Valera was willing to plunge his country into civil war and thereby subject Nora and the children in April 1922 to 'the premier terror of Errorland' (*FW* 62.25) (a phrase that yokes together de Valera as President of Dail Eireann, his parsimonious role in the Treaty negotiations, and the ensuing terror that accompanied the breakdown of order). 'The devil era' (*FW* 473.8), which is interpreted, significantly, in the context of the Treaty negotiations as 'a slip of time between a date and a ghostmark' (*FW* 473.8–9), had begun.

Hugh Kenner has suggested that the figure being waked in *Finnegans Wake* may be a participant in that conflict.[13] Certainly there are enough references to figures and events, as well as to fratricide, violence to the person, and decidedly sinister encounters, to support Kenner's opinion that *Finnegans Wake* is a Civil War text. When Michael Collins was murdered in 1922 by Irregulars, a note appeared on his grave: 'Move over, Mick, make room for Dick', Dick being Richard Mulcahy, Collins's successor. Throughout *Finnegans Wake* this notice recurs in different guises: 'Move up. Mumpty! Mike room for Rumpty!' (*FW* 99.19–20). Erskine Childers (1870–1922), whose father Hugh Culling Eardley Childers (1827–96) was nicknamed 'Here

198

Comes Everybody', is also given some prominence in the text. Author of the thriller *The Riddle of the Sands* (1903), Childers took part in the Howth gun-running in July 1914; he later joined de Valera's Republican side in the Civil War, and, having been caught with a pistol in his possession (given him by Michael Collins when the two were on the same side), was executed in November 1922 by a Free State firing squad. He is mentioned as 'chilldays embers' (473.9), and as 'hailed chimers' ersekind' (596.5), where there is a play on his (and HCE's) Englishness; he is possibly being referred to in the first question in the Picture Gallery chapter in the phrase 'made a summer assault on our shores and begiddy got his sands full' (*FW* 132.20–1), and he is there when the Document is being scrutinized in Chapter 5 as 'the eternal chimerahunter . . . the sensory crowd in his belly coupled with an eye for the goods trooth bewilderblissed by their night effluvia with guns like drums' (*FW* 107.14–17).

The stress on the Civil War context of *Finnegans Wake* emphasizes the less ambiguous period preceding the Troubles: the 'Surrection!' (*FW* 593.2–3) of Easter Week 1916, 'our hour or risings' (*FW* 598.13), and the Proclamation of the Republic, 'Eireweeker to the wohld bludyn world' (*FW* 593.3). The last chapter of *Finnegans Wake* is ushered in with a celebration of a new dawn, part of which takes its cue from 1916. 'Surrection!' is both resurrection and insurrection; 'Eireweeker' is at the same time Eire, Easter Week, HCE, ear, and weaker; 'the whole bludyn world' invokes the papal address 'Urbi et Orbi' given at Easter and therefore linked with the 1916 Declaration of the Republic from the General Post Office; 'Surrection' also picks up the phrase in Chapter 1 used after the 'erection' of the wall – 'For whole the world to see' (*FW* 6.11–12). Throughout the final chapter are references to the wider nationalist struggle for Irish independence: Sinn Fein, a slogan which did service for Joyce's own ideological perspective, 'oursouls alone', is mentioned at 614.14 and 623.28–9; Patrick Pearse appears at 620.24; at 614.17 Parnell's insistence that 'newmanmaun set a marge to the merge of unnotions' is dusted down again (compare its earlier formulation at 292.26–7); 'A Nation Once Again', the unofficial nineteenth-century Irish national anthem and rallying call written by Thomas Davis in the 1840s, appears as 'Innition wons agame' at 614.17–18; while Michael Dwyer, the 1798 rebel, has a walk-on part at 600.18. The celebration of Easter 1916, however, is short-lived, and with the *ricorso* we are back to the opening chapter with 'snake wurrums everyside' (*FW* 19.12), 'sneaks' (*FW* 19.13), 'Racketeers and bottloggers' (*FW* 19.19), the ante- and post-bellum period, as it were, of 'Bloody wars' (*FW* 14.9) and 'Killallwho' (*FW* 15.11). Indeed, in the very last words of the chapter the Sinn Fein slogan, 'Ourselves alone', becomes simply 'a lone' (*FW* 628.15). And if *Finnegans Wake* – caught as it is between 1916 and 1923 – is concerned in no small measure with the theme of loss, then part of that loss turns on the historical failure of the Irish revolution to bring forth a new Ireland.

In searching for a clue to Joyce's politics in *Finnegans Wake* we might well recall Shaun's cautionary note in his portrait of Shem in Chapter 7: 'not even then could such an antinomian be true to type' (*FW* 172.17–18). Possibly in reaction to his Jesuit education and Catholic upbringing, Joyce maintained an aloofness from politics. As an undergraduate, Stephen Dedalus did not sign Czar Nicholas II's petition for peace; as an established Irish writer, Joyce did not join the newly formed Irish Academy of Letters; he even declined an invitation to a St Patrick's Day party which the Irish Ambassador was to attend, for fear that his presence might be misconstrued as a tacit endorsement of the Free State. According to Ellmann, in matters of politics Joyce 'refused to commit himself publicly in any way' (*JJ* 708). But this is not quite correct, for from the moment of his exile from his native country in 1904, there developed a parallel and increasingly public commitment to writing. Unlike many British writers of the 1930s, such as Edward Upward, W. H. Auden, Christopher Isherwood, or George Orwell, Joyce was unimpressed by the often naive way writing was opposed to action. For the writer, writing was the most effective instrument for reshaping and changing the world – hence the significance (in part at

least) of the image in *Finnegans Wake* of the telescope, which could 're-present' reality. At the same time, his commitment to writing went hand in hand with a Flaubertian desire to refine himself out of existence and to make the paraphrase of his work formidable and, with his final work, perhaps impossible.

In the late eighteenth century Edmund Burke voiced his opposition to Grattan's Protestant Parliament on the grounds that, if the connection with Westminster were broken, the precarious rights of Irish Catholics – which were few enough under English law – would be further eroded. Joyce's view – and it is one that he never seems to have radically altered – was that genuine freedom for the Irish people was not to be equated simply with breaking the cross-channel link. Like Stephen, he understood that he was a servant of two masters, Britain and Rome. Historically, with the establishment of the Free State in 1922 the links with the Crown were broken, but the

other tyranny continued and indeed – at least in the field of censorship and social legislation – flourished. 'Healiopolis' in the figure of Tim Healy – the same person whom the nine-year-old Joyce had attacked in 'Et Tu, Healy' – was now in charge at the Viceregal Lodge (A2) in Phoenix Park. If Joyce was a republican, then it was of the Parnellite Home Rule variety; that is, he desired to break the connection with Britain – but not entirely (after all, he was in receipt of a Civil List pension and continued to travel with a British passport). It is against this background that we should interpret his remarks in *Finnegans Wake* about 'Freestouters and publicranks' (*FW* 329.31); that is, he is not saying a plague on all your houses, whether Free Stater or Republican; he is expressing impatience with the narrowing of the political options available for his country.

He was equally irritated with the Border and with the Border issue. In the encounter between the attacker and the adversary, 'the boarder incident prerepeated itself' (*FW* 81.32–3), while in the portrait of Shem in Chapter 7 Shaun declares: 'He even ran away with hunself and became a farsoonerite, saying he would far sooner muddle through the hash of lentils in Europe than meddle with Irrland's split little pea' (*FW* 171.4–6). To muddle through rather than meddle with – here is the characteristic Joycean note, now augmented with the familiar opposition between Europe as opportunity and Ireland as backward and provincial. It is not the whole story of course, for what is *Finnegans Wake* doing if it is not meddling with 'Irrland's split little pea'? Indeed, throughout his writings Joyce strikes at the narrow definitions of Irish identity increasingly apparent from the 1880s onwards.

In the choice of names for his main characters Joyce betrays a political stance. Take

26 The intimidating border crossing today at Aughnacloy, County Tyrone, with the British Army endeavouring to keep Ireland a 'split little pea'. Joyce favoured a 'disunited kingdom' (*FW* 188.16–17). *Photograph Dan Harper.*

the hero's name in *Finnegans Wake*. In the summer of 1923, soon after he began writing *Finnegans Wake*, Joyce was on holiday in Bognor Regis, and while there he must have been reading the Ward Lock guide to the area.

Sidlesham Church, a mile northward of the old mill, is an Early English structure, not unworthy of notice, and an examination of the surrounding tombstones should not be omitted if any interest is felt in deciphering curious names. For such a comparatively small spot there would seem to be an unusually large number of singular appellations, striking examples being Earwicker, Glue, Gravy, Boniface, Anker, and Northeast.[14]

Open *Finnegans Wake* at page 30, and lo and behold the same series of names is there.

Discard the theory, we are told, that would link Earwicker with 'such pivotal ancestors as the Glues, the Gravys, the Northeasts, the Ankers and the Earwickers of Sidlesham' (*FW* 30.6–7). Joyce delights in this mixture of casualness, definiteness, and clue-dropping – and the 'singular appellations' are too good to use only once: 'Glue on to him, Greevy! Bottom anker, Noordeece!' (*FW*. 375.3).

In a text so full of Irishness, Joyce's choice not of an Irish surname but of one gleaned from a West Sussex guidebook is another political point. Who now, Joyce seems to be saying, can tell the difference between Mutt and Jute, the indigenous Irish from the foreign invader? 'Become a bitskin more wiseable, as if I were you' (*FW* 16.24–5). Conversely, who now can claim proprietorial or exclusive rights to English, given the writing of *Finnegans Wake* and given the way Joyce – like the Gaelic-speaking Festy King – 'murdered all the English he knew' (*FW* 93.2)?

As Chapter 1 of *Finnegans Wake* reminds us, human history in general and European and British history in particular has been a history of warfare, of 'wills gen wonts' (*FW* 4.1). From a textbook which Joyce almost certainly used at school, he would have learnt the following question and answer:

What great events mark the opening of the nineteenth century? The Union of Great Britain and Ireland; Buonaparte, afterwards Napoleon the emperor of the French, chosen first consul for life; the battles of Copenhagen and Alexandria . . . naval victory off Trafalgar . . . war in Spain and Portugal . . . battle of Waterloo – final conflict with the French, 1815.[15]

The pacifist Joyce thought otherwise. Listen to the sounds of guns and wailing that constitute the 'nightmare' of history: 'Brékkek Kékkek Kékkek Kékkek! Kóax Kóax Kóax! Ualu Ualu Ualu! Quaouauh!' (*FW* 4.2–3). What better place to capture the essence of human history than a museum dedicated to war? Casting a shadow over the whole text is the Willingdone, a monument to war. In Joyce's notebooks for *Finnegans Wake* there is a list of foreign words for peace, for *paix* – *Hoping, Takiya, Hoa bink, Thai bink, Soc, Kuam samakkhi, berdamai, ju jen pen suk, shanti, sainte, sianta, al-solhe, soulhe, soulk, Khagagouthioun, dama.*[16] As the first three words of the last chapter indicate, *Finnegans Wake* is a call for peace: 'Sandhyas! Sandhyas! Sandhyas!' (*FW* 593.1).

Samdhi, like *Shantih*, is Sanskrit for peace: the first chapter begins with the fall of human history, the last chapter with an expression of hope, a turning of the page of human history, a coda to what has gone before. Peace in Joyce – the contrast with the

'Shantih' of the last line of *The Waste Land* is instructive – is never associated with some higher realm of consciousness, but is invariably located in time and place. It is in keeping, therefore, that the opening to the last chapter mimes the Easter Rising, and that hope for the future is shadowed by the hopes for the future in the past.

MEMEMORMEE!

According to Mulligan in *Ulysses*, Stephen has the 'cursed jesuit strain . . . only it's injected the wrong way' (*U* 1.209). In *Finnegans Wake*, Shem is described by Shaun as 'an Irish emigrant the wrong way out' (*FW* 190.36). '(S)elf exiled in upon his ego' (*FW* 184.6–7), Joyce had time to reflect on his past life in Dublin. Ireland was his 'wastobe land, a lottuse land, a luctuous land, Emerald-illuim' (*FW* 62.11–12). It was not Eliot's Waste Land of postwar Europe; it was a 'was to be' land, a lotus land, where time stood still and people forgot the journey they were on; it was the Emerald Isle. But it was also a 'lottuse', a lot of use; luscious but also luctuous, mournful, luck used; 'illuim', Ilium or Troy, site of destruction from within, ill you in/him, Troy the dispersal point (*illim* in Latin is an adverb meaning 'from that place') for Joyce's Odyssean wanderings round Europe but never the home to return to. Ireland produced these mixed feelings of attachment and hostility in Joyce. Indeed, he felt that Ireland had risen against him, did him hurt, 'poor jink' (*FW* 62.17), that he was made a 'curse for them' so that they (the Irish), 'all saints of incorruption of an holy nation', might in some convoluted way convince him of their proper sins.

In his early years abroad when writing *Dubliners*, Joyce entertained the notion

blind stomach, a deaf heart, a loose liver, two fifths of two buttocks . . .

(*FW* 169.13–18)

According to Shaun, Shem is a sham:

So low was he that he preferred Gibsen's tea-time salmon tinned, as inexpensive as pleasing, to the plumpest roeheavy lax or the friskiest parr or smolt troutlet that ever was gaffed between Leixlip and Island Bridge and many was the time he repeated in his botulism that no junglegrown pineapple ever smacked like the whoppers you shook out of Ananias' cans, Findlater and Gladstone's, Corner House, Englend.

(*FW* 170.26–32)

It is an honest admission, to prefer tinned food to the fresh produce. For Shaun it is a further example of Shem's lowness; for the reader this kind of detail strengthens sympathy for 'Jymes' (*FW* 181.27), the

that he would write a chapter of 'the moral history' of his race. (*Letters* II. 134) By the time he came to *Finnegans Wake*, his project was even more ambitious: the story not only of the Irish but of the human race. Exile removed him from the day-to-day irritations with Irish life and politics, and enabled him to observe his country less passionately and as if he were hearing voices or peering through a telescope. But this was not all to the good. Whereas *A Portrait* is a semi-autobiographical work, the portrait he presents of himself in *Finnegans Wake* is at one level highly detailed but at another level excessively detached. Shem's 'bodily getup', for example, is described thus:

fortytwo hairs off his uncrown, eighteen to his mock lip, a trio of barbels from his megageg chin (sowman's son), the wrong shoulder higher than the right, all ears, an artificial tongue with a natural curl, not a foot to stand on, a handful of thumbs, a

28 The Irishmen Thomas MacGreevy and Beckett in London in the early 1930s. A graduate of Trinity College and a fellow Irishman in exile, Beckett was then lecturing at the Ecole Normale when Joyce met him for the first time in 1928. The following year Beckett was one of the twelve disciples who wrote in praise of 'Work in Progress' in *Our Exagmination round His Factification for Incamination of Work in Progress*. 'Sam knows miles bettern me how to work the miracle. And I see by his diarrhio he's dropping the stammer out of his silenced bladder since I bonded him off more as a friend and as a brother. . . . He'll prisckly soon hand tune your Erin's ear for you' (*FW* 467.18–32). MacGreevy also contributed an essay to *Our Exagmination* and, like Beckett, was a guest at the celebrated 'Déjeuner Ulysse' given by Adrienne Monnier in 1929 to celebrate the French translation of Joyce's book. *Courtesy of Mrs Margaret Farrington and Elizabeth Ryan.*

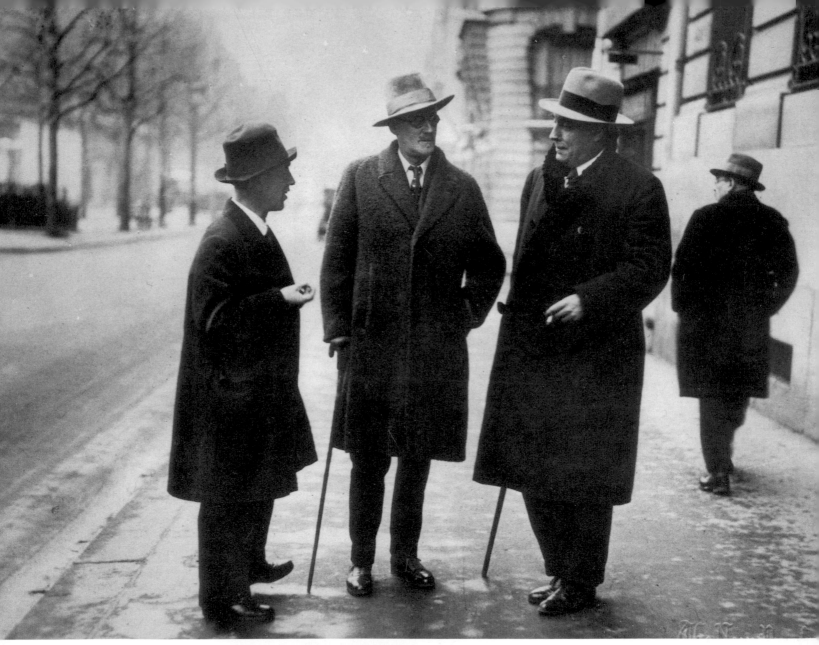

29 'Three Irish Beauties' in Paris *c.* 1929: James Stephens, Joyce, and John Sullivan. From November 1929 onwards Joyce devoted considerable energies to championing the Irish tenor Sullivan, for the banned writer saw in him the banned singer, prevented by the 'Italian ring' from making it to the top (*JJ* 620). Joyce was also very fond of James Stephens, author of *The Insurrection in Dublin* (1916) as well as delightful fiction such as *The Charwoman's Daughter* (1912) and *The Crock of Gold* (1912). By November 1929 Stephens had become 'so much a part of Joyce's phantasmagoria that Joyce could freely beguile himself with the fancy of transferring authorship' of *Finnegans Wake* to him – Stephens, after all, had been born on the same day as Joyce (*JJ* 619). *Courtesy of the University of Southern Illinois Library.*

30 Portrait of Joyce by Jo Davidson. First published in *Pastimes of James Joyce* (1941). *Courtesy of the Beinecke Rare Book and Manuscript Library, Yale University.*

sinner myself, and even liked his faults. Hundreds of pages and scores of characters in my books came from him.

(*Letters* I. 312)

The beginning of *A Portrait* bears the imprint of Joyce's earliest memories of his father. 'His father told him that story: his father looked at him through a glass: he had a hairy face' (*P* 7). At the end of *Finnegans Wake*, Joyce returns to his earliest memories in a remarkable passage which links the death of his father and the female voice and final soliloquy of Anna Livia Plurabelle:

I done me best when I was let. Thinking always if I go all goes. A hundred cares, a tithe of troubles and is there one who understands me? One in a thousand of years of the nights? All me life I have been lived among them but now they are becoming lothed to me. And I am lothing their little warm tricks. And lothing their mean cosy turns. And all the greedy gushes out through their small souls. And all the lazy leaks down over their brash bodies. How small it's all! And me letting on to meself always. And lilting on all the time. I thought you were all glittering with the noblest of carriage. You're only a bumpkin. I thought you the great in all things, in guilt and in glory. You're but a puny. Home! My people were not their sort out beyond there so far as I can. For all the bold and bad and bleary they are blamed, the seahags. No! Nor for all our wild dances in all their wild din. I can seen meself among them, allaniuvia pulchrabelled. How she was handsome, the wild Amazia, when she would seize to my other breast! And what is she weird, haughty Niluna, that she will snatch from my ownest hair! For 'tis they are the stormies. Ho hang! Hang ho! And the clash of our cries till we spring to be free.

'poorjoist' (*FW* 113.36). But by comparison with *A Portrait*, this style of writing lacks a personal tension, for exile distanced Joyce not only from his native country but also from the material of his writing, leaving him with nothing better to do than write 'the mystery of himsel in furniture' (*FW* 184.9–10).

The death of his father in December 1931 prompted one of the most moving sequences in *Finnegans Wake*. In a letter to Harriet Shaw Weaver just after his death, Joyce reflected on his relationship with his father:

My father had an extraordinary affection for me. He was the silliest man I ever knew and yet cruelly shrewd. He thought and talked of me up to his last breath. I was very fond of him always, being a

Auravoles, they says, never heed of your name! But I'm loothing them that's here and all I lothe. Loonely in me loneness. For all their faults. I am passing out. O bitter ending! I'll slip away before they're up. They'll never see. Nor know. Nor miss me. And it's old and old it's sad and old it's sad and weary I go back to you, my cold father, my cold mad father, my cold mad feary father, till the near sight of the mere size of him, the moyles and moyles of it, moananoaning, makes me seasilt saltsick and I rush, my only, into your arms. I see them rising! Save me from those therrble prongs! Two more. Onetwo moremens more. So. Avelaval. My leaves have drifted from me. All. But one clings still. I'll bear it on me. To remind me of. Lff! So soft this morning, ours. Yes. Carry me along, taddy, like you done through the toy fair! If I seen him bearing down on me now under whitespread wings like he'd come from Arkangels, I sink I'd die down over his feet, humbly dumbly, only to washup. Yes, tid. There's where. First. We pass through grass behush the bush to. Whish! A gull. Gulls. Far calls. Coming, far! End here. Us then. Finn, again! Take. Bussoftlhee, mememormee! Till thousendsthee. Lps. The keys to. Given! A way a lone a last a loved a long the

(*FW* 627.13–628.16)

The ending to *Finnegans Wake* is normally seen in terms of Anna Livia Plurabelle and her final thoughts on life as she passes out to sea, but to my mind it is at least as much to do with the son–father, father–son relationship. Joyce goes back to his father, to 'corksown blather' (*FW* 197.5), and he rushes into his arms. 'Avelaval': *Ave et Vale*, Hail and Farewell. All kinds of memories are stirred for him, both as a son and as a father. 'Carry me along, taddy, like you done through the toy fair!' This is inspired by a memory of his own days as a father carrying Giorgio through a toy fair in Trieste to compensate for not giving his son a rocking chair. It is mixed with a wish to see his own father again. The distant past calls; he thinks the memory is coming back to him, but it is stopped short by the thought that the relationship with his father is at an end: 'End here.' No further developments are possible. 'Us then.' The portrait is complete. But then comes the thought of Finn 'again', the *ricorso*, the resurrection, the encouragement to be drawn from Ireland's playful and ubiquitous mythological figure. 'Take.' His childhood memory and language returns, movingly captured through ALP's hushed Irish voice: 'Bussoftlhee' – But softly. But soft Lee – we are back in his father's city. Ever since Mutt's 'Bussave a sec' heard in the opening chapter of *Finnegans Wake*, this tender moment has been coming: 'Bussave a sec . . . Bussoftlhee'. It is a 'soft morning', too, an Irish expression that Joyce, in common with most Irish emigrants, must have missed hearing in exile. 'ours'. The word 'mememormee!' prompts another chain of associations: memory, me, me, more me, as the child presses his father to pick him up. Remember me, Joyce says to his father, till 'thousendsthee', till thousand years, till thou sends for me in thy kingdom. 'Lps' – more tender now even than lips, kiss. 'The keys to' – the keys to my heart, the keys to Heaven, in the words of Jesus's farewell to St Peter. 'Given'. And then the *ricorso*: 'A way a lone a last a loved a long the' back to 'riverrun, past Eve and Adam's' and the whole cycle of the Fall of Man again. 'They lived und laughed ant loved end left' (*FW* 18.19–20): und, ant, end; lived, laughed, loved, left. This is Joyce at his most lyrical and his most profound, the story of the human race here at one with the history of Joyce and his father.

This is Joyce's farewell to his father, to Ireland, and, as it turned out, to writing. *Ulysses* begins with the death of his mother; *Finnegans Wake* ends with thoughts of his father. Nora, too, is never far away in this final passage. The question – 'is there one who understands me?' – is reminiscent of a pleading tone Joyce adopted in his early courting letters to Nora. In August 1904, for example, he asks her: 'Can you not see the simplicity which is at the back of all my disguises?' (*Letters* II. 49). In *Ulysses* there is an answer to this question, for, as Molly declares, 'nobody understands his cracked ideas but me' (*U* 18.1407). In this mixing of voices and contexts, Molly/Nora is both addressee and solution. In another letter to Nora, this time in October 1909, Joyce speaks of loathing Ireland and the Irish (*Letters* II. 255). The thought too is repeated here in this final sequence: 'All me life I have been lived among them but now they are becoming lothed to me.' Nora can also be heard in moments of self-accusation on Joyce's part as when he writes 'I thought you were great in all things, in guilt and in glory. You're but a puny.'

From exile in Europe in the inter-war years, Joyce looked back to the Land of Youth where he had spent his childhood. In this regard the word 'moyles' is especially suggestive. When Yeats's Oisin, the son of Finn, arrives on the Island of Forgetfulness, the 'moil' of his centuries filled him:

> Wrapt in the wave of that music, with weariness more than of earth,
> The moil of my centuries filled me; and gone like a sea-covered stone
> Were the memories of the whole of my sorrow and the memories of the whole of my mirth,

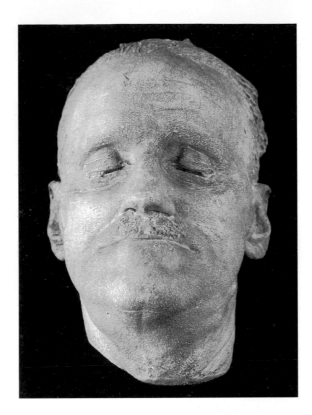

32 Joyce's death mask. *Photograph Bord Failte. Courtesy of the James Joyce Museum, Joyce Tower, Sandycove, Co. Dublin.*

> And a softness came from the starlight and filled me full to the bone.[17]

The word 'moyles' possibly also recalls a stanza in Francis Fahy's 'Galway Bay':

> A prouder man I'd walk the land in health and peace of mind,
> If I might toil and strive and moil, nor cast one thought behind;
> But what would be the world to me, its rank and rich array,
> If memory I lost of thee, my poor old Galway Bay.

It would be appropriate in the closing moments of *Finnegans Wake* for Joyce to remember the birthplace of Nora, and to invoke a song that is unashamedly nostalgic

33 'Yssel that the limmat?' (*FW* 198.13) Is that the Sihl or the Limmat? Isn't that the limit? Carola Giedion-Welcker's photo of Joyce in Zurich in 1938. This is one of Stephen James Joyce's favourite shots of his grandfather. *Courtesy Zurich James Joyce Foundation.*

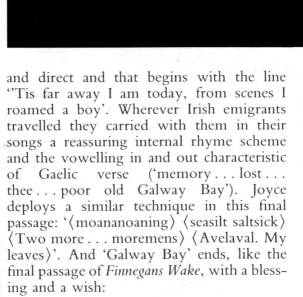

34   Sunrise at Howth. *Photograph Dan Harper.*

and direct and that begins with the line ''Tis far away I am today, from scenes I roamed a boy'. Wherever Irish emigrants travelled they carried with them in their songs a reassuring internal rhyme scheme and the vowelling in and out characteristic of Gaelic verse ('memory . . . lost . . . thee . . . poor old Galway Bay'). Joyce deploys a similar technique in this final passage: '⟨moananoaning⟩ ⟨seasilt saltsick⟩ ⟨Two more . . . moremens⟩ ⟨Avelaval. My leaves⟩'. And 'Galway Bay' ends, like the final passage of *Finnegans Wake*, with a blessing and a wish:

> The blessings of a poor old man be with
>   you night and day,
> The blessings of a lonely man whose
>   heart will soon be clay;
> 'Tis all the Heaven I'd ask of God upon
>   my dying day –
> My soul to soar for evermore above
>   you, Galway Bay.

But the strongest association of the word 'moyles' is with Moore's 'Silent, O Moyle! Be the Roar of Thy Water'. Fionnuala, whose name is related to Fionn, was transformed into a swan and forced to wander in exile from Ireland until the coming of Christianity, until Christ's return. She is Lir's daughter, 'murmuring mournfully' (mememormee). 'When shall the Swan, her death-note singing, Sleep with wings in darkness furl'd?' 'When will that day-star, mildly springing, Warm our Isle with peace and love?' It is Joyce's hope for his country: 'I see them rising!' The Easter Rising, Tim Finnegan waking from the dead, his father's arms rising, the 'moananoaning' giving way to the 'riverrun' that begins the whole human saga again, from the indefinite stutter of the series of 'a's in the last sentence – 'A way a lone a last a loved a long' – to the hope that is contained in the definite article, ironically by itself one of the least definite words in the language.

209

NOTES

CHAPTER ONE: JOYCE AND VICTORIAN IRELAND (I)

1 T. S. Eliot, '*Ulysses*, Order, and Myth', in Frank Kermode (ed.), *Selected Prose of T. S. Eliot* (London: Faber and Faber, 1975), 178.
2 Grattan Freyer, 'A Letter From Ireland', *Scrutiny*, vol. 6, no. 4 (March 1938), 382.
3 Eileen Joyce Schaurek, in *Evening Herald* (Dublin), 16 July 1963. Cited in E. H. Mikhail (ed.), *James Joyce: Interviews and Recollections* (London: Macmillan, 1990), 69.
4 It might be helpful at this stage if I indicate where I stand on the issue of Joyce's relationship to the fictional portraits he presents of himself in his writing. In *Time and Western Man* (1927) Wyndham Lewis claimed that 'Joyce is fundamentally autobiographical', that *A Portrait* gives 'you a neat, carefully-drawn picture of Joyce from babyhood upwards' (p. 117). In anchoring Joyce to a provincial, shabby-genteel Irish background, Lewis was hoping to place him and thereby discredit his achievement. From the opposite end of the spectrum, Hugh Kenner in *Dublin's Joyce* (1956) and *Ulysses* (1980) has tended to stress the gulf that separates Stephen Dedalus from Joyce, a move that William Empson in *Using Biography* (1984) characterizes as the 'Kenner Smear' (p. 204). My own view – and it is the one on show throughout this study – is that we need a flexible approach, one that avoids the twin errors of reductionism and of seeing no author behind the writing. Joyce relishes playing with identities – his own, his past identity, his wife's, his wife's past identity, his friends', his rivals 'and enemies' – and, to my mind, it is the critic's task to ensure these identities are kept in play. We need an approach that Laurence Sterne would have approved, where wit and judgement go hand in hand, where we neither slavishly seek biographical equivalents nor assume that Joyce is always the 'poisoner of his word' (*FW* 463.13).
5 Kevin Sullivan, *Joyce Among the Jesuits* (New York: Columbia University Press, 1958), 14.
6 Cited in Mikhail, *James Joyce*, 65.
7 The subtitle to Herbert Howarth's *The Irish Writers 1880–1940* (London: Rockliff, 1958) is 'Literature Under Parnell's Star'.
8 Katharine O'Shea, *Charles Stewart Parnell: His Love Story and Political Life*, 2 vols (London: Cassell, 1914), II. 240.
9 The use of the word 'auditors' can be compared with its appearance in the manuscript of 'The Dead'. Gabriel runs through in his mind the speech he is to give: 'He was undecided about the lines from Robert Browning for he feared they would be above the heads of his auditors' (see *The James Joyce Archive* vol. 4: Dubliners *Drafts and Manuscripts*, p. 467). The word is not quite right here, being stiffly formal and a little overdone, and before publication Joyce changed it to the more neutral 'hearers' (*D* 179).
10 For a recent survey of the presence of Parnell in *Ulysses*, see Andrew Enda Duffy's 'Parnellism and Rebellion: The Irish War of Independence and Revisions of the Heroic in *Ulysses*', *James Joyce Quarterly*, vol. 28, no. 1 (Fall 1990), 179–95.
11 Cited in F. S. L. Lyons, *Charles Stewart Parnell* (London: Fontana/Collins, 1978), 374–5.
12 Wyndham Lewis, *Time and Western Man* (London: Chatto and Windus, 1927), 108.

CHAPTER TWO: JOYCE AND VICTORIAN IRELAND (2)

1 Cited in E. H. Mikhail, *James Joyce: Interviews and Recollections* (London: Macmillan, 1990), 3.
2 Hugh Kenner, '*Ulysses*' (London: Allen and Unwin, 1980), 66.

3 See Bruce Bradley, *James Joyce's Schooldays* (Dublin: Gill and Macmillan, 1982), 75.

4 According to Conor Cruise O'Brien, Kathleen Sheehy's son, the conversation between Gabriel and Miss Ivors in 'The Dead' is based on this family altercation. See his *States of Ireland* (St Albans: Panther, 1974), 80n.

5 Ibid., 62.

6 Ulick O'Connor (ed.), *The Joyce We Knew* (Cork: Mercier, 1967), 23–4.

7 For details on the biographical background to *Exiles*, see John MacNicholas, *James Joyce's 'Exiles': A Textual Companion* (New York and London: Garland, 1979), 5–16.

8 Mary and Padraic Colum, *Our Friend James Joyce* (London: Gollancz, 1959), 205–6.

9 Matthew Hodgart and Mabel Worthington, *Song in the Work of James Joyce* (New York: Columbia University Press, 1959), 9.

10 I am indebted at this point to Ruth Bauerle. See her remarkable companion, *The James Joyce Songbook* (New York and London: Garland, 1982), 189. 'Compressed in this brief passage is not merely a description of HCE, but the whole scene from *A Portrait*: a phrase from the song, twilight in the kitchen in dear dirty Dublin, and Simon Dedalus, puzzling and frightening his children.'

11 For a modern biography of Moore, see Terence de Vere White, *Tom Moore: The Irish Poet* (London: Hamish Hamilton, 1977). Moore's audience in Britain and Ireland was probably more diverse in its range of sympathies than sometimes imagined. The list of subscribers to volume 3 (numbers 5 and 6) of *Irish Melodies*, for example, contained: serving officers in the British army, Irish bishops, the Dean of St Patrick's, the Provost of Trinity College Dublin, the Beef-Steak Club Dublin, the Harmonic Society ('3 sets'), Maria Edgeworth's father Richard Lovel Edgworth (sic), and Lady Morgan. In addition, of the 618 subscribers or so, some 275 were women – from places as far apart as Weymouth, Sundbury, Tooting, Blackheath, Cork, and Strabane. Perhaps women were more prepared to sympathise with Moore's sense of displacement, and did not so much overlook as relish the words of disaffection.

12 Byron in Leigh Hunt's *Tatler*, 15 January 1831. Cited in Leslie Marchand, *Byron: A Portrait* (London: Futura, 1976), 385. The playful Byron had enormous respect for his friend Moore. In a letter dated 8 December 1813 he writes: 'I have you by rote and by heart: of which *ecce signum!* When I was at — on my first visit, I have a habit, in passing my time a good deal alone, of – I won't call it singing, for that I never attempt except to myself – but of uttering to what I think tunes, your 'Oh breathe not,' 'When the last glimpse,' and 'When he who adores thee,' with others of the same minstrel; – they are my matins and vespers. I assuredly did not intend them to be overheard, but, one morning, in comes, not La Donna, but Il Marito, with a very grave face, saying, 'Byron, I must request you won't sing any more, at least of *those* songs'. I stared, and said, 'Certainly, but why?' – 'To tell you the truth,' quoth he, 'they make my wife *cry*, and so melancholy, that I wish her to hear no more of them.' See Thomas Moore, *Letters and Journals of Lord Byron: With Notices of His Life* (London: John Murray, 1838), 197.

13 The *Nation*, which was founded in 1842 by Charles Gavan Duffy, John Blake Dillon, and Thomas Davis, was associated with the cause of Young Ireland. It made an important contribution to Irish culture, not least in its popularizing of new nationalist ballads. In contrast with his contemporaries Yeats and John Eglinton, Joyce never felt impelled to join in the 'deDavisization' of Irish literature. Perhaps he remembered that the *Nation* had published the work of James Clarence Mangan, who was, according to Joyce, 'the most significant poet of the modern Celtic world, and one of the most inspired singers that ever used the lyric form in any country' (James Joyce, *The Critical Writings*, 179). Perhaps his passing (dismissive) references to Davis in his imaginative works were enough. For further discussion of Davis's influence on the development of Irish literature, see Malcolm Brown, *The Politics of Irish Literature: From Thomas Davis to W. B. Yeats* (London: Allen and Unwin, 1972), and Thomas Kinsella's essay, 'The Irish Writer', in W. B. Yeats and Thomas Kinsella, *Davis, Mangan, Ferguson: Tradition and the Irish Writer* (Dublin: Dolmen Press, 1970).

14 This version of 'The Croppy Boy', written in 1845 by 'Carroll Malone' (W. B. McBurney), first appeared in the *Nation* on 4 January 1845. See Georges-Denis Zimmermann, *Songs of Irish Rebellion: Political Street Ballads and Rebel Songs 1780–1900* (Dublin: Allen Figgis, 1967), 228–9. Joyce copied out this song for Giorgio (see *Letters* III. 334–5), but there are several differences in the versions. Joyce calls the priest Father Breen, and he also omits the crucial verse about the croppy boy being the last of his 'name and race'.

15 Mikhail, *James Joyce*, 64.

CHAPTER THREE: JOYCE, NORA AND THE
WEST OF IRELAND

1 Brenda Maddox, *Nora: A Biography of Nora Joyce*

(London: Hamish Hamilton, 1988). The American edition carries the misleading subtitle 'The Real Life of Molly Bloom' (Boston: Houghton Mifflin, 1988).

2 'It became my delight to rouse him to these outbursts, for I was the poet in the presence of his theme'. W. B. Yeats, *Autobiographies* (London: Macmillan, 1977), 96.

3 Thomas Barnacle died in July 1921 and is buried in an unmarked grave in Rahoon Cemetery. He was nursed through his last illness by his estranged wife, Annie. The following April Nora returned to Galway with her children to visit her mother.

4 Maddox, *Nora*, 19, 29.

5 Ibid., 245, 200, 299, 426.

6 Ibid., 17.

7 'I admire very much the personality of your... of... your wife' (*E* 74). In his discussion with Richard, Robert hesitates before bringing himself to say the word that refers to Bertha. Joyce manages to capture in this pause (a) his own elopement with Nora (they did not marry until 1931), (b) the awkwardness and perhaps sneers of fellow Dubliners who did not know how to refer to Nora, and (c) a heightened moment in the play itself that anticipates Richard's reply: 'I am afraid that that longing to possess a woman is not love' (*E* 78).

8 Marilyn French, *The Book as World: James Joyce's 'Ulysses'* (London: Sphere, 1982), 44, 53.

9 Bonnie Kime Scott, *Joyce and Feminism* (Bloomington: Indiana University Press; Sussex: Harvester, 1984), 6, 203.

10 See Julia Kristeva, *Desire in Language: A Semiotic Approach to Literature and Art*, ed. Leon Roudiez, trans. A. Jardine, T. Gora, and L. Roudiez (Oxford: Blackwell, 1984), *passim*.

11 Julia Kristeva, *The Kristeva Reader*, ed. Toril Moi (Oxford: Blackwell, 1986), 42, 86, 122.

12 Christine van Boheemen, *The Novel as Family Romance: Language, Gender, and Authority from Fielding to Joyce* (Ithaca and London: Cornell University Press, 1987), 136.

13 Frances Restuccia, *Joyce and the Law of the Father* (New Haven and London: Yale University Press, 1989). I am indebted to Christine Froula's insightful review of this book in the *James Joyce Quarterly*, vol. 27, no. 4 (Summer, 1990), 871–5.

14 Sandra Gilbert and Susan Gubar, *No Man's Land: The Place of the Woman Writer in the Twentieth Century*, vol. I: *The War of the Words* (New Haven and London: Yale University Press, 1988), 261.

15 Shari Benstock, 'Nightletters: Woman's Writing in the *Wake*', in Bernard Benstock (ed.), *Critical Essays on James Joyce* (Boston: G. K. Hall, 1985), 230.

16 For a recent study contextualizing the French side to this debate, see Geert Lernout, *The French Joyce* (Ann Arbor: University of Michigan Press; 1990).

17 Malcolm Salaman, 'What It Must Be Like to Be Beautiful' in *Illustrated English Magazine* no. 17 (1897), 134.

18 Katherine Leeds, 'In Praise of Mystery', in Mrs F. Harcourt Williamson (ed.), *The Book of Beauty* (London: Hutchinson, 1896), 111. For a study of Joyce's reading, see, *inter alia*, Richard Brown, *James Joyce and Sexuality* (Cambridge: Cambridge University Press, 1985).

19 'You have been to my young manhood what the idea of the Blessed Virgin was to my boyhood,' Joyce confessed to Nora in 1909 (*Letters* II. 242).

20 See Karen Lawrence's essay, 'Joyce and Feminism', in Derek Attridge (ed.), *The Cambridge Companion to James Joyce* (Cambridge: Cambridge University Press, 1990), 237–58. The quotation here appears on page 253.

21 The contrast with the 'single' style of 'Nausicaa' is worth noting at this point – though both 'Nausicaa' and 'Penelope' exhibit different aspects of the art of weaving and deception. Joyce told Budgen that 'Nausicaa' is written in a 'namby-pamby jammy marmalady drawersy (alto là!) style with effects of incense, mariolatry, masturbation, stewed cockles, painter's palette, chit chat, circumlocution, etc., etc.' (*Letters* I. 135). If Joyce had a particular Victorian novelette in mind it may well have been the one Gerty MacDowell recalls during the episode, namely Maria Cummins's *The Lamplighter* (1854). Chapter 20 begins in a style not unlike 'Nausicaa': 'It was the twilight of a sultry September day, and, wearied with many hours' endurance of an excessive heat, unlooked for so late in the season, Emily Graham sat on the front piazza of her father's house, inhaling a delicious and refreshing breeze, which had just sprung up. The western sky was still streaked with brilliant lines of red, the lingering effects of a gorgeous sunset, while the moon, now nearly at the full, and triumphing in the close of day, and the commencement of her nightly reign, cast her full beams upon Emily's white dress, and gave to the beautiful hand and arm, which, escaping from the draperied sleeve, rested on the side of her rustic armchair, the semblance of polished marble' (1904 edn, pp. 117–18). It may be a coincidence that the main character of *The Lamplighter* is called Gertrude (until Chapter 16 she is known as Gerty), and she harbours a secret attachment to a man called Willie (in 'Nausicaa' Gerty dreams of becoming Mrs Reggy Wylie). And if this were not enough, a little later than the passage just quoted, Gertrude is reintroduced into the narrative in a

phrase almost identical to the one used of Bloom in 'Nausicaa': 'At length, some one emerges from behind the high fence which screens the garden from public gaze, and approaches the gate.... The present Gertrude – for it is she – has now become a young lady' (p. 118). 'Leopold Bloom (for it is he) stands silent' (*U* 13.744–5). For a more extended discussion, see Kimberly Devlin's essay 'The Romance Heroine Exposed: "Nausicaa" and *The Lamplighter*', *James Joyce Quarterly*, vol. 22 no. 4 (Summer 1985), 383–96.

CHAPTER FOUR: *DUBLINERS*, TOPOGRAPHY, AND SOCIAL CLASS

1 Frank Budgen, *James Joyce and the Making of 'Ulysses'* (London: Oxford University Press, 1972), 69. It has to be remembered that in Joyce's day, as one of his contemporaries at university recalls (also in topographical terms), Dublin was very largely a face-to-face community: 'Between Abbey Street and College Green, a five minutes' walk, one could meet every person of importance in the life of the city at a certain time in the afternoon.' See Mary Colum, *Life and Dream* (Dublin: Dolmen Press, 1966), 83.
2 Cyril Connolly, *The Selected Essays of Cyril Connolly*, ed. Peter Quennell (New York: Stansky Moss/Persea Books, 1984), 181.
3 Margot Norris, in Derek Attridge (ed.), *The Cambridge Companion to James Joyce* (Cambridge: Cambridge University Press, 1990), 168.
4 Raymond Williams, *Orwell* (London: Fontana/Collins, 1971), 23–4.
5 George Orwell, *Collected Essays, Journalism and Letters of George Orwell* Vol. II, ed. Sonia Orwell and Ian Angus (Harmondsworth: Penguin, 1970), 105.
6 This valuable, problematic essay can be found in Georg Lukács, *Writer and Critic*, ed. and trans. Arthur Kahn (London: Merlin Press, 1970). Lukács grounds his distinction between narration and observation in the development of nineteenth-century European capitalism and in the way writers after the 1848 revolutions became increasingly marginalized from and in society. 'Description is the writer's substitute for the epic significance that has been lost' (p. 127). 'Description debases characters to the level of inanimate objects' (p. 133). 'The method of observation and description developed as part of an attempt to make literature scientific, to transform it into an applied natural science, into sociology' (p. 140). According to Lukács, Balzac and Tolstoy narrate, Flaubert and Zola describe. In his specific comments on Joyce and modernism in *The Meaning of Con-*

temporary Realism (1962), Lukács has less to contribute.
7 D. A. Chart, *The Story of Dublin* (London: Dent, 1907), 295.

CHAPTER FIVE: JOYCE AND EDWARDIAN DUBLIN

1 D. A. Chart, *The Story of Dublin* (London: Dent, 1907), 126.
2 Hugh Kenner, 'Notes Toward An Anatomy of "Modernism"', in E. L. Epstein (ed.), *A Starchamber Quiry: A James Joyce Centennial Volume 1882–1982* (New York and London: Methuen, 1982), 35.
3 Joseph O'Brien, *Dear Dirty Dublin: A City in Distress, 1899–1916* (Berkeley and Los Angeles: University of California Press, 1982).
4 James Malton, *A Picturesque and Descriptive View of the City of Dublin* (London, 1792–9; repr. Dublin: Dolmen Press, 1979), ii.
5 Frank Budgen, *James Joyce and the Making of 'Ulysses'* (1934; London: Oxford University Press, 1972), 195.
6 Constantine Curran, *James Joyce Remembered* (London: Oxford University Press, 1968), 41.
7 Peter Costello, *Leopold Bloom: A Biography* (Dublin: Gill and Macmillan, 1981). Louis Hyman in *The Jews of Ireland* (London and Jerusalem: Israel Universities Press, 1972) discusses various Blooms (and Blums who changed their names) who lived in Dublin at the turn of the century and who may have been used by Joyce in his construction of Bloom. See pp. 170–6.
8 Joyce's interest in South Africa continued to find expression in *Finnegans Wake*. His most famous – and in many ways his most percipient – remark is his belief in 'everyman his own goaldkeeper and in Africa for the fullblacks' (*FW* 129.31–2). But for the most part the references revert to the colonial encounter in the late nineteenth century, especially between the British and the Boers: 'vying with Lady Smythe to avenge MacJobber' (178.22–3) includes a reference to the Battle of Ladysmith, while 'Avenge Majuba!' was a rallying cry in the Boer War; 'Oom Bothar' (200.14) refers to Louis Botha, a Boer general. The battle of Spion Kop in 1900, led by the Dublin Fusiliers, is appropriately mentioned in the Willingdone Museum in the phrase 'spy on' (10.1), while in the next line the word 'Capeinhope', with its echoes of the Cape of Good Hope and Wellington's horse Copenhagen, mixes by extension the Napoleonic with the Boer Wars. Later in the book the global village idea returns with a reference to the 'Cape of Good Howthe' (312.19–20). Joyce was also alert to the Boers' demands for *onse taal*, 'our language' – 'the flowing taal that brooks no brooking' (246.36–247.1) – and at

one point he humorously fuses the British national anthem with the Boers' own national anthem, *Die Stem* – 'Good savours queen with the stem of swuith Aftreck!' (240.17) (I am indebted to Pieter Bekker for these references.)

9 For a definition of 'serial' relationships, see Jean-Paul Sartre, *Critique of Dialectical Reason*, trans. Alan Sheridan-Smith (London: New Left Books, 1976), especially pp. 256–69. Sartre defines a group as an ensemble each of whose members is determined by the others in reciprocity; a series, on the other hand, is an ensemble each of whose members is determined in alterity by the others. One example he uses to illustrate the concept of seriality is waiting for a bus, where the individual is defined according to other people in the queue: 'The Other is me in every Other and every Other in me and everyone as Other in all the Others'. Another example – relevant to my discussion of Joyce and the Jews (see pp. 186–96) – is the Jew, 'the perpetual being-outside-themselves-in-the-other'. For an interesting application of Sartre's idea to modern literature including Joyce, see Fredric Jameson, 'Seriality in Modern Literature', *Bucknell Review*, vol. 18 (Spring 1970), 63–80.

10 Eugen Sandow, *Strength and How To Obtain It* (1897; London: Gale and Polden, 1900), 7, 10, 11. (Joyce's insertion of 'Physical' into the title is one of his rare lapses – if it is a lapse that is.) For further discussion of Joyce and popular culture, see Cheryl Herr, *Joyce's Anatomy of Culture* (Urbana and Chicago: University of Illinois Press, 1986).

11 Sandow, *Strength*, 86.

12 Ibid., 90. It should not be forgotten that whatever he thinks himself, Bloom, at five feet nine-and-a-half inches and of 'full build' (*U* 17.2003), is not in the context of turn-of-the-century Dublin a small man. In terms of height, he would qualify for the Dublin Metropolitan Police.

CHAPTER SIX: *ULYSSES* AND THE UNMAKING OF MODERN IRELAND

1 This is the phrase Joyce used in the schema for *Ulysses* which accompanied his letter to Carlo Linati in September 1920. The schema is reproduced as a foldout in Richard Ellmann, *Ulysses on the Liffey* (London: Faber, 1972).

2 Hugh Kenner, '*Ulysses*' (London: Allen and Unwin, 1980), 34. For further discussion of the opening phrase 'Stately, plump' see Fritz Senn's essay, ' "Stately, plump", for example: Allusive Overlays and Widening Circles of Irrelevance', *James Joyce Quarterly*,

vol. 22, no. 4 (Summer 1985), 347–54.

3 Mary and Padraic Colum, *Our Friend James Joyce* (London: Gollancz, 1959), 112.

4 E. M. Tillyard, *The English Epic and its Background* (London: Chatto and Windus, 1954), 12.

5 Oliver St John Gogarty, *It Isn't This Time Of Year At All: An Unpremeditated Autobiography* (London: MacGibbon and Kee, 1954), 71.

6 Matthew Arnold, *On the Study of Celtic Literature* (London: Smith, Elder, 1867), 97–102, 103.

7 When Joyce enrolled as an undergraduate at the Royal University, Matthew Arnold's brother Thomas was Professor of English. For further discussion of Matthew Arnold's place in the development of modern Anglo-Irish literature, see W. J. McCormack, *Ascendancy and Tradition in Anglo-Irish Literary History from 1789 to 1939* (Oxford: Clarendon Press, 1985), 219–38, and S. Deane, *Celtic Revivals: Essays in Modern Irish Literature 1880–1980* (London: Faber and Faber, 1985), 17–27.

8 The actual model for Haines, Samuel Chevenix Trench, was not English by background. He was Anglo-Irish, and Irish Irelander by choice. When he lived at the Tower he was known as Dermott Trench. A keen supporter of the Irish Literary Revival, he assisted AE in the editing of the *Irish Homestead* and belonged to a theatre group responsible in October 1901 for staging Douglas Hyde's Irish play *Casadh an t-Sugain* (The Twisting of the Rope). See Colum, *Our Friend James Joyce*, 64–5.

9 These lines are from Yeats's poem, 'Remorse For Intemperate Speech'. See *W. B. Yeats: The Poems*, ed. Richard Finneran (London: Macmillan, 1983), 255.

10 For further discussion of Joyce and *The Countess Cathleen*, see my paper 'Close-Up: *The Countess Cathleen*' in the forthcoming proceedings of the Twelfth International James Joyce Symposium (ed. George Sandelescu *et al*) (Gerrards Cross: Colin Smythe).

11 E. H. Mikhail (ed.), *James Joyce: Interviews and Recollections* (London: Macmillan, 1990), 62.

12 Georg Lukács, *The Theory of the Novel*, trans. Anna Bostock (London: Merlin, 1971): 'The novel is the epic of an age in which the extensive totality of life is no longer directly given, in which the immanence of meaning in life has become a problem, yet which still thinks in terms of totality' (p. 56). 'The epic gives form to a totality of life that is rounded from within; the novel seeks, by giving form, to uncover and construct the concealed totality of life' (p. 60).

13 W. B. Yeats, *The Letters of W. B. Yeats*, ed. Allan Wade (London: Rupert Hart-Davis, 1954), 469.

14 For a survey of books which deal with the rise of the Abbey Theatre, see my *Yeats: A Guide Through the*

Critical Maze (Bristol: Bristol Classical Press, 1989), 51–8.

15 Lady Gregory, *The Collected Plays of Lady Gregory* Vol. 1, ed. Ann Saddlemyer (Gerrards Cross: Colin Smythe, 1970), 262.

16 D. H. Greene and E. M. Stephens, *J. M. Synge 1871–1909* (New York, Macmillan), 84, 96.

17 James Stephens, *The Insurrection in Dublin* (Dublin: Scepter, 1966), 87: '[This ideal of freedom] rides Ireland like a nightmare, thwarting or preventing all civilising or cultural work in this country, and it is not too much to say that Ireland cannot even begin to live until that obsession and fever has come to an end, and her imagination has been set free to do the work which imagination alone can do – Imagination is intelligent kindness – we have sore need of it.'

18 'Heteroglossia' is 'the base condition governing the operation of meaning in any utterance. It is that which insures the primacy of context over text.' For a definition of 'heteroglossia' and a discussion of the term, see Mikhail Bakhtin, *The Dialogic Imagination: Four Essays*, ed. Michael Holquist (Austin and London: University of Texas Press, 1983), 428. In a more recent study, *Dialogism: Bakhtin and His World* (London: Routledge, 1990), Holquist cautions: 'Heteroglossia is a plurality of relations, not just a cacophony of different voices' (p. 111).

19 *The Critical Writings of James Joyce*, ed. Ellsworth Mason and Richard Ellmann (New York: Viking, 1966), 71.

20 AE (George Russell), *The Living Torch*, ed. Monk Gibbon (New York: Macmillan, 1938), 137–8.

21 W. B. Yeats, *Essays and Introductions* (New York: Collier, 1977), 160, 195, 189.

22 Finneran (ed.), *W. B. Yeats: The Poems*, 21, 74.

23 Ibid., 364.

24 W. B. Yeats, *Autobiographies* (London: Macmillan, 1977), 326.

25 Constantine Curran, *James Joyce Remembered* (London: Oxford University Press, 1968), 34.

26 I am indebted at this point to Peter de Voogd's 'A Daintical Pair of Accomplasses'. See forthcoming proceedings of the Twelfth International James Joyce Symposium.

27 Patrick McGee, *Paperspace: Style as Ideology in Joyce's 'Ulysses'* (Lincoln and London: University of Nebraska Press, 1988), 37–8.

28 The use of the word 'arranged' here stems from David Hayman's identification of the figure of The Arranger in *Ulysses*, that figure who seems to work independently of the narrator. See David Hayman, *'Ulysses': The Mechanics of Meaning*, revised edn (Madison, Wisconsin: University of Wisconsin, 1982),

88–104. For further discussion of this concept, see Kenner, *'Ulysses'*, 61–71, and James McMichael, *Ulysses and Justice* (Princeton: Princeton University Press, 1991), *passim*.

CHAPTER SEVEN: *FINNEGANS WAKE* AND EXILE IN EUROPE

1 E. H. Mikhail (ed.), *James Joyce: Interviews and Recollections* (London: Macmillan, 1990), 46.

2 See Thomas Faerber and Markus Luchsinger, *Joyce in Zürich* (Zurich: Unionsverlag. 1988), 14. Carola Giedion-Welcker's comment can be found in Willard Potts (ed.), *Portraits of the Artist in Exile* (San Diego and New York: Harvest/Harcourt Brace Jovanovich, 1986), 277.

3 More details of Joyce's links with Paris can be found in Jean-Michel Rabaté's essay, 'Joyce the Parisian', in Derek Attridge (ed.), *The Cambridge Companion to James Joyce* (Cambridge: Cambridge University Press, 1990), 83–102.

4 Ezra Pound, *Literary Essays of Ezra Pound*, ed. T. S. Eliot (London: Faber and Faber, 1968), 3.

5 Samuel Beckett, 'Dante . . . Bruno. Vico . . . Joyce', in Samuel Beckett *et al.*, *Our Exagmination Round His Factification For Incamination of 'Work in Progress'* (London: Faber and Faber, 1961), 14.

6 Patrick Parrinder, *James Joyce* (Cambridge: Cambridge University Press, 1984), 214.

7 Louis Hyman, *The Jews of Ireland* (London and Jerusalem: Israel Universities Press, 1972), 176. For a discussion of the Limerick episode see Hyman, pp. 210–17. Father Creagh's prejudice is even more remarkable when set against the small numbers of Jews prepared to settle in that city. In 1861 there was one Jew, in 1871 two, in 1881 four, in 1896 130. The boycott, however, lasted two years and drove out eighty members of the Jewish community, leaving some forty behind.

8 Ira B. Nadel, *Joyce and the Jews: Culture and Texts* (London: Macmillan, 1989), 1. My discussion in this section is (partly) indebted to Nadel's work, but the approach I adopt is different. To my mind, Joyce – whether in the area of gender, race, or nationality – invariably problematizes the concept of identity and refuses the comfort of a fixed position. Thus, Bloom represents both Everyman and the Other of western civilization, a deliberate commingling of identities. Joyce, the 'Europasianised Afferyank' (*FW* 191.4), highlights the overdetermination in such matters, not either/or but both/and. In this regard *Ulysses* is about meeting the self, or as the philosophical Stephen puts

it: 'What went forth to the ends of the world to traverse not itself, God, the sun, Shakespeare, a commercial traveller, having itself traversed in reality itself becomes that self' (*U* 15.2117–19).

9 Mary and Padraic Colum, *Our Friend James Joyce* (London: Gollancz, 1959), 56. Colum took Joyce to see the grandsons of Morris Harris, one-time Vice-President and Treasurer of the Jewish congregation in Dublin. They had inherited an antique shop on Nassau Street, were brought up as Jews even though their father, John Sinclair, was a Protestant. For further details, see Hyman, *The Jews of Ireland*, 148–9 and 181.

10 For an account of this episode with Martha Fleischmann, see Brenda Maddox, *Nora* (London: Hamish Hamilton, 1988), 215–19, and Richard Ellmann, *Four Dubliners: Oscar Wilde, William Butler Yeats, James Joyce, Samuel Beckett* (New York: George Braziller, 1988), 73–8.

11 John Garvin, *James Joyce's Disunited Kingdom and the Irish Dimension* (Dublin and London: Gill and Macmillan; New York: Barnes and Noble, 1977), *passim*.

12 Sean O'Faolain, *De Valera* (Harmondsworth: Penguin, 1939), 173. For a more sympathetic and authoritative account of de Valera's politics in the early 1920s, see the opening chapters of Joseph Lee's *Ireland 1912–1985* (Cambridge: Cambridge University Press, 1989).

13 Hugh Kenner, *A Colder Eye: The Modern Irish Writers* (Harmondsworth: Penguin, 1983), 290.

14 *Ward Lock Guide to Worthing and South-West Sussex* (London: Ward Lock, 1906), p. 40 of 'Bognor' section.

15 Richmal Mangnall, *Historical and Miscellaneous Questions* (adapted for the use of schools by Rev. Ingram Cobbin) (London and Glasgow: Charles Griffin, n.d.), 120. In *A Portrait*, Stephen thinks of the great men in history 'whose names were in Richmal Magnall's [*sic*] Questions' (p. 53). The question-and-answer format is put to comic use in 'Ithaca'.

16 *Finnegans Wake*: Buffalo Notebooks VI B. 22 in *The James Joyce Archive* vol. 34 (ed. Michael Groden *et al.*) (New York and London: Garland Press, 1977–9), p. 150.

17 *W. B. Yeats: The Poems*, ed. Richard Finneran (London: Macmillan, 1983), 378.

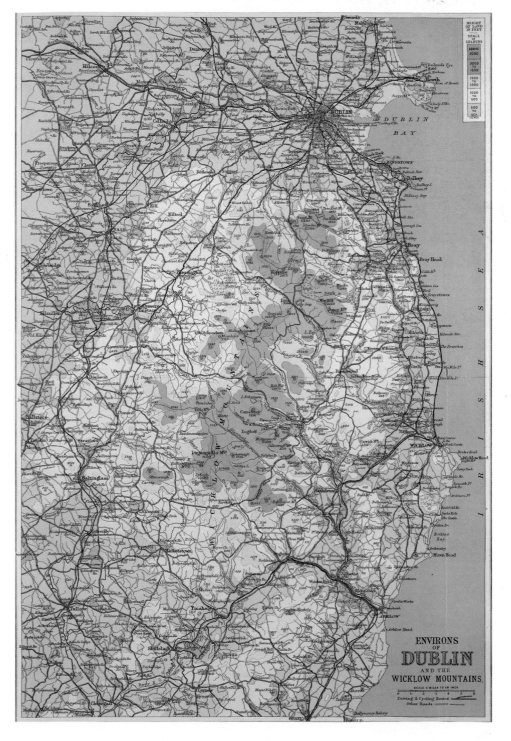

The river Liffey from source to sea. Map of Dublin and its Environs. *Copyright © Bartholomew 1990. Reproduced with permission.*

Following page shows a detail of the above map.

Chronology of the Life and Times of James Joyce

1882   James Joyce born on 2 February in Rathgar, Dublin, the eldest surviving son of John Joyce and Mary Joyce (*née* Murray). May: the Chief Secretary of Ireland and his Under-Secretary assassinated in the Phoenix Park, Dublin.

1884   Birth of Stanislaus Joyce. November: the Gaelic Athletic Association formed to promote Irish sport.

1886   Gladstone's Home Rule Bill defeated at Westminster.

1887   March: the *Times* of London, making use of letters forged by Richard Pigott, launches an attack on Parnell, leader of the Irish Parliamentary Party. May: the Joyce family moves to Martello Terrace, Bray, Co. Wicklow.

1888   Joyce enrols at Clongowes Wood, Salins, Co. Kildare. Death of Matthew Arnold. Birth of T. S. Eliot.

1889   Death of Gerard Manley Hopkins, the Jesuit poet who taught at the Royal University, Dublin. (He is buried in the Jesuit plot at Glasnevin Cemetery). Yeats's *The Wanderings of Oisin* published.

1890   Parnell, cited in a divorce case involving Captain O'Shea, driven from office. Death of Cardinal Newman, first Rector of the National University of Ireland.

1891   Death of Parnell. Joyce writes 'Et Tu Healy', a poem attacking those like Timothy Healy who betrayed Parnell.

June: Joyce withdrawn from Clongowes probably for financial reasons. Shaw's *The Quintessence of Ibsenism* and Wilde's *The Picture of Dorian Gray* published.

1892   Publication of Yeats's play, *The Countess Cathleen*.

1893   April: Joyce enters Belvedere College, Dublin. The family, continuing their financial decline, move back into Dublin. The Gaelic League founded to promote the Irish language.

1894   Joyce accompanies his father to sell off remaining property in Cork. Wilde's *Salome*, with illustrations by Aubrey Beardsley, published. The appearance of George Moore's *Esther Waters* coincides with the demise of the three-decker novel.

1895   The trial of Oscar Wilde.

1896   Joyce is stirred by Father Cullen's sermons during the annual November retreat at Belvedere.

1897   Yeats's *The Tables of the Law: The Adoration of the Magi* published, stories which Joyce learnt by heart.

1898   Joyce leaves Belvedere and enters the Royal University (now University College, Dublin) to read modern languages.

1899   Yeats's *The Wind Among the Reeds* published. Joyce refuses to sign a petition denouncing Yeats's play *The Countess Cathleen* for heresy.

1900   Joyce reads a lecture on 'Drama and Life' to the Literary and Historical Society, publishes an essay on 'Ibsen's New Drama' in the *Fortnightly Review*, and writes a (non-extant) play entitled 'A Brilliant Career' during a trip to Mullingar. Death of Wilde in Paris.

1901   January: Queen Victoria dies; is succeeded by Edward VII. October: Joyce publishes 'The Day of the Rabblement', an essay attacking the newly flourishing Irish dramatic movement.

1902   March: Joyce's younger brother George dies of peritonitis at the age of fifteen. Joyce graduates from university and in October meets Yeats for the first time; he reads him some poems and 'epiphanies', and perhaps tells Yeats: 'I have met you too late. You are too old.' December: Joyce goes to Paris to study medicine. Begins reviewing for the Dublin *Daily Express*. Yeats's *Cathleen ni Houlihan* performed in Dublin. Lady Gregory's *Cuchulain of Muirthemne* published.

1903   March: Joyce meets Synge in Paris. April: Joyce is called home, where his mother is dying of cancer. He remains in Dublin, and, as he did to his dying brother Charles in early 1902, he sings to his mother the lines 'Who Goes With Fergus' from Yeats's play *The Countess Cathleen*. His mother dies in August. July: Edward VII visits Ireland. Moore's collection of short stories, *The Untilled Field*, published.

1904   January: Joyce writes 'A Portrait of the Artist', an essay-story dealing with aesthetics. He submits it to *Dana*, a freethinking magazine edited by John Eglinton (pseudonym of W. K. Magee) and Fred Ryan, but it is rejected. He begins writing *Stephen Hero*. In the spring he teaches for a short while at the Clifton School, Dalkey, an experience he makes use of when writing the 'Nestor' episode of *Ulysses*. On 10 June he meets Nora Barnacle and is attracted to her immediately: they walk out together for the first time probably on 16 June, the day Joyce made famous in *Ulysses*. July and August: prompted by George Russell (AE), Joyce writes 'The Sisters', 'Eveline', and 'After the Race', and places them in the *Irish Homestead*, a weekly magazine supporting Horace Plunkett's Irish Agricultural Organization Society. Also in July/August, Joyce writes 'The Holy Office', a stinging attack on the hypocrisy of his contemporaries. August: at the height of his singing career, he shares a platform with John McCormack at a concert given at the Antient Concert Rooms in Dublin. September: he stays for a brief period with Oliver St John Gogarty in the Martello Tower at Sandycove, scene of the opening episode of *Ulysses*. On 8 October he departs with Nora for the continent and finds employment teaching at a Berlitz School in Pola. 1 November: Shaw's *John Bull's Other Island* opens at the Royal Court in London. 27 December: the opening night of the newly formed Abbey Theatre includes a performance of Yeats's *On Baile's Strand*, the first play in his Cuchulain cycle.

1905   March: Joyce moves to Trieste to take up a teaching post at the Berlitz School. Son Giorgio born on 27 July. Stanislaus joins them in October. Joyce completes all but one of the stories of *Dubliners* and submits them to Grant Richards for publication, but without success. November: Arthur Griffith launches the Sinn Fein policy. Publication of Moore's novel, *The Lake*, and Synge's play, *In the Shadow of the Glen*.

1906   May: first number of Griffith's *Sinn Fein* appears. By June Joyce has almost completed *Stephen Hero*, the bulk of which was written between October 1904 and June 1906. July: Joyce takes family to Rome, where he works as a foreign correspondent in a bank. Rome reminds him of 'a man who lives by exhibiting to travellers his grandmother's corpse'. September: Joyce conceives – but does not write – another story for *Dubliners*, to be called 'Ulysses'.

1907 January: Synge's *Playboy of the Western World* prompts a riot at the Abbey Theatre when it is first staged. February: defeated by the experience of Rome and failing to secure a job in Marseilles, Joyce returns to Trieste. Early May: *Chamber Music* published by Elkin Mathews. Joyce writes articles for *Il Piccolo della Sera*, a Triestine newspaper. Lucia, their daughter, is born on 26 July. That summer Joyce contracts rheumatic fever, and while convalescing he writes 'The Dead'. November: Elkin Mathews rejects *Dubliners*. In 1907 Joyce decides to re-shape *Stephen Hero* and, by the end of November, has rewritten the first chapter.

1908 By April the third chapter of *A Portrait* has been finished. Then follows the darkest period of the 'seven lost years' of *A Portrait*, about which we know little. September: Patrick Pearse opens St Enda's school for boys in Rathfarnham, Dublin.

1909 March: Joyce writes an article on Wilde for *Il Piccolo della Sera*. The same month Synge dies of cancer at the age of thirty-seven. July: Joyce, in search of an Irish publisher for *Dubliners* and to investigate the possibility of a post at University College, returns to Ireland with his son Giorgio. August: he visits Nora's family in Galway and listens to Nora's mother singing 'The Lass of Aughrim', the song that Bartell D'Arcy sings in 'The Dead'. September: he returns to Trieste with his sister Eva. October: a subsequent visit to Dublin in connection with the Volta cinema project.

1910 Returns to Trieste on 2 January with his sister Eileen. Maunsel and Company postpone publication of *Dubliners*. Death of Edward VII in May; succeeded by George V.

1911 Home Rule Bill passed in House of Commons, but rejected in the Lords.

1912 Joyce's last journey to Ireland. Visits Nora's family in Galway and cycles out to Oughterard, some 17 miles from Galway, to see the graveyard where he imagined Michael Furey was buried. This visit inspired his poem, 'She Weeps Over Rahoon'. His attempt to persuade George Roberts of Maunsel to publish *Dubliners* again proves unsuccessful, this time because the printer refuses to handle the unpatriotic sheets. On his way home to Trieste he composes the vitriolic poem, 'Gas from a Burner'.

1913 Ulster Volunteer Force and Irish Volunteers established. Dublin lockout of workers. On Yeats's suggestion, Ezra Pound writes to Joyce seeking material to publish.

1914 On 2 February the serial publication of *A Portrait* begins in the *Egoist*. Joyce begins writing *Exiles* and *Ulysses*. June: *Dubliners* is published by Grant Richards in London. August: outbreak of the First World War.

1915 January: Stanislaus Joyce arrested and interned by the Austrian authorities for his outspoken Irredentist views. June: Joyce and his family move to neutral Zurich. Finishes *Exiles*. With the help of Yeats, Pound, and Edmund Gosse, Joyce is awarded pension from the Royal Literary Fund, to be followed in 1916 by a Civil List pension.

1916 Easter Rising in Dublin by the Irish Volunteers under Patrick Pearse and the Irish Citizen Army under James Connolly. Francis Sheehy Skeffington summarily executed by British army captain. May: execution of leaders of Rising (de Valera's American background saves him); Casement hanged for his part in gun-running episode. December: *A Portrait* published by B. W. Huebsch in New York. Yeats's *Reveries Over Childhood and Youth*, the first volume of his autobiography, published by Macmillan.

1917 February: Joyce receives his first gift from

221

Harriet Shaw Weaver. March: Russian Revolution. August: Joyce's first eye operation. July: de Valera, in prison in England, elected as Sinn Fein candidate in East Clare. November: Yeats's *The Wild Swans at Coole* published by the Cuala Press. On doctor's advice, Joyce winters in Locarno.

1918   March: *Little Review* in New York begins serialization of *Ulysses* (this continues until stopped by a court action in December 1920). April: Joyce takes over management of English Players; row with Henry Carr, an English actor, after performance of Wilde's *The Importance of Being Earnest*. May: *Exiles* published in London and New York. June: Nora plays Cathleen in Synge's *Riders to the Sea*. In the autumn Joyce considers having an affair with Martha Fleischmann, who lives in a flat opposite and whom he mistakenly imagines to be Jewish. December: Sinn Fein wins landslide victory in general election.

1919   January: War of Independence (the Anglo-Irish War) begins; ends July 1921. April: de Valera elected President of Dail Eireann. October: Joyce and family return to Trieste.

1920   Joyce meets Pound, and in July moves to Paris. Black-and-Tan atrocities in Ireland. George Clancy, Mayor of Limerick and 'Davin' in *A Portrait*, murdered at home by Black and Tans. October: Terence MacSwiney, Mayor of Cork, dies in Brixton Prison on hunger strike.

1921   Sylvia Beach agrees to publish *Ulysses* in Paris. June: rift between Joyce and Budgen develops – lasts for three years. December: Anglo-Irish Treaty signed in London. Sinn Fein split, when de Valera refusing to sign.

1922   *Ulysses* appears on 2 February, Joyce's fortieth birthday. Civil War in Ireland between those who accepted the Treaty and the Republicans, who did not. April: Nora and children, on a visit to her family in Galway, come under fire from both sides. August: death of Arthur Griffith. Michael Collins killed in an ambush in County Cork. November: Erskine Childers, convicted of possessing an illegal weapon, is executed. Mussolini marches on Rome. Eliot's *The Waste Land* published.

1923   March: Joyce begins writing *Finnegans Wake*. May: end of Civil War in Ireland. Joyce spends summer vacation at Bognor Regis, Sussex.

1924   First fragment of 'Work in Progress' published in *Transatlantic Review* in Paris. Severe eye trouble. French translation of *A Portrait* appears.

1925   Several more fragments of 'Work in Progress' published. Yeats's *A Vision* published, 1925–6.

1926   Publication of a pirated edition of *Ulysses* in the United States. First German translation of *A Portrait*. First French translation of *Dubliners*.

1927   The first of seventeen instalments of 'Work in Progress' published in *transition* (edited by Eugene Jolas in Paris). *Pomes Penyeach* published by Shakespeare and Company. First German translation of *Ulysses*.

1928   *Anna Livia Plurabelle* published by Crosby Gaige in New York. First German translation of *Dubliners*. Yeats's *The Tower* published.

1929   *Tales Told of Shem and Shaun* published by Black Sun Press in Paris. *Our Exagmination round his Factification for Incamination of Work in Progress* published by Shakespeare and Company. First French translation of *Ulysses*, honoured by a special 'Déjeuner Ulysse', hosted by Sylvia Beach and Adrienne Monnier.

1930   *Haveth Childers Everywhere* published in Paris and New York. Joyce undergoes an eye operation in Zurich. May: Beckett refused access to Joyce household and accused of trifling with Lucia's feelings. Marriage of Giorgio Joyce and Helen Kastor Fleischman. Joyce's promotion of

Irish tenor, John Sullivan.

1931   Marriage of James and Nora Joyce at Kensington Registry Office on 4 July. September: rift between Joyce and Sylvia Beach over an American publication of *Ulysses*. Death of John Joyce on 29 December.

1932   15 February: Stephen James Joyce born, son of Giorgio and Helen Joyce; 'Ecce Puer' written same day. Lucia has her first breakdown caused by schizophrenia. Paul Léon becomes Joyce's secretary. De Valera, leader of Fianna Fail, comes to power in Ireland (continues as Taoiseach until 1948).

1933   Lucia hospitalized in Switzerland. Court in New York lifts ban on *Ulysses*. *Ulysses* published by the Odyssey Press in Hamburg. Yeats's *The Winding Stair* published. Hitler becomes German Chancellor.

1934   *Ulysses* published in the United States by Random House. May: Giorgio and his family leave for the United States, where they remain until November 1935. In June, *The Mime of Mick Nick and the Maggies* published.

1935   Lucia stays with relatives in Ireland and with Harriet Shaw Weaver in England, but her health continues to decline. She is admitted to St Andrew's Hospital, Northampton for blood tests.

1936   Joyce's *Collected Poems* published in New York. Spanish Civil War begins. Joyce's final estrangement from Harriet Shaw Weaver.

1937   *Storiella as She is Syung*, the last fragment of 'Work in Progress' to be published. New constitution of Eire approved.

1938   'Work in Progress' completed; in July Joyce reveals its title: *Finnegans Wake*. Douglas Hyde becomes first President of Ireland. May: Yeats's *New Poems* published.

1939   Death of Yeats on 28 January. May: *Finnegans Wake* published by Faber and Faber in London and the Viking Press in New York. When war is declared, Joyce is preoccupied with Lucia and her continuing hospitalization. De Valera pursues a policy of neutrality for Ireland.

1940   Joyce forced to flee France; moves to Zurich.

1941   On 13 January Joyce dies in Zurich from a perforated duodenal ulcer. Two days later he is buried in the Fluntern Cemetery in Zurich. On 25 January the Irish Minister of Supplies, Sean Lemass, declares, 'We in this country have a right to be neutral if we so decide.'

1944   The extant MS of *Stephen Hero* published.

1949   Ireland (now Eire) formally declares itself a republic and ceases to be a member of the British Commonwealth.

1951   10 April: Nora Joyce dies in Zurich.

Dramatis Personae in Joyce's Life and Work

FAMILY

Giorgio Joyce (1905–76)

Joyce's son. In 1930 he married Helen Kastor Fleischman, and two years later Stephen, their son, was born. The marriage was never very happy, Helen suffering several nervous collapses. Giorgio remarried in 1954.

John Joyce (1849–1931)

Joyce's father. The model for Simon Dedalus in *Ulysses*, for Earwicker in *Finnegans Wake*, and for several others besides, his stories and sayings appear throughout Joyce's work. A native of Cork City, he moved to Dublin in 1874–5. In 1880 he married Mary Murray, and the same year obtained employment in the office of the Collector of Rates. The father of ten children, he was a heavy drinker and ruined the family financially. James's attitude to his father was, like most things, mixed. He blamed him for his mother's death, but, in the words of Maria Jolas, he 'talked of fatherhood as if it were motherhood', the highest tribute he could pay his father or his father's influence.

Lucia Joyce (1907–82)

Joyce's daughter. The model for Molly Bloom's daughter, Milly, and for Issy in *Finnegans Wake*, Lucia was destined for an artistic career, but she suffered from schizophrenia and in 1932 had a complete mental breakdown. For a time her distraught father refused to accept that she was incurable. In 1936 she became a patient at the Delmas clinic in Ivry outside Paris, where she stayed until 1951. She was then transferred to St Andrew's Hospital, Northampton, where she spent the remaining years of her life.

Mary Joyce (née Murray) (1859–1903)

Joyce's mother. Daughter of an agent for wines and spirits from Longford, Mary Murray sang in the choir at a church in Rathgar and had, in the words of Richard Ellmann, a 'slightly old-fashioned courtliness of manner'. Her father, knowing that John Joyce was a heavy drinker who had already broken off two engagements, was against the marriage, but Mary was prepared to indulge Joyce's boisterousness. In the opening episode of *Ulysses* Joyce paints a poor picture of his relationship with his mother but, as his letters to her from Paris in 1902–3 show, he was actually very tender and devoted to her. Within a year of her death, Joyce replaced his mother with another important female presence, that of Nora.

Nora Joyce (née Barnacle) (1884–1951)

Joyce's wife. Daughter of a seamstress and a baker, Nora left school in April 1896 at the age of twelve and was taken on as a helper in the local Presentation Convent in Galway. Information about her life before her move to Dublin in 1904 is sketchy. She may have worked in a laundry and in Gorman's bookbindery. She had several boyfriends – Michael Feeney, William Mulvagh, and Michael Bodkin, the last of whom died of tuberculosis in February 1900. In 1904 she left Galway for Dublin, where she found work as a domestic at Finn's hotel. She first met Joyce in Nassau Street on 10 June 1904, and they first walked out together probably on 16 June. On 8 October of the same year they departed for the continent. They had two children Giorgio and Lucia, for whose sake they later married in 1931 in London. Nora Joyce is buried in the Fluntern Cemetery in Zurich. For a recent, controversial account of her life, see Brenda Maddox, *Nora: A Biography of Nora Joyce* (1988).

Stanislaus Joyce (1884–1955)

Joyce's brother. Stanislaus is the model for Maurice in *Stephen Hero* and *A Portrait* and for Shaun and the Shaun figures in *Finnegans Wake*. He was very close to Joyce and in 1905 joined the Joyce household in the Austro-Hungarian port of Trieste. He was interned by the Austrians during the First World War because of his forthright Irredentist views advocating the union or re-covery of all Italian-speaking districts with Italy. After the war the two brothers drifted apart. Joyce did not like Stanislaus's surveillance; Stanislaus objected to always playing second fiddle. In the 1920s Stanislaus was among the first to criticize 'Work in Progress', arguing that it was 'the last word in modern literature', being 'the witless wandering of literature before its final extinction'. His memories of James Joyce can be found in *My Brother's Keeper: James Joyce's Early Years* (1958) and in *The Dublin Diary of Stanislaus Joyce* (1962).

FRIENDS AND CONTEMPORARIES IN IRELAND

John Francis Byrne (1879–1960)

Joyce's closest friend at university and model for Cranly in *A Portrait*. Their friendship cooled after Joyce sent Byrne a photo-postcard from Paris in December 1902 referring in dog-Latin to the Paris whores, but was restored in 1909 when Joyce returned to Dublin. On that visit Joyce was extremely agitated by rumours of Nora's intimacy with Vincent Cosgrave during the summer of 1904, but was reassured by Byrne that these were groundless. Byrne was then living in 7 Eccles Street, the house that Joyce was later to assign to Leopold Bloom in *Ulysses*. In later life, Byrne wrote a memoir of Joyce, *Silent Years* (New York: Farrar, Straus and Young, 1953).

Padraic Colum (1881–1972)

Poet and playwright, Colum's early volume of verse *Wild Earth* (1907) won him high praise. We are told in 'Scylla and Charybdis' that Yeats admired his line, 'As in wild earth a Grecian vase', though Joyce is probably mocking both the emptiness of the line and the judgement of Yeats. His early plays – *The Land* (1905), *The Fiddler's House* (1907), and *Thomas Muskerry* (1910) – are realistic portrayals of rural life in the Irish midlands, and as such ran counter to the Abbey ideals of Yeats and Lady Gregory. An account of his friendship with Joyce can be found in *Our Friend James Joyce* (1958), which he wrote with his wife Mary Colum. He is one of the few Irish writers who knew Joyce both in his Dublin days and in the inter-war years when he was in Paris. In 1928 Colum wrote a preface for an American de luxe edition of *Anna Livia Plurabelle*, was present at the secret baptism of Joyce's grandson, visited Lucia in hospital, and collaborated with Joyce in assisting refugees from the Nazis.

John Eglinton (1868–1961)

The pseudonym of William K. Magee, the leading essayist in Ireland during the early years of this century – Yeats called him 'our one Irish critic'. Eglinton believed that it is 'by a "thought movement" rather than by a "language move-ment" that Ireland will have to show that it holds the germs of true nationality'. He attempted to broaden the discussion of Irish identity, attacked outdated or sentimental views of nationalism, and put forward the thesis of the 'De-Davisisation of Irish literature' – that is, that literature should eschew propaganda. Joint-editor with Fred Ryan of *Dana*, he also wrote *Bards and Saints* (1906), a collection of thoughtful essays on Irish literature and culture, and *Irish Literary Portraits* (1935), a series of vignettes of the major figures of the Literary Revival, including Yeats and Joyce.

Oliver St John Gogarty (1878–1957)

Joyce's friendship with Gogarty began in 1903 when his friendship with Byrne cooled. At that time a medical student at Trinity College, Dublin, Gogarty was a master of wit, won prizes for poetry, and had a natural ear for parody, all of which recommended themselves to Joyce. When he was living in the Martello Tower at Sandycove, which he rented from the Secretary of State for War, he invited Joyce to stay. Joyce arrived on 9 September 1904, but on the night of 14 September, after an incident with a gun fired by the other occupant, Samuel Chevenix Trench, he decided to leave. The friendship with Gogarty thereafter deteriorated, and Joyce paints an unflattering portrait of him as 'Buck' Mulligan in *Ulysses* (he is also used as a model for 'Blazes' Boylan, for Ignatius Gallagher in 'A Little Cloud', and for Robert Hand in *Exiles*). An account of their friendship – and enmity – can be found in J. B. Lyons, *James Joyce and Medicine* (Dublin: Dolmen, 1973).

Lady Gregory (1852–1932)

Playwright and folklorist, Lady Gregory was closely involved with Yeats in the foundation of the Abbey Theatre. She helped Joyce find work as a reviewer and invited him, without success, to her country estate at Coole in the west of Ireland. Joyce was never averse to financial support but resisted any attempt to patronize him. In 1903 he wrote an uncomplimentary review of her *Poets and Dreamers*, and in *Ulysses* he calls her an 'old hake'. Lady Gregory was above such bickering and thought *A Portrait* a model autobiography. For a recent biography, see Mary Lou Kohfeldt, *Lady Gregory: The*

Woman Behind The Irish Renaissance (London: André Deutsch, 1985).

Thomas Kettle (1880–1916)

A friend of Joyce at university, where both were active in the Literary and Historical Society. As MP for East Tyrone from 1906 to 1910, Kettle was a prominent figure in Irish political life. In 1909 he married Mary Sheehy, the sister of Eugene and Richard Sheehy and Joyce's possible secret adolescent love. Kettle lent his support to Joyce's candidature for a post at University College, Dublin in 1909, and he became a model for Robert Hand in *Exiles*. In 1907 he wrote a complimentary review of *Chamber Music*, but was highly critical of the draft of *Dubliners* he saw in 1912 (especially the outspokenness of 'An Encounter') and threatened to denounce it if published. Thereafter, their friendship waned. In 1916 Kettle was killed in action during the First World War. His political writings can be found in *The Day's Burden: Studies, Literary and Political and Miscellaneous Essays* (Dublin and London: Maunsel and Company, 1918). A recent biography of Kettle has been written by J. B. Lyons: *Enigma of Tom Kettle: Irish Patriot, Essayist, Poet, British Soldier, 1880–1916* (Sandycove, Co. Dublin: Glendale Press, 1983).

George Moore (1852–1933)

Novelist, art critic, and man of letters, Moore was the Irish novelist from whom Joyce arguably learnt most. Both *Dubliners* and *A Portrait* betray an unacknowledged but important debt to Moore's collection of stories *The Untilled Field* (1903) and to his symbolist novel *The Lake* (1905), respectively. Moore spent his childhood at his family's estate in County Mayo. He returned to Ireland in 1901 from sojourns in Paris and England and threw himself into the Irish Literary Revival, but by 1911 his enthusiasm for Ireland was over, and he returned to London. There he wrote *Hail and Farewell* (1911–14), an idiosyncratic account of the Revival, which is especially critical of Yeats and Lady Gregory. (Yeats's reply came in *Dramatis Personae*, 1935, in which he refers to Moore's 'coarse palate', and celebrates Lady Gregory's patrician qualities.) Joyce is scathing about Moore as a novelist, and in 'Scylla and Charybdis' links his name with that of Edward Martyn, the Catholic playwright who criticized Yeats's *The Countess Cathleen* for its lack of religious orthodoxy. 'Did you hear Miss Mitchell's joke about Moore and Martyn? That Moore is Martyn's wild oats?' When they met in London in 1929, Joyce was, according to Moore, 'courteous, respectful, and I was the same. He seemed anxious to accord me the first place. I demurred, and declared him first in Europe. We agreed that our careers were not altogether dissimilar.' 'Paris', commented Joyce, 'has played an equal part in our lives.' (See *JJ* 617).

George Russell (AE) (1867–1935)

Poet, painter, economist, editor, essayist, novelist, and theosophist, Russell first introduced Joyce to Yeats in 1902 with the words, 'The first spectre of the new generation has appeared. His name is Joyce.' He was closely associated with the *Irish Homestead* – the 'pig's paper' as it is called in *Ulysses* – and in 1905 became its editor. In 1904 Russell was responsible for publication of the first three stories of *Dubliners* to be written. Earlier the same year, 1904, Russell refused to include Joyce's poetry in his verse anthology, *New Songs*. Joyce attacks him in 'The Holy Office' and mercilessly plays on his pseudonym in the 'Scylla and Charybdis' episode of *Ulysses*, that episode where 'the truth is midway', which in Russell's case lies somewhere between his own name and his pseudonym. For his biography, see Henry Summerfield, *That Myriad-Minded Man AE* (Gerrards Cross: Colin Smythe, 1975).

Francis Sheehy Skeffington (1878–1916)

A friend of Joyce at university. Together they published a pamphlet in 1901, which contained their two essays: Joyce's 'The Day of the Rabblement' and Skeffington's 'A Forgotten Aspect of the University Question'. At one time Joyce suggested they found a newspaper together. They frequently met at the Sheehy family house, and Skeffington, the disputatious pacifist, became the model for MacCann in *A Portrait*. In 1903 Skeffington married Hanna Sheehy and adopted her name. He was also a close friend of Fred Ryan (1874–1913), who was co-editor of *Dana* and active in the Irish theatre, in socialist circles, and, later, in the Egyptian nationalist movement. During Easter Week 1916, when trying to prevent looting, Sheehy Skeffington was arrested and summarily executed by Captain Bowen-Colthurst (a relative of Elizabeth Bowen). Hanna refused compensation from the British government and later became a leading member of Sinn Fein. Sheehy Skeffington's papers are housed in the National Library in Dublin. For his biography, see Leah Levenson, *With Wooden Sword: A Portrait of Francis Sheehy-Skeffington, Militant Pacifist* (Boston, Mass: Northeastern University Press, 1983).

John Millington Synge (1871–1909)

The Abbey Theatre's leading playwright, author of *Riders to the Sea* (1904), and *The Playboy of the Western World* (1907). Joyce, who had met Synge in Paris in 1902–3, was intially hostile to his work, but in time came to value his celebration of rural life. 'The Dead' was written in the aftermath of the *Playboy* riots in January 1907, for Synge too has a part to play, with Nora, in this story of Joyce's unresolved tension with the west of Ireland. In 1912 Joyce visited the Aran Islands with Nora and warmed to the place where Synge had discovered 'every symbol of the cosmos'. For an account of his life, see David Greene and Edward Stephens, *J. M. Synge 1871–1909* (New York: Macmillan, 1959; Collier Books, 1961).

William Butler Yeats (1865–1939)

Poet, dramatist, and prose writer, Yeats was the leading figure with whom Joyce had to contend. When Joyce met him in 1902 to show him his 'epiphanies' and his poems, Yeats already had an international reputation. Joyce knew by heart not only the lines 'Who Goes with Fergus' from *The*

Countess Cathleen, the play his contemporaries at university had denounced, but also the whole of two occult stories by Yeats, 'The Adoration of the Magi' and 'Tables of the Law'. Joyce also admired *The Wind Among the Reeds* (1899). Joyce, who had learnt Norwegian in order to read Ibsen, dismissed the backward-looking direction of Yeats's work at the Abbey Theatre, but still felt impelled when in Trieste to translate the plays of Yeats and Synge into Italian – and he submitted without success his own play *Exiles* to the Abbey for consideration. Yeats played an important role in advancing Joyce's career. It was Yeats who gave Ezra Pound Joyce's name in 1913, and this led to *A Portrait* being serialized in the *Egoist*. In spite of his often dismissive attitude in *Ulysses* and *Finnegans Wake*, Joyce's admiration for Yeats's work continued throughout his life: one evening at Fouquet's in 1935 Joyce spent a couple of hours reciting Yeats's verse by heart. (*Letters* I. 371–2) When Yeats died in 1939, Joyce commented in private that of the two Yeats was the greater writer. For a recent biography, see A. Norman Jeffares, *W. B. Yeats: A New Biography* (London: Hutchinson, 1988). For a guide to books about Yeats, see my *Yeats: A Guide Through the Critical Maze* (Bristol: Bristol Classical Press, 1989).

FRIENDS AND CONTEMPORARIES IN EUROPE

Sylvia Beach (1887–1962)

Bookseller, librarian, and publisher, Sylvia Beach published the first edition of *Ulysses*. An American feminist, she made Paris her home. In November 1919 she opened an English bookshop on the rue Monsieur-le-Prince and called it Shakespeare and Company. In July 1921 she moved her shop to 12 rue de l'Odéon, across the street from La Maison des Amis des Livres, the lending library of her friend, Adrienne Monnier. In the 1920s and 1930s Shakespeare and Company became a literary shrine and numbered among its visitors Valery Larbaud, Paul Valéry, Jules Romains, George Antheil,

Robert McAlmon, Ernest Hemingway, John Dos Passos, Archibald MacLeish, T. S. Eliot, and Stephen Spender. Sylvia Beach's relationship with Joyce was often full of tension, and ten years almost to the day after she had handed Joyce a copy of *Ulysses* she relinquished her claims and agreed to an American edition. For her biography, see Noel Riley Fitch, *Sylvia Beach and the Lost Generation: A History of Literary Paris in the Twenties and Thirties* (Harmondsworth: Penguin, 1985).

Samuel Beckett (1906–89)

Like Joyce, Beckett was born in Dublin but chose to live most of his life away from Ireland. They first met in autumn 1928 when Beckett was a *lecteur* at the Ecole Normale. Beckett was one of the twelve disciples who wrote in praise of 'Work in Progress' in *Our Exagmination round His Factification for Incamination of 'Work in Progress'* (1929). He was also present at the 'Déjeuner Ulysse' in June 1929 to mark the French translation of *Ulysses*. His relationship with Joyce was temporarily interrupted in the early 1930s when it was thought he had trifled with Lucia's affections. Contact resumed in June 1932 when Beckett wrote 'Home Olga', a ten-line acrostic on Joyce's name. Beckett ran errands for Joyce, acted as his amanuensis, and in time came to be called by Joyce 'Beckett' rather than 'Mr Beckett'. In early January 1938, Beckett, on his way home from a Left Bank café, was stabbed by a pimp, and taken to hospital. Joyce immediately took charge, and, at his own expense, had Beckett moved to a private room and their own doctor put on to the case. For Beckett's biography see Deirdre Bair, *Samuel Beckett* (1978). See also Eoin O'Brien's carefully researched and beautifully illustrated book on Beckett's Ireland, *The Beckett Country: Samuel Beckett's Ireland* (Dublin: The Black Cat Press; London: Faber and Faber 1986).

Frank Budgen (1882–1971)

An English painter who became a close friend of Joyce in Zürich in 1918. Their conversations during the period 1918–20 form the basis of his book *James Joyce and the Making of Ulysses* (first published in 1934), which is an excellent introduction to *Ulysses*. In Zurich, he and Joyce met nearly every day and enjoyed drinking and singing music-hall numbers. Joyce involved Budgen in his secretive and voyeuristic affair with Martha Fleischmann in the winter of 1918–19. In 1920 Joyce moved to Paris and Budgen returned to London. In June 1921, after a quarrel while Budgen was visiting Paris, they did not see each other for several years. Their friendship revived, however, and whenever Budgen was in Paris he called on Joyce.

Eugene (1894–1952) and Maria Jolas (1895–1987)

Born in New Jersey of a French father and German mother and educated in Lorraine near the German border, Eugene Jolas was ideally placed to become founder and editor of *transition*, the literary avant-garde magazine, which from its inception in 1927 until its demise in 1938, was – especially in the early years – associated with 'Work in Progress'. Maria Jolas (née McDonald), also an American by birth, was an important figure for the last period of Joyce's life from 1927 until his death. She warned him of the perilous condition of Lucia and advised him to consult Jung about her; in 1940 she tried to persuade him to take refuge in the United States. An account of Eugene Jolas and Joyce's work in *transition* can be found in Dougald McMillan, *Transition: The History of a Literary Era 1927–38* (London: Calder and Boyars, 1975). Maria Jolas's article, 'The Joyce I Knew and the Women around Him', appeared in *The Crane Bag*, vol. 4, no. 1 (1980). See also Marc Dachy, *Eugène Jolas Sur James Joyce* (Paris: Plon, 1990).

Paul Léon (1893–1942)

A Russian-Jewish refugee, Paul Léon moved to Paris in 1921 after spending 1918–21 in London as an exile following the Bolshevik Revolution.

His friendship with Joyce began in 1928, and by the end of 1929 he was in effect Joyce's unpaid secretary, a role he played until 1940. Léon dealt with Joyce's correspondence and business matters, scrutinized Joyce's texts and manuscripts, and collaborated in editorial decisions (Maria Jolas called him Joyce's *alter ego*). On the fall of Paris in June 1940, Léon and his wife went to Saint-Gérand-le-Puy to be with the Joyces (who had moved there the previous December). In September he returned to Paris, rescued part of Joyce's library, and deposited Joyce's papers with the Irish Ambassador to Occupied France. The following August he was arrested by the Gestapo, and after a nine-month period of imprisonment was murdered on his way to a concentration camp in Silesia.

Harriet Shaw Weaver (1874–1961)

Feminist, social reformer, and later Marxist, she first came into contact with Joyce as editor of the *Egoist*, the magazine that serialized *A Portrait* in 1915. The Egoist Press, which she ran almost single-handed, published three editions of *A Portrait* and one each of *Ulysses*, *Exiles*, *Dubliners*, and *Chamber Music*. She became Joyce's patron and supported him financially throughout his inter-war years in Paris. In the 1920s Joyce was particularly anxious to explain to her 'Work in Progress', and took care to explicate passages, and defend himself against adverse comments from Wyndham Lewis and others. In the 1930s she was increasingly involved with Lucia Joyce's welfare, and in 1951, when Lucia was transferred to a hospital in Northampton, Weaver became her legal guardian. Weaver also paid for Joyce's funeral in Zurich and became his literary executor. Her relationship with Joyce was never easy – she disliked his drinking habits especially – but once her loyalty was given she never reneged on her commitment. For her life, see Jane Lidderdale and Mary Nicholson, *Dear Miss Weaver* (New York: Viking, 1970).

FURTHER READING

JOYCE'S TEXTS

The Critical Writings of James Joyce, ed. Ellsworth Mason and Richard Ellmann (New York: Macmillan, 1959; repr. New York: Viking, 1966).

'Dubliners': Text, Criticism, and Notes, ed. Robert Scholes and A. Walton Litz (New York: The Viking Press, 1969; repr. 1979).

Exiles (New York: The Viking Press, 1951).

Finnegans Wake (London: Faber and Faber, 1939; repr. 1971).

Giacomo Joyce, ed. Richard Ellmann (London: Faber and Faber, 1968).

James Joyce Poems and Shorter Writings, ed. Richard Ellmann, A. Walton Litz and John Whittier Ferguson (London: Faber and Faber, 1991).

'A Portrait of the Artist as a Young Man': Text, Criticism, and Notes, ed. Chester Anderson (New York: The Viking Press, 1968).

Stephen Hero, ed. John Slocum and Herbert Cahoon (New York: New Directions, 1944; repr. 1963).

Ulysses, Garland edition (Harmondsworth: Penguin, 1986).

Ulysses: A Critical and Synoptic Edition, ed. Hans Walter Gabler *et al.* (New York and London: Garland Press, 1984).

The James Joyce Archive, ed. Michael Groden *et al.*, 63 vols (New York and London: Garland Press, 1977–9).

The Essential James Joyce, ed. Harry Levin (1948; repr. Harmondsworth: Penguin, 1975).

Letters of James Joyce, ed. Stuart Gilbert (London: Faber and Faber, 1957).

Letters of James Joyce Vols II and III, ed. Richard Ellmann (London: Faber and Faber, 1966).

Selected Letters of James Joyce, ed. Richard Ellmann (New York: The Viking Press, 1975).

BIOGRAPHICAL STUDIES

Anderson, Chester, *James Joyce* (London: Thames and Hudson, 1967).

Bair, Deirdre, *Samuel Beckett* (London: Jonathan Cape, 1978).

Bradley, Bruce, *James Joyce's Schooldays* (Dublin: Gill and Macmillan, 1982).

Curran, Constantine, *James Joyce Remembered* (London: Oxford University Press, 1968).

Dachy, Marc, *Eugène Jolas Sur James Joyce* (Paris: Plon, 1990).

Dawson, Hugh, 'Thomas MacGreevy and Joyce' in the *James Joyce Quarterly*, vol. 25, no. 3 (Spring 1988), 305–21.

Ellmann, Richard, *James Joyce*, revised edn (London: Oxford University Press, 1982).

Faerber, Thomas and Marcus Luchsinger, *Joyce in Zürich* (Zurich: Unionsverlag, 1988).

Freund, Gisèle, *Three Days with Joyce* (New York: Persea Books, 1985).

Freund, Gisèle and V. B. Carleton, *James Joyce in Paris: His Final Years* (London: Cassell, 1966).

Gorman, Herbert, *James Joyce: A Definitive Biography* (London: John Lane The Bodley Head, 1941; repr. 1949).

Hutchins, Patricia, *James Joyce's Dublin* (London: Grey Walls Press, 1950).

—— *James Joyce's World* (London: Methuen, 1957).

Joyce, Stanislaus, *My Brother's Keeper: James Joyce's Early Years*, ed. Richard Ellmann (New York: The Viking Press, 1958).

—— *The Dublin Diary of Stanislaus Joyce*, ed. George Harris Healey (London: Faber and Faber, 1962).

Maddox, Brenda, *Nora: A Biography of Nora Joyce* (London: Hamish Hamilton, 1988).

McDougall, Richard, *The Very Rich Hours of Adrienne Monnier* (New York: Charles Scribner's Sons, 1976).

Melchiori, Giorgio (ed.), *Joyce in Rome* (Rome: Bulzoni Editore, 1984).

Mikhail, E. H. (ed.), *James Joyce: Interviews and Recollections* (London: Macmillan, 1990).

Paris, Jean, *Joyce: par lui-même* (Paris: Editions du Seuil, 1969).

Potts, Willard (ed.), *Portraits of the Artist in Exile: Recollections of James Joyce by Europeans* (Dublin: Wolfhound Press, 1979).

Power, Arthur, *Conversations with James Joyce*, ed. Clive Hart (Chicago: University of Chicago Press, 1974).

Sheehy, Eugene, *May It Please the Court* (Dublin: Fallon, 1951).

Sullivan, Kevin, *Joyce Among the Jesuits* (New York: Columbia University Press, 1958).

REFERENCE BOOKS AND GUIDES

Atherton, James, *The Books at the Wake: A Study of Literary Allusions in James Joyce's 'Finnegans Wake'* (Carbondale and Edwardsville: Southern Illinois University Press, 1974).

Bauerle, Ruth, *The James Joyce Songbook* (New York and London: Garland, 1982).

Bidwell, Bruce and Linda Heffer, *The Joycean Way: A Topographic Guide to 'Dubliners' and 'A Portrait of the Artist as a Young Man'* (Dublin: Wolfhound Press, 1981).

Blamires, Harry, *The Bloomsday Book: A Guide Through James Joyce's 'Ulysses'* (London: Methuen, 1966; repr. 1989).

Delaney, Frank, *James Joyce's Odyssey: A Guide to the Dublin of 'Ulysses'* (St Albans and London: Granada, 1983).

Gifford, Don, *Joyce Annotated: Notes for 'Dubliners' and 'A Portrait of the Artist as a Young Man'* (Berkeley and London: University of California Press, 1982).

Gifford, Don and Robert Seidman, *Notes for Joyce: An Annotation of James Joyce's 'Ulysses'*, revised edn (Berkeley and London: University of California Press, 1989).

Glasheen, Adeline, *Third Census of 'Finnegans Wake': An Index of Characters and their Roles* (Berkeley: University of California Press, 1977).

Hart, Clive, *A Concordance to 'Finnegans Wake'* (Minneapolis: University of Minnesota Press, 1963).

Hart, Clive and Leo Knuth, *A Topographical Guide to James Joyce's 'Ulysses'*, revised and corrected edn (Colchester: A Wake Newslitter Press, 1981).

Hodgart, Matthew and Mabel Worthington, *Song in the Work of James Joyce* (New York: Columbia University Press, 1959).

Igoe, Vivien, *James Joyce's Dublin Houses and Nora Barnacle's Galway* (London: Mandarin, 1990).

MacNicholas, John, *James Joyce's 'Exiles': A Textual Companion* (New York and London: Garland, 1979).

McHugh, Roland, *Annotations to 'Finnegans Wake'* (London: Routledge and Kegan Paul, 1980).

Nicholson, Robert, *The 'Ulysses' Guide: Tours Through Joyce's Dublin* (London: Methuen, 1988).

Rose, Danis and John O'Hanlon, *Understanding 'Finnegans Wake': A Guide to the Narrative of James Joyce's Masterpiece* (New York and London: Garland, 1982).

Steppe, Wolfhard and Hans Walter Gabler, *A Handlist to James Joyce's 'Ulysses'* (New York and London: Garland, 1985).

Thornton, Weldon, *Allusions in 'Ulysses'* (Chapel Hill: University of North Carolina Press, 1968).

CRITICAL STUDIES

Attridge, Derek and Daniel Ferrer (eds), *Post-Structuralist Joyce: From the French* (Cambridge: Cambridge University Press, 1984).

Attridge, Derek (ed.), *The Cambridge Companion to James Joyce* (Cambridge: Cambridge University Press, 1990).

Benstock, Bernard, *James Joyce: The Undiscover'd Country* (Dublin: Gill and Macmillan; New York: Barnes and Noble, 1977).

—— (ed.), *Critical Essays on James Joyce* (Boston: G. K. Hall, 1985).

Bishop, John, *Joyce's Book of the Dark: 'Finnegans Wake'* (Madison: University of Wisconsin Press, 1986).

Boheemen, Christine van, *The Novel as Family Romance: Language, Gender and Authority from Fielding to Joyce* (Ithaca, NY: Cornell University Press, 1987).

Budgen, Frank, *James Joyce and the Making of 'Ulysses'*

(1934; reissued as *James Joyce and the Making of 'Ulysses', And Other Writings* intro. Clive Hart. London: Oxford University Press, 1972).

Card, James van Dyck, *An Anatomy of 'Penelope'* (London and Toronto: Associated University Presses, 1984).

Deane, Seamus, *Celtic Revivals: Essays in Modern Irish Literature 1880–1980* (London: Faber and Faber, 1985).

Ellmann, Richard, *Eminent Domain: Yeats Among Wilde Joyce Pound Eliot and Auden* (New York: Oxford University Press, 1970).

—— *Ulysses on the Liffey* (London: Oxford University Press, 1972).

Empson, William, *Using Biography* (London: Chatto and Windus/The Hogarth Press, 1984).

French, Marilyn, *The Book as World: James Joyce's 'Ulysses'* (London: Sphere, 1982).

Garvin, John, *James Joyce's Disunited Kingdom and the Irish Dimension* (Dublin and London: Gill and Macmillan; New York: Barnes and Noble, 1977).

Gilbert, Stuart, *James Joyce's 'Ulysses': A Study* (1930; New York: Knopf, 1952).

Goldberg, S. L., *The Classical Temper: A Study of James Joyce's 'Ulysses'* (London: Chatto and Windus, 1961).

Groden, Michael, *'Ulysses' in Progress* (Princeton: Princeton University Press, 1977).

Hart, Clive, *Structure and Motif in 'Finnegans Wake'* (London: Faber and Faber, 1962).

Hart, Clive and David Hayman (eds), *James Joyce's 'Ulysses': Critical Essays* (Berkeley and Los Angeles: University of California Press, 1974).

Hayman, David, *'Ulysses': The Mechanics of Meaning*, revised edn (Madison, Wisconsin: University of Wisconsin Press, 1982).

Henke, Suzette and Elaine Unkeless (eds), *Women in Joyce* (Brighton, Sussex: Harvester Press, 1982).

Howarth, Herbert, *The Irish Writers, 1880–1940: Literature under Parnell's Star* (London: Rockliff, 1958).

Kain, Richard M., *Fabulous Voyager: James Joyce's 'Ulysses'* (Chicago: Chicago University Press, 1947).

Kenner, Hugh, *Dublin's Joyce* (London: Chatto and Windus; Bloomington, Ind.: Indiana University Press, 1956).

—— *Joyce's Voices* (Berkeley: University of California Press; London, Faber and Faber, 1978).

—— *'Ulysses'*, (London: Allen and Unwin, 1980; revised edn, Baltimore and London: Johns Hopkins University Press, 1987).

Lawrence, Karen, *The Odyssey of Style in 'Ulysses'* (Princeton: Princeton University Press, 1981).

Lernout, Geert, *The French Joyce* (Ann Arbor: University of Michigan Press, 1990).

Levin, Harry, *James Joyce* (London: Faber and Feber, 1942).

Litz, A. Walton, *The Art of James Joyce: Method and Design in 'Ulysses' and 'Finnegans Wake'* (London: Oxford University Press, 1961).

Manganiello, Dominic, *Joyce's Politics* (London: Routledge and Kegan Paul, 1980).

Martin, Augustine (ed.), *James Joyce: The Artist and the Labyrinth* (London: Ryan, 1990).

McCabe, Colin, *James Joyce and the Revolution of the Word* (London: Macmillan, 1978).

McCormack, William J., *Ascendancy and Tradition in Anglo-Irish Literary History from 1789 to 1939* (Oxford: Clarendon Press, 1985).

McCormack, William J. and Alistair Stead (eds), *James Joyce and Modern Literature* (London: Routledge and Kegan Paul, 1982).

McGee, Patrick, *Paperspace: Style as Ideology in Joyce's 'Ulysses'* (Lincoln, Nebraska: University of Nebraska Press, 1988).

Norris, Margot, *The Decentered Universe of 'Finnegans Wake'* (Baltimore: Johns Hopkins University Press, 1976).

Parrinder, Patrick, *James Joyce* (Cambridge: Cambridge University Press, 1984).

Peake, Charles, *James Joyce: The Citizen and the Artist* (London: Arnold, 1977).

Pierce, David, 'The Politics of "Finnegans Wake"', *Textual Practice*, vol. 2, no. 1 (Winter 1988), 367–80.

Restuccia, Frances L., *Joyce and the Law of the Father* (New Haven and London: Yale University Press, 1989).

Scott, Bonnie Kime, *Joyce and Feminism* (Bloomington: Indiana University Press; Brighton: Harvester Press, 1984).

Senn, Fritz, *Joyce's Dislocutions: Essays on Reading as Translation*, ed. John Paul Riquelme (Baltimore: Johns Hopkins University Press, 1984).

Torchiana, Donald, *Backgrounds for Joyce's 'Dubliners'* (Boston and London: Allen and Unwin, 1986).

Watson, George, *Irish Identity and the Literary Revival:*

Synge, Yeats, Joyce and O'Casey (London: Croom Helm, 1979).

HISTORICAL STUDIES AND BACKGROUND INFORMATION

Arnold, Matthew, *On the Study of Celtic Literature* (London: Smith, Elder, 1867).

Brown, Terence, *Ireland: A Social and Cultural History 1922–79* (Glasgow: Fontana, 1981).

Busby, Roy, *British Music Hall: An Illustrated Who's Who from 1850 to the Present Day* (London and New Hampshire: Paul Elek, 1976).

Cahill, Susan and Thomas Cahill, *A Literary Guide to Ireland* (Dublin: Wolfhound Press, 1979).

Chart, D. A., *The Story of Dublin* (London: Dent, 1907).

Clarke, Desmond, *Dublin* (London: Batsford, 1977).

Costello, Peter, *Leopold Bloom: A Biography* (Dublin: Gill and Macmillan, 1981).

Craig, Maurice, *Dublin 1660–1860* (Dublin: Allen Figgis, 1969).

Cullen, L. M., *Life in Ireland* (London: Batsford, 1968).

—— *The Emergence of Modern Ireland 1600–1900* (London: Batsford, 1981).

Fitch, Noel Riley, *Sylvia Beach and the Lost Generation: A History of Literary Paris in the Twenties and Thirties* (Harmondsworth: Penguin, 1985).

Fitzpatrick, Samuel, *Dublin: A Historical and Topographical Account of the City* (London: Methuen, 1907).

Gorham, Maurice, *Ireland from Old Photographs* (London: Batsford, 1971).

—— *Dublin from Old Photographs* (London: Batsford, 1983).

Herr, Cheryl, *Joyce's Anatomy of Culture* (Urbana and Chicago: University of Illinois Press, 1986).

Hyman, Louis, *The Jews of Ireland: From the Earliest Times to the Year 1910* (London and Jerusalem: Israel Universities Press, 1972).

Lee, Joseph, *Ireland 1912–1985: Politics and Society* (Cambridge: Cambridge University Press, 1989).

Lyons, F. S. L., *Charles Stewart Parnell* (Glasgow: Collins, 1977).

Malton, James, *A Picturesque and Descriptive View of the City of Dublin* (London, 1792–9; revised edn, Dublin: Dolmen Press, 1978).

McDougall, Richard, *The Very Rich Hours of Adrienne Monnier* (New York: Charles Scribner's Sons, 1976).

Muirhead, L. Russell, *Ireland: The Blue Guide Series* (London: Benn, 1949).

Nadel, Ira, *Joyce and the Jews: Culture and Texts* (London: Macmillan, 1989).

O'Brien, Joseph, *Dear Dirty Dublin: A City in Distress, 1899–1916* (Berkeley and Los Angeles: University of California Press, 1982).

O'Shea, Katharine, *Charles Stewart Parnell: His Love Story and Political Life*, 2 vols (London: Cassell, 1914).

Pearl, Cyril, *Dublin in Bloomtime: The City James Joyce Knew* (New York: The Viking Press, 1969).

Pearsall, Ronald, *Edwardian Popular Music* (London, North Pomfret and Vancouver: David and Charles, 1975).

Power, Arthur, *Conversations with James Joyce*, ed. Clive Hart (Chicago: University of Chicago Press, 1974).

Watters, Eugene and Matthew Murtagh, *Infinite Variety: Dan Lowrey's Music Hall 1879–97* (Dublin: Gill and Macmillan, 1975).

JOURNALS

European Joyce Studies (James Joyce Foundation, Zurich).

James Joyce Broadsheet (University of Leeds).

James Joyce Literary Supplement (University of Miami).

James Joyce Quarterly (University of Tulsa).

Joyce Studies: An Annual (University of Texas at Austin).

INDEX

Numbers in italics refer to pages on which illustrations appear.

PLAN OF
DUBLIN

Scale of ½ a Mile

Tramway Routes shown thus ═══════

The Plan is divided into half Mile Squares